Cornell Studies in Classical Philology

EDITED BY

Frederick M. Ahl, Kevin Clinton, John E. Coleman,
Judith R. Ginsburg, G. M. Kirkwood, Gordon R. Messing,
Phillip Mitsis, Alan J. Nussbaum,
Pietro Pucci, Winthrop Wetherbee

VOLUME XLVIII

Epicurus' Ethical Theory:
The Pleasures of Invulnerability
by Phillip Mitsis

Momentary Monsters: Lucan and His Heroes
by W. R. Johnson

Epicurus' Scientific Method
by Elizabeth Asmis

The Rhetoric of Imitation: Genre and Poetic Memory
in Virgil and Other Latin Poets
by Gian Biagio Conte, edited by Charles Segal

Seneca's *Hercules Furens*:
A Critical Text with Introduction and Commentary
by John G. Fitch

From Myth to Icon:
Reflections of Greek Ethical Doctrine in Literature and Art
by Helen F. North

Odysseus Polutropos:
Intertextual Readings in the *Odyssey* and the *Iliad*
by Pietro Pucci

THE TOWNSEND LECTURES

Artifices of Eternity: Horace's Fourth Book of Odes
by Michael C. J. Putnam

Epicurus' Ethical Theory

THE PLEASURES OF INVULNERABILITY

PHILLIP MITSIS

CORNELL UNIVERSITY PRESS

ITHACA AND LONDON

International Standard Book Number 0-8014-2187-X
Library of Congress Catalog Card Number 88-47746
Printed in the United States of America
*Librarians: Library of Congress cataloging information
appears on the last page of the book.*

*The paper in this book is acid-free and meets the guidelines for
permanence and durability of the Committee on Production Guidelines
for Book Longevity of the Council on Library Resources.*

To my parents

Contents

Acknowledgments ix

Introduction 1

1. Pleasure, Happiness, and Desire 11

Pleasure, Feelings, and the Satisfaction of Desire 19
Pleasure and Belief 40
Kinetic and Katastematic Pleasures 45
Pleasure, *Ataraxia,* and *Aponia* 51

2. Justice and the Virtues 59

Justice, Psychic States, and the Unity of Virtue 70
Epicurean Contracts 79
Conclusion 92

3. Friendship and Altruism 98

Associationist and Contractual Friendships 104
Friendship and Pleasure 112
Friendship, Happiness, and Invulnerability 117
Conclusion 127

4. Reason, Responsibility, and the Mechanisms of Freedom 129

Rationality and Responsibility 132
Indeterminism and the Swerve 153
Varieties of Reduction 160

Bibliography 167
Index Locorum 177
Index of Modern Scholars 182

Acknowledgments

A Prescott W. Townsend grant from the Cornell Department of Classics made it possible for me to finish a penultimate draft of this book in Oxford (1984–85). I am grateful to Sir Kenneth and Audrey Dover for helping to make my stay there as pleasant as possible. A National Endowment for the Humanities fellowship at the National Humanities Center (1987–88) enabled me, under almost embarrassingly idyllic conditions, finally to put this project to rest.

For their generosity in offering valuable criticism of this study, I am deeply indebted to Julia Annas, Elizabeth Asmis, John Coleman, Gail Fine, David Furley, Gordon Kirkwood, David Konstan, Tony Long, Matt Neuburg, Martha Nussbaum, Pietro Pucci, John Rist, Anne Scott, David Sedley, Christopher Shields, Richard Sorabji, Gisela Striker, and Jennifer Whiting. I also thank Cornell University Press's anonymous reader, Neil Beshers, and Bernhard Kendler and Marilyn Sale for suggesting helpful changes in overall presentation. Matt Neuburg proofread the galleys with painstaking care, a keen knowledge of Greek language and Classical literature, and a rigorous insistence on consistent conventions of citation. Finally, I acknowledge a special and long-standing debt of gratitude to Terry Irwin for carefully guiding and watching over this study from its very beginnings.

An earlier and slightly different version of chapter 3 was published as "Epicurus on Friendship and Altruism," in *Oxford Studies in Ancient Philosophy* 5, ed. J. Annas (Oxford, 1987), pp. 127–53.

P.M.

Ithaca, New York

Epicurus' Ethical Theory

Introduction

Practice [my ethical teachings] and all that is associated with them by day and by night . . . and you will live as a god among men. For a man living amidst immortal goods is in no way like a mortal animal.

Epicurus, *Epistola ad Menoeceum* 135

Perhaps the most characteristic, albeit problematic, element of Hellenistic ethical thought is a deeply held conviction that individuals can banish all contingency from their lives and, with the help of reason alone, aspire to a condition of divine invulnerability, self-sufficiency, and happiness. This theme or ambition is by no means completely new among Greek moral philosophers. At various times in Plato's dialogues, for instance, Socrates and his interlocutors had inquired into the conditions and requirements of such a godlike state and rigorously examined whether attempting to lead a completely self-sufficient life would be desirable, even if it were possible. Sometimes Plato seems attracted to the life governed solely by reason and its consequent rewards of self-sufficiency and invulnerability. Only by identifying ourselves entirely with the rational part of our souls, he seems to suggest, can we hope to escape the incursions of chance and the terrors of unstable and erratic lives. At other times, however, Plato appears to concede that to live such a life, we would have to pay too high a price, give up our attachments to far too many intrinsically valuable goods and activities. Pursuing the good life will involve risks, he argues, and our successes or failures may therefore not always depend solely on us. Plato is not alone in this attempt to discover whether we would be both better off and happier trying to insulate ourselves from worldly contin-

1

gencies: Aristotle's ethical theory features a similar attempt to gauge the extent to which those things which he believes make our lives valuable, such as friendships and strong moral commitments, also make us vulnerable to chance.

Nonetheless, the relentless and often rather theatrical preoccupation with invulnerability among Hellenistic philosophers has indicated to many the beginnings of a new era in Greek ethical thinking. Initially, it might be tempting to suggest that Hellenistic moral thinkers somehow lost what Momigliano aptly describes as their predecessors' "indefinable touch of irony and sadness"[1] and that their ethical theories suffer from a corresponding impoverishment in intellectual dexterity and moral sensitivity. Plutarch, obviously offended by what he takes to be so much vulgar posturing on the part of Epicureans, recounts an incident that exemplifies the sometimes extreme forms that these Hellenistic ambitions could take: "Colotes himself, for another, while hearing a lecture of Epicurus on natural philosophy, suddenly cast himself down before him and embraced his knees [in supplication]; and this is what Epicurus himself writes about it in a tone of solemn pride: 'You, as one revering my remarks on that occasion, were seized by a desire . . . to embrace me by clasping my knees and lay hold of me to the whole extent of the contact that is customarily established in revering and supplicating [gods and deified monarchs]' " (*Adversus Colotem* 1117b–c). Clearly, there are few signs here of either a developed sense of irony or a tragic awareness of life's vulnerability. As Martha Nussbaum observes, it is almost impossible to imagine Aristotle and his students carrying on in this fashion.[2] Few can fail to share Plutarch's distaste for such pretensions, and we can readily join him in wondering how any sensible thinker could tolerate,

1. A. Momigliano, *The Development of Greek Biography* (Cambridge, 1971), p. 65.
2. M. Nussbaum, "Therapeutic Arguments: Epicurus and Aristotle," in *The Norms of Nature*, ed. M. Schofield and G. Striker (Cambridge, 1986), p. 58. Also worth reading is the wry account of this aspect of Epicureanism by Ch. Theodorides in *Epikouros: Hē alēthinē opsē tou archaiou kosmou* (Athens, 1981), pp. 184–86. In a letter to his mother, Epicurus writes, "For these things that I gain are nothing small or of little force, things of the sort that make my state equal to a god's, and show me as a man who not even by his mortality falls short of the imperishable and blessed nature. For while I am alive, I know joy to the same degree as the gods" (Arrighetti, *Epicuro opere*, frag. 72.29–40).

much less aspire to, this kind of unblushing, self-indulgent smugness. At first glance, then, there might appear to be little that could be morally attractive, much less philosophically interesting, motivating such unappealing displays.

Various reasons have been suggested for this Hellenistic preoccupation with individuals' achieving complete control over the conditions of their happiness. Few of them, though, have had any immediate connection with these philosophers' stated theoretical aims. In his magisterial *Die Philosophie der Griechen* (1880), Zeller offered what is still perhaps the most pervasive and certainly the most resilient explanation of this aspect of Hellenistic ethical thinking. Relying on Hegel's periodization of Greek thought, Zeller argued that after the death of Aristotle (322 B.C.), philosophers were especially concerned with personal invulnerability because they were attempting to combat feelings of anxiety over an unsettled and threatening political world. Hellenistic ethical thought, in his view, is in many ways a direct and immediate reaction to a crumbling social world—a world in which the old communal certainties of life in Greek cities were disrupted, with the consequence that individuals began to turn inward to salvage some remnants of personal contentment, stability, and tranquillity. Zeller also diagnosed a corresponding narrowing of these philosophers' aims. He argued that, given the declining demands of Hellenistic political life, philosophy lost many of its previous theoretical and practical ambitions and became valued merely as a guide to personal well-being, safety, and contentment.

Many recent historians of Hellenistic politics would probably claim, however, that Hegel's neat periodization of Greek intellectual life is far too schematic. For example, it is not at all clear that the traditional concerns of public life in Greek cities were so radically modified after the death of Alexander. It is even less clear from literary or historical texts that there were any sudden, widespread feelings of a new powerlessness in the face of contemporary political realities. More important, though, the founders of the three main schools of Hellenistic philosophy—Epicurus, Zeno, and Pyrrho— all fail to register the slightest hints of anxiety or dismay at any dissolution of traditional political practices. To the contrary, they seem much more concerned that entrenched institutions of the polis and traditional political ambitions were continuing to dominate the moral outlook of their contemporaries. Thus the historical underpinnings of Zeller's thesis no longer seem secure enough to warrant any easy inferences from changes in political climate to changes in the goals and styles of philosophers.

Zeller's historicist explanation, though forcefully presented, also neglects the more systematic, philosophical foundations of Hellenistic philosophers' commitment to invulnerability. Much recent work has shown that the Stoics, for example, elaborated sophisticated views of logic, dialectic, philosophy of language, and psychology and attempted to demonstrate the ways in which their ethical theory was systematically tied to their corresponding inquiries in these fields. Consequently, few contemporary scholars would still refuse to treat the Stoics as serious moral thinkers capable of defending a complex and challenging ethical option.

Though few would find in Zeller's reductive historicism an adequate explanation of Stoic concerns with invulnerability and moral autonomy, Epicurus' ethical writings, for the most part, have yet to receive the same kind of serious philosophical appreciation. The Epicurean ethical corpus is often treated merely as an archaic self-help manual—a group of unconnected aphorisms meant only to offer guidance in times of personal or political crisis. Indeed, scholars have asserted that Epicurean ethical texts, although they may be of some interest to social historians, psychologists, or perhaps those concerned with the formation of ancient political ideologies, can hardly pretend to more serious philosophical consideration. The very popularity and egalitarianism of Epicureanism, many would claim, give sufficient indication that we are dealing not with considered moral thinking but with simple moral recipes for those uninitiated in philosophical theorizing.

Such judgments might seem warranted, because Epicureans deny that they have any intrinsic need of, or even interest in, logic or dialectic. Similarly, they seem to content themselves with a fairly rudimentary philosophy of language. Thus Epicurean ethical theory might appear to lack the more rigorous theoretical underpinnings of Stoic moral thought. At the same time, Epicurean methods of argument often appeal directly to moral beliefs and to emotional attitudes in ways that are foreign to most contemporary philosophers. Although this is characteristic of many ancient philosophical texts, the special stridency and rhetorical urgency of Epicurean ethical writing have often seemed better suited to clever propagandists than to philosophers interested in carefully fashioned arguments.

In the chapters that follow, I wish to demonstrate why such deflationary judgments about Epicurus' ethics mistake both the nature and the goals of his arguments. Structuring my account around his demand for invulnerability, I hope to show both the strengths and the limitations of a moral theory with this type of commitment. Such a focus allows us better to understand Epicurus' ethics and to see that he holds nuanced and defensible positions on a fairly wide range of ethical issues. This breadth becomes more readily apparent when one views his ethical doctrines in the larger context of ancient and modern ethical debates. Accordingly, in considering particular arguments, I generally proceed dialectically, measuring Epicurean doctrines against both their ancient and modern alternatives. This approach has been common and fruitful in the study of other areas of ancient ethics—especially Plato, Aristotle, and, more recently, the Stoics—but studies of Epicurus' ethics, at least in this respect, have fallen somewhat behind. In part, no doubt, this is because few have thought that his doctrines merit this kind of systematic, philosophical examination.

Although there have been good recent studies of particular problems in Epicurus' ethics, still the best and most concerted attempt to treat his ethical theory as a whole and rigorously to test its philosophical claims is J. M. Guyau's *La morale d'Epicure* (1886). Guyau was a convinced utilitarian, attempting to win converts to Bentham and Mill in France. Consequently, his account of Epicurus is both a spirited defense of a contemporary ethical option and a partisan tract written with particular philosophical objectives. Although few can claim to have achieved his sense of intellectual excitement in discussing Epicureanism, however, Guyau's account is marred at key junctures by serious anachronisms or doctrinal distortions. New work on the papyrological discoveries at Herculaneum, a greater awareness of the differences between ancient and modern ethical goals and methods of arguments, an increasing sense of the important role that particular rhetorical contexts play in ancient philosophical writings—all make possible a more complex and considerably more sophisticated account of Epicurus' ethical project.

My interpretive procedures are, I hope, easily recognizable and fairly straightforward. It will perhaps be helpful, however, to describe two features of my arguments in greater detail. In bringing Epicurean doctrines into dialectical confrontation with both ancient and modern alternatives, I clearly run two considerable risks. The first is more easily dealt with since, for the purposes of this study, I need only issue a brief disclaimer. I often argue that Epicurus' theory takes its shape by confronting certain philosophical options. For instance, his theory of friendship seems to display conflicting allegiances to egoism and to a richer, more vulnerable conception of human happiness that includes friendship as an essential component. We know that Aristotle and the Platonic Socrates defended different poles of this opposition, and it is illuminating to examine Epicurus' doctrines in the light of his predecessors' particular agreements and disagreements. This procedure is especially important because it helps to isolate elements in Epicurus' theory that are rooted in specifically Greek concerns and methods of argument. Nevertheless, this should not be taken to imply that I necessarily see any direct lines of philosophical influence emanating to Epicurus from specific precursors. Although his interest in philosophical polemics suggests that he had a wide acquaintance with Platonic and Aristotelian writings, a consensus about the extent of Epicurus' knowledge of Platonic and Peripatetic ethics has not begun to emerge, even after several detailed studies. Since my own aims are not strictly historical, I normally describe considerations that I take to be motivating Epicurus' theories as, say, "Aristotelian" or "akin to Aristotle's," if comparisons with Aristotle help to clarify the particular form of an Epicurean argument. Those who are more confident about Plato's or Aristotle's role in Hellenistic philosophy may view the positions I reconstruct as evidence of historical influence. Those who are more skeptical, however, need not view these positions as being tied to any particular historical figure. Clearly, it is possible that in Epicurus' discussion of altruism, for example, his worry about the proper place of friendship in the good life reflects and responds to a common tradition of Greek ethical speculation.

A second danger is less easily dealt with. By continually introducing contemporary ethical concerns and arguments into my discussion, I run a certain risk of anachronism. Contemporary accounts of altruism, moral obligation, and materialistic reduction, for example, often have distinct points of departure from those of ancient discussions and conceal different theoretical assumptions. But just as often, it is precisely the recognition of such differences that helps to isolate what is really distinctive and hence ultimately valuable in ancient discussions. Thus I have tried, whenever possible, to identify such theoretical divergences when introducing contemporary formulations into an ancient context. Nonetheless, I remain painfully aware of how easily the goal of balancing philosophical rigor with historical faithfulness eludes even the most accomplished interpreters of Greek thought. Since the main goal of this book is to help reclaim a more respected place for Epicurean theory in the history of Greek ethics, I perhaps can be excused for any anachronisms that tempt either more high-flying philosophers or more careful and informed historians to attend more seriously to Epicurus' ethics.

It will perhaps be useful at this point to sketch the main outlines of my argument. The first three chapters form a unit and present the main doctrines of Epicurean ethics thematically and in the same order followed by Cicero in the first book of *De finibus* (*On Ends*). I have done this partly because this book provides the most thorough and systematic presentation of Epicurean ethics surviving from antiquity but also because it offers a helpful and often extremely reliable theoretical backdrop for reconstructing and understanding the arguments that Epicurus actually used to support his ethical doctrines. Epicurus' surviving ethical writings consist of a few isolated sayings in such collections as his *Principal Doctrines* (*Kuriai doxai*) and the *Vatican Sayings* (*Gnomologium vaticanum*). In addition, there survives a brief, protreptic letter, *The Letter to Menoeceus* (*Epistola ad Menoeceum*), which summarizes in a general way many of his key ethical doctrines. Thus the interpreter of Epicurus' ethics is faced with only a few of his conclusions, with little in the way of supporting argument. Cicero's account often can help unite these isolated and fragmentary bits of evidence by enabling us to explain their wider, systematic connections. There are dangers in this procedure, of course, since Cicero sometimes can be a hostile or unsympathetic witness, especially when criticizing Epicureanism in *De finibus* II. It is no doubt this feature of the *De finibus* that has led some scholars to shy away from Cicero's testimony and to search elsewhere for help in reconstructing Epicurus' arguments. Unfortunately, there are few other places where one can plausibly look. Lucretius gives precious little information about Epicurean ethical doctrines or their supporting arguments, and other sources, if not even more overtly hostile than Cicero, give extremely little sustained, systematic exposition. Thus we are forced to turn to Cicero in search of evidence, and we must therefore come to terms as best we can with his philosophical vocabulary, methods of exposition, and general intellectual outlook. My discussion of the virtues (chapter 2) and friendship (chapter 3) relies heavily on Cicero's account, and the results of this reliance can perhaps be best assessed there.

I begin, however, with the difficult problem of Epicurean hedonism, arguing that we should resist the temptation of assimilating Epicurus' view of pleasure to some well-known modern versions. My main purpose in this chapter is to set his hedonism in its original intellectual context, that is, within the main traditions of Greek eudaemonist ethics. Epicurus analyzes pleasure not primarily as a subjective state of consciousness or mental event but rather as the overall healthy condition or functioning of a natural organism, because he is attempting to demonstrate how pleasure can serve as the objective, natural goal that structures our actions and consequently gives an overall unity and organization to our lives. This is the main role that happiness (*eudaimonia*) plays in Greek ethical theorizing, and by identifying pleasure with happiness, Epicurus tries to show how pleasure can fulfill this same function. Since much of this evidence can, and will continue to, be read in a variety of ways, I have little doubt that difficulties still remain with my overall account. This problem is especially obvious in those cases where I have been unable to tie up, even to my own satisfaction, all the loose ends of the surviving evidence. I have tried to indicate to readers, though, where bits of refractory evidence remain and to explain why there are some reasons for doubting my overall story. Nonetheless, I remain convinced that a coherent account of Epicurus' hedonism can begin to emerge only when scholarly approaches are shifted in some of the directions that I have suggested.

In the next two chapters, I turn to a series of problems that arise for all eudaemonist theorists in antiquity: the extent to which their theory of the final good can accommodate such other-directed elements as justice and friendship. For Epicurus, these problems arise in an especially acute form because of his commitment to invulnerability. In chapter 2, I analyze a tension in Epicurus' treatment of the virtues first as invulnerable psychic states and then, especially in the case of justice, as a set of external requirements that are formulable in rules. Epicurus' contribution on this topic is of particular contemporary relevance because it shows why agent-centered and rule-governed accounts of morality need not always be mutually exclusive.

In the next chapter, I turn to Epicurus' discussion of friendship and give an account of the competing tensions registered there. In describing such tensions, my intent is not to show that Epicurus is simply confused or that we can can thereby dismiss his views more easily; rather, I would argue that such tensions often are of great philosophical interest. I claim, for example, that Epicurus' account of friendship is an uneasy compromise between a strict egoism that would give individuals total control over the conditions of their happiness and a more complex view that includes altruism as an essential component in a good life. It is precisely his attempts to cope with these competing demands that make Epicurus' account philosophically challenging. In the same chapter, I also delineate the particular nuances of Epicurus' commitment to invulnerability and assess its effects on his conception of the good life.

A final chapter takes up the problems that Epicurus' atomism pose for his ethical theory. Two doctrines readily associated with atomism—namely, determinism and mechanism—might seem to threaten the Epicurean conception of individual autonomy and invulnerability. I begin by discussing the moral psychology and theory of voluntary action that underlie Epicurus' conception of invulnerability. A better appreciation of his thinking on these issues will show why some standard versions of indeterminism do not really fit his model of autonomous action. Moreover, a proper understanding of his nonreductionist materialism allows us to understand his reasons for thinking that his ethical doctrines not only are compatible with but, in fact, require his physical theories.

An earlier draft of this book concluded with a chapter on Epicurean attempts to combat the fear of death. Several readers have persuaded me that, although these issues are important, a general discussion of the ethical problems posed by death is not immediately pertinent to the particular argument of this book. I have restricted myself, therefore, to occasionally mentioning some of Epicurus' views on death in passing, especially in the footnotes. Readers interested in a more connected account may consult the admirable discussions either of A. A. Long and David Sedley in *The Hellenistic Philosophers* (Cambridge, 1987, pp. 149–54) or of David Furley, "Nothing to Us?" in *The Norms of Nature* (ed. M. Schofield and G. Striker, Cambridge, 1986, pp. 75–91). I venture some criticisms of their accounts in "Epicurus on Death and the Duration of Life," in *Proceedings of the Boston Area Colloquium on Ancient Philosophy*, vol. 4, ed. J. J. Cleary (Lanham, 1988), pp. 295–314, with a response by Gisela Striker.

One final note. Readers will quickly notice an inordinate number of footnotes, some of them quite lengthy, in comparison with the main body of the text. My justification is that I have tried to present the main lines of Epicurus' arguments as clearly as possible and to make them readily accessible to a nonspecialist audience. This approach has necessitated keeping discussions of scholarly controversies, textual problems, quotations from original texts, and so forth mostly in the notes. Without some such procedure, the discussion easily could have become completely bogged down in scholarly details of interest primarily to specialists.

1

Pleasure, Happiness, and Desire

Like most other Greek moralists,[1] Epicurus thinks that the central aims of an ethical theory are to describe the nature of happiness (*eudaimonia*) and to delineate the methods by which one achieves it (*ta poiounta tēn eudaimonian; Ad Menoeceum* 122). Perhaps the most important and certainly the most controversial feature of his ethical theory is his identification of pleasure (*hēdonē*) with our ultimate and final goal (*telos*), happiness (*eudaimonia*). By equating pleasure with happiness, Epicurus places his discussion of pleasure not only at the very center of his ethics but also squarely within the tradition of Greek ethical eudaemonism.[2] Many critics, both ancient and modern, have supposed that his entire ethical project stands or falls with his justification of pleasure as our *telos*. On the whole, this supposition is reasonable, since Epicurus tries to show how the content of morality, including friendship and altruism, can be derived from his analysis of pleasure. He manifestly believes, moreover, that he can justify a life of virtue by showing how it is inextricably linked to a life of pleasure.

At the same time, however, even Epicurus' most sympathetic

1. The Cyrenaics are an instructive exception, however (cf. D. L. II.87–88). They claim that happiness is desirable not for its own sake but for the sake of particular individual episodes of pleasure. Thus, happiness is not our final goal (*telos eudaimonias diapherein*). This claim poses interesting challenges for Epicurean hedonism, which I address in the last section of this chapter.

2. See G. Striker, "Epikur," in *Klassiker der Philosophie* I, ed. O. Höffe (Munich, 1981) pp. 108–14.

critics have been quick to admit that several obvious inconsistencies afflict his account of pleasure. Because Epicurus' attempts to formulate a coherent ethical system and thereby give plausible answers to central questions about happiness seem crippled from the outset, it is tempting to dismiss his ethical theory as a whole.[3] By sometimes denying that he even needs any arguments for showing that pleasure is the *telos* of every rational action (*De fin.* I.30), Epicurus seems merely to have aggravated and provided additional fuel for his critics' attacks. As Zeller complains, echoing a long tradition of obvious irritation, "No other system troubled itself so little about the foundations on which it rested."[4] If we are to believe his critics, then, Epicurus offers us obviously defective accounts of pleasure and happiness, without even so much as the courtesy of an argument.

Although it generally is agreed that Epicurus' claims about pleasure are mistaken, it is not at all clear exactly what conception of pleasure critics mean to ascribe to him. Following Guyau,[5] there has been a widespread tendency to assimilate the Epicurean account of pleasure to hedonist theories in the British empiricist tradition. These comparisons have not always been explicit, but scholars, however consciously, have often relied on this empiricist conception of pleasure in approaching Epicurean hedonism. Such comparisons can be fundamentally misleading, however, and consequently have skewed our picture of Epicurus' general theoretical aims.

3. See G. Bonelli, *Aporie etiche in Epicuro* (Brussels, 1979), for a recent and extreme statement of such a view.

4. E. Zeller, *Stoics, Epicureans, and Sceptics*, trans. Reichel (London, 1880), p. 418.

5. J. M. Guyau, *La morale d'Epicure et ses rapports avec les doctrines contemporaines* (Paris, 1886). Guyau's sense that his study of Epicurean ethics had an important role to play in discussions of the dominant systematic ethical doctrine of his day, utilitarianism, often gives his book an air of intellectual engagement and excitement that subsequent accounts have found difficult to match. Sometimes, though, he is too ready to see correspondences between Epicurus' ethical concerns and those of his contemporaries. I will argue that the divergences between Epicurus and modern hedonists are in many ways more revealing than the similarities. Cf. J. Annas, "Doing without Objective Values: Ancient and Modern Strategies," in *The Norms of Nature*, ed. M. Schofield and G. Striker (Cambridge, 1986), pp. 3–29, for discussion and a fruitful example of this type of methodological approach.

Recently, scholars have become increasingly cautious about glossing over or explaining away disparities in the aims and methods of ancient and modern moral philosophers. This interpretive caution has not only made possible impressive gains in our historical understanding but also has begun to clarify some characteristic goals and assumptions that differentiate ancient from contemporary moral theorists. Sometimes this has had a salutary effect on recent discussions of moral topics as well. For example, the recognition that ancient eudaemonism offers an important and distinctive alternative to modern teleological and deontological defenses of morality has reinvigorated contemporary treatments of moral psychology, the virtues, and problems of ethical justification.

In marked contrast, ancient discussions of pleasure have had, for the most part, an almost negligible influence on current thinking about pleasure. And this situation will no doubt remain until we begin to gain a better understanding of deeply rooted differences in ancient and modern methods of approaching the problem of pleasure. In any case, without a clearer understanding of these divergences there can be little reason to hope for an adequate appreciation of the distinctive philosophical aims and methods of ancient hedonism.

With respect to Epicureanism, we have many reasons to be wary of the anachronism of treating Epicurus as a somewhat crude forerunner of Locke, Bentham, or Sidgwick. Given the tenacity and prevalence of such comparisons, however, a few brief initial caveats may be in order. The British hedonists' view of pleasure depends on a series of interrelated claims in epistemology and the philosophy of mind that cannot confidently be attributed to Epicurus, or indeed to any ancient thinker. One crucial element in Sidgwick's[6] account of pleasure, for instance, is the Cartesian assumption that mental happenings are transparent states directly open to introspection. Descartes' particular picture of a private, inner mental life, when

---

6. In general, when speaking of the doctrines of British hedonism I refer to Sidgwick's formulations, since he gives the clearest account of classic utilitarian doctrine. His discussion is particularly useful because he thinks it is methodologically valuable to consider historically important alternatives to his views. See J. B. Schneewind, *Sidgwick's Ethics and Victorian Moral Philosophy* (Oxford, 1977), for further discussion.

combined with the view that pleasure itself is something mental, gives rise to Sidgwick's assumption that pleasure is a special, uniform, internal "feeling" directly open to our introspection.[7] Given these initial assumptions about pleasure, the hedonist's project becomes the fairly straightforward one of discovering which activities tend to maximize this feeling overall. For several reasons, however, the attribution of this type of hedonic project to Epicurus is problematic.

To begin with, it is worth noticing how this issue is often prematurely decided by translations that render *hēdonē* and *voluptas* as "the feeling of pleasure." Whereas speakers of English may be encouraged by such expressions as "I *feel* pleasure when doing x" to conceive of pleasures, at least initially,[8] as falling into a single class of uniform and commensurable feelings, speakers of Greek normally would have more difficulty viewing various pleasures as instances of a particular quality or type of "feeling."[9] This linguistic

7. See J. C. B. Gosling, *Pleasure and Desire* (Oxford, 1969), p. 52, for contemporary empiricist accounts of pleasure and their roots in the British hedonist tradition. M. F. Burnyeat has shown how dangerous it is to attribute this initial Cartesian claim to Greek thought as a whole ("Idealism and Greek Philosophy: What Descartes Saw and Berkeley Missed," *Philosophical Review* 91 [1982], 3–40). See W. Lyons, *The Disappearance of Introspection* (Cambridge, 1986), for discussion of the role that claims about introspection play in psychological theories and, consequently, moral psychologies.

8. T. Penelhum ("The Logic of Pleasure," *Philosophy and Phenomenological Research* 17 [1956–57], 488) suggests that we tend to take the noun 'pleasure' as the name of a private episode, analogous to a feeling. This is partly because 'pleasure,' like most nouns, suggests that there is some entity to which it refers. However, one need only think of Ryle's discussions of expressions such as 'enjoy,' 'like,' 'to be amused,' and so on to see how quickly this initial tendency becomes problematic (see G. Ryle, *Dilemmas* [Cambridge, 1954] pp. 54–67; "Pleasure," *Aristotelian Society Supplementary Volume* 28 [1954], 135–46).

9. Cf. Gosling, *Pleasure and Desire*, p. 24. I take up this linguistic issue in greater detail below and in my forthcoming commentary on *De finibus* I, II (ad loc. *De fin.* I.23). Of the modern translations of Epicurean texts that I have checked, every one uses "pleasure" and "the feeling of pleasure" interchangeably, with no apparent reasons from context. I claim here only that it is unclear that Epicurus considers pleasure a "feeling" in the sense required by hedonists like Sidgwick. Clearly, Epicurus thinks pleasure is a *pathos* (*Ad Men.* 129: *kai epi tautēn [hēdonēn] katantōmen hōs kanoni tōi pathei pan agathon krinontes*). But Greek philosophers use *pathos* for a wider range of states than can be plausibly characterized as "feelings" in Sidgwick's sense; see J. C. B. Gosling and C. C. W. Taylor, *The Greeks on Pleasure* (Oxford, 1982), p. 347. Cf. J. Brunschwig, "The Cradle Argument in Epicureanism and Stoicism," in

claim is complicated and clearly requires further argument. Nor would I want to argue that linguistic practices necessarily set inflexible limits to philosophical theorizing. But for the moment, by rendering *hēdonē* with a sufficiently neutral equivalent like "pleasure," we can perhaps avoid unfairly prejudicing the issue.[10] The importance of this will soon become apparent.

At *Ad Menoeceum* 128–29, Epicurus insists that pleasure is the *archē* and the *telos*, the beginning and the end, of the blessed life (*tou makariōs zēn*), because our pursuit of pleasure governs and unifies all of our rational choices and gives a structure to our lives as a whole. A bit earlier in the letter (*Ad Men.* 128), Epicurus had just claimed that the end (*telos*) belonging to the blessed life (*tou makariōs zēn*) consists in bodily health and tranquillity of mind (*ataraxia*). We do all things, he explains, to free ourselves from both physical pain and mental disturbance. This identification of *hēdonē* with freedom from pain and disturbance is Epicurus' most distinctive, though most problematic, claim about the nature of pleasure.[11] Most scholars have taken his assertion that *aponia* and *ataraxia* are the highest possible pleasures to be a clean contradiction or "a simple fraud";[12] others, perhaps more sympathetically, have found it symptomatic of an ambivalence in Epicurus' commitment to hedonism.[13] Sidgwick, aligning himself with the former group, im-

---

The Norms of Nature, ed. M. Schofield and G. Striker (Cambridge, 1986), p. 115, for a contrasting view about *pathē*.

10. P. Merlan, *Studies in Epicurus and Aristotle* (Wiesbaden, 1960), p. 1, claims that the Epicurean use of *hēdonē* is sui generis and warns that translations can be misleading. He then suggests, however, that the undisturbed condition of *ataraxia* is a state to which Epicureans idiosyncratically apply the term *hēdonē*, "the feeling of pleasure" (p. 2). See J. Mewaldt, *Epikur, Philosoph der Freude* (Stuttgart, 1949), for the claim that the German equivalent of Epicurus' *hēdonē* is *Freude*, and the defense of Merlan, who argues that Epicurus is not a philosopher of pleasure but a philosopher of joy (p. 15).

11. See Cicero, *Tusc. disp.* III.47: "At idem ait non crescere voluptatem dolore detracto summamque esse voluptatem nihil dolore." Cf. U. 419, and for criticism *De fin.* II.29–30.

12. Cicero at *De fin.* II.29–30 reflects the general reaction: "Quam haec sunt contraria!" See Gosling and Taylor, *The Greeks on Pleasure*, p. 350. Cf. Plato, *Republic* 583c–85a.

13. Cf. M. Hossenfelder, "Epicurus—Hedonist malgré lui," in *The Norms of Nature*, ed. M. Schofield and G. Striker (Cambridge, 1986), pp. 245–63, and his fuller account in *Die Philosophie der Antike 3: Stoa, Epikureismus, und Skepsis*, vol. 3 of

mediately dismissed this "paradox of Epicurus" for its obvious opposition "to common sense and common experience."[14] And indeed, given Sidgwick's conception of pleasure as a feeling that we are to maximize, such a charge would clearly seem justified.

Other Epicurean arguments are equally difficult to reconcile with this empiricist account of pleasure. Another conspicuous feature of Epicurus' theory, for example, is his attempt to demonstrate how pleasure can meet several formal requirements for happiness. Among Greek ethical theorists, disputes tend to arise not so much over there being such formal conditions or requirements, about which there is fairly widespread agreement; rather, disputes generally arise either about the relations among these formal requirements or about the contents that will satisfy them.[15] Accordingly, in order to show how pleasure can meet the formal requirements of a theory of happiness,[16] Epicurus claims that in pursuing pleasure as our final good (see *De fin.* I.29), we will be happy and, consequently, invulnerable to chance (*Ad Men.* 131a),[17] self-sufficient (*Ad Men.* 130; *SV* 44, 77), and in complete possession of all the goods necessary for fully satisfying our natures (*Ad Men.* 131a).[18] In sharp

---

Geschichte der Philosophie, ed. W. Röd (Munich, 1985). Hossenfelder argues that Epicurus adopts a eudaemonist ethical framework whose principles eventually pressure him into embracing hedonism as "a last resort." Epicurus, he claims, "would have preferred to be a Stoic" (p. 245). While I am sympathetic to Hossenfelder's attempt to show the importance of eudaemonist principles in Epicurean ethics, I doubt that Epicurus is a hedonist *malgré lui*. I will argue that Epicurus' theory of pleasure, properly understood, offers several plausible answers to the "eudaemonist problems" that Hossenfelder thinks Epicurus must solve.

14. H. Sidgwick, *The Methods of Ethics* (London, 1907), p. 125.

15. See T. H. Irwin, "Stoic and Aristotelian Conceptions of Happiness," in *The Norms of Nature*, ed. M. Schofield and G. Striker (Cambridge, 1986), p. 206, for a discussion of these formal conditions. In what follows, I am greatly indebted to his account. See also Domenico Pesce, *Saggio su Epicuro* (Bari and Rome, 1974), p. 69, and *De fin.* I.29: "quod omnium philosophorum sententia tale debet esse ut ad id omnia referri oporteat."

16. Epicurus' theory is not nearly as explicit as Aristotle's about the relations among (or, for that matter, even the necessity of satisfying) these formal criteria. Indeed, he sometimes denies the need for any justification at all of his claims about the *telos*. Yet these formal conditions appear prominently throughout his discussions of pleasure, and he certainly relies on such considerations when identifying happiness with *hēdonē*.

17. I discuss in greater detail the evidence for this requirement in chapter 3.

18. Aristotle gives an account of these formal criteria at *EN* 1097a15, except

contrast, any attempt to fill this kind of formal inventory would seem distinctly odd to Hobbes, Locke, and their successors.[19] Hedonists of this stripe would argue that individuals attempting to maximize and intensify a particular feeling of pleasure may have good hedonic reasons for rejecting all such formal constraints. In their view, the intensity of particular episodes of pleasure might easily outweigh in overall hedonic benefit the fact that they threaten an individual's self-sufficiency or leave one vulnerable to forces outside of one's own control. Similarly, in applying this hedonic strategy to the conduct of our life as a whole, they might claim that a few years of enjoying such intense episodes could easily outweigh the risks of living either an incomplete or a dependent life overall.[20]

If the way that we take our pleasures is strictly a subjective matter, as it evidently appears to be for adherents of this theory, Epicurean attempts to give us a surefire recipe for happiness might seem amusingly and misguidedly pedantic. By claiming to have discovered those needs and desires that are *natural* for all of us as properly functioning human beings to satisfy (*Ad Men.* 127; *KD* 29; *SV* 21), Epicurus would appear to these hedonists merely to be making an

---

for the requirement that our happiness be up to us. Voluntariness is clearly an important condition for him as well, but the voluntariness of happiness is not strictly an independent formal requirement for Aristotle, since it must be adjusted and made compatible with completeness—that is, some goods necessary for our happiness may not be entirely under our own control. For the Epicurean, in contrast, happiness must be entirely within our control as well as complete (cf. *Ad Men.* 122). J. Annas examines the importance of completeness as a formal constraint for Epicurean happiness in "Epicurus on Pleasure and Happiness," *Philosophical Topics* 16 (1987), 5–21. She convincingly demonstrates how this demand for completeness pressures Epicurus in the direction of admitting nonhedonic values into his account of the final good.

19. An interesting exception is Mill, who gets into trouble trying to formulate his principle of utility precisely because he feels the need to account for several of these formal conditions. This point is brought out well by Annas, "Epicurus on Pleasure and Happiness"; for further discussion of the difficulties that these formal requirements present for both Mill and Epicurus, see chapter 3: Friendship, Happiness, and Invulnerability.

20. Such a view is closer to that of the Cyrenaics (D. L. II.87), who argue that happiness is desired not for its own sake but for the individual pleasures that it contains. The Epicurean, in showing that pleasure can meet the requirements for a theory of happiness, tries to argue that pleasure can serve to structure a whole life rationally. On such a view, pleasure, like happiness, must be stable, permanent, and with fixed limits; cf. Hossenfelder, "Epicurus—Hedonist malgré lui."

illegitimate attempt to bolster his idiosyncratic view of pleasure.[21] Thus, the Epicurean appeal to nature[22] by way of the formal conditions of happiness can hold few, if any, attractions for proponents of a Benthamite felicific calculus.

Given these manifest differences in aim and method, as well as the high degree of implausibility of central Epicurean doctrines in the context of British empirical hedonism, I want to suggest a more oblique approach to Epicurus' theory of pleasure. If we begin by assuming that Epicurus takes *hēdonē* to be a readily identifiable feeling that individuals can measure introspectively and then attempt to maximize, we no doubt will find his theory confused and disappointing. If we try to sort out the distinctive features of Epicurus' theory and examine them within the larger framework of Greek eudaemonism,[23] however, we will find that his account of pleasure merits more sympathetic consideration.[24] And since his

21. For attempts to make a similar move without appealing to nature, see J. Griffin's account of 'informed desires' and his objections (*Well-Being: Its Meaning, Measurement, and Moral Importance* [Oxford, 1986], pp. 11–17).

22. It is instructive to compare Sidgwick's hostility to this procedure: "How then are we to distinguish 'natural impulses'—in the sense in which they are to guide rational choice—from the unnatural? Those who have occupied themselves with this distinction seem generally to have interpreted the Natural to mean either the *common* as opposed to the rare or exceptional, or the *original* as opposed to what is later in development; . . . But I have never seen any ground for assuming broadly that Nature abhors the exceptional, or prefers the earlier time to the later" (p. 81). For a subtle and important discussion of the interplay of these two claims in Epicurus's theory of pleasure, see Brunschwig, "The Cradle Argument." G. Arrighetti discusses the epistemological dimension of this Epicurean appeal to nature and shows how it is meant to combat skepticism about the *telos* of action ("Devoir et plaisir chez Epicure," in *Proceedings of the VIIth Congress of the International Federation of the Societies of Classical Studies*, ed. J. Harmatta [Budapest, 1984], p. 386).

23. Here it is important to remember that within the context of Greek ethical thought, Epicurus cannot merely assume that pleasure and happiness are identical (cf. G. Vlastos, "Happiness and Justice in the *Republic*," in *Platonic Studies* [Princeton, 1973], p. 111). For British hedonists this connection seems much more obvious, and they can identify happiness and pleasure almost without argument (see R. Brandt, *Encyclopedia of Philosophy*, "Happiness"; Sidgwick, p. 405). See G. Vlastos, "Happiness and Virtue in Socrates' Moral Theory," *Proceedings of the Cambridge Philological Society* 30 (1984),181, for an important discussion of the respective meanings of 'happiness' and *eudaimonia*; also, M. Ring, "Aristotle and the Concept of Happiness," in *The Greeks and the Good Life*, ed. D. Depew (Fullerton, Calif., 1980), pp. 69–71.

24. That is, it merits consideration not only because of his attempt to meet the formal demands of eudaemonism but also because his theory of pleasure offers some plausible answers to questions about the content of happiness.

analysis of pleasure plays a crucial role in the rest of his ethical theory, it may be possible, as I will argue in later chapters, to attribute to him more nuanced accounts of the virtues, of altruism, and of human action in general.

Pleasure, Feelings, and the Satisfaction of Desire

At this point, it might be helpful to distinguish two contrasting theoretical approaches to problems of pleasure and of hedonistic explanation. Since it is fairly common to find elements from both theories conflated in discussions of Epicureanism, a brief, though inevitably somewhat schematic, overview of the diverging commitments of these two approaches may prove useful.

As a rough preliminary, we might broadly distinguish dispositional accounts of pleasure from theories that treat pleasure as a special type of private episode or feeling. The latter view, held in various forms by the British hedonists, rests on two fundamental assumptions about pleasure. It holds, first, that pleasure is a particular feeling whose presence can be verified by introspection, and second, that pleasant sensations are more or less similar in kind, although they may differ in intensity or duration. As a consequence, pleasures can be ranked on a uniform scale, and our pursuit of pleasure involves the relatively uncomplicated procedure[25] of testing various pursuits and activities to discover which produce the greatest levels of intensity and duration of this feeling overall.

Since pleasure is separable from the activities that give rise to it, the pleasantness of a feeling can be assessed ultimately only by the individual experiencing the feeling. Agents may make mistakes about the overall hedonic value of a present, occurrent feeling, of course, since when estimating its strength they must compare it with other feelings that they are no longer experiencing. As Sidgwick remarks, "in so far as any estimate of pleasantness involves comparison with feelings only represented in idea, it is liable to be erroneous through imperfections in the representation—still, no

25. That is, *theoretically* uncomplicated. This procedure may conceal considerable difficulties in practice.

one is in a position to controvert the preference of the sentient individual, so far as the quality of the present feeling alone is concerned."[26] In this view, then, pleasure is essentially subjective and separable from its sources.

In contrast to the empiricist view, dispositional theories treat pleasure not as an immediately felt quality but as the realization of a perceived good or the satisfaction of a desire.[27] Proponents of this kind of motivational analysis, familiar from Aristotle, tend to focus more intently on the question of whether a particular desire is satisfied.[28] If I have been hungry and thirsty, but then am able to satisfy my desires for food and drink, I will find my present condition a pleasant one to the extent that I have managed to satisfy these desires. Similarly, if all of my desires have been completely satisfied, I will be in a state of pleasant satisfaction overall.

A further moral sometimes is drawn here. If a certain desire cannot be satisfied, either in principle (such as a desire to live in a past century) or as a matter of contingent empirical fact (say, because of the scarcity of a desired good), then the desire itself is to be viewed as frustrating and painful. Or if each attempt at satisfying a desire—for example, the desire for tobacco or cocaine—merely provokes a stronger craving, then these particular kinds of addictive desires are not for genuinely pleasurable activities.

This outlook on desires indicates another difference between these two theories in matters of hedonic strategy. Hedonists pursuing the intensity of a particular feeling might try to strengthen

26. Sidgwick, p. 128. Cf. Gosling and Taylor, pp. 347–48, for the ascription to Epicurus of a similar conception of the incorrigibility of judgments about the pleasantness of occurrent states. See Ryle, *Dilemmas* (Cambridge, 1954), p. 58, for criticism of this general claim.

27. See Gosling, *Pleasure and Desire*, chs. 2, 3, and 10, for a much more detailed and nuanced treatment of these issues. I am greatly indebted to his discussion in what follows.

28. This is by no means the case for all dispositionalist theories, however. Some, for instance, might focus exclusively on the manner in which a particular desire is being satisfied. I should emphasize that I am giving an account of only one possible version of the dispositionalist theory, because of its special relevance to Epicurean concerns. Nonetheless, I think this contrast between empirical and motivational views of pleasure, however broadly drawn, offers a useful backdrop for examining Epicurus' theory.

their desires or cravings in order to yield higher degrees of this pleasurable feeling.[29] They might even cultivate desires that are in principle unsatisfiable in order to experience individual intense episodes of a particular feeling. Dispositional theorists, on the other hand, generally avoid claiming that the intensity of a pleasurable feeling can serve as a criterion to rank pleasures. This reluctance is due to their disinclination to think of pleasures as essentially similar in kind or measurable on a uniform scale. Satisfaction, not degrees of intensity, serves as their criterion for assessing the pleasures of different activities. A necessary first step for those pursuing a pleasant life overall will consequently be to foster the types of desires that will be satisfiable. Moreover, agents must structure and coherently order their desires to ensure that none remains unsatisfied and that no particular group of desires will be mutually frustrating.

For the dispositionalist, finding procedures for ranking various pleasures becomes more problematic. The empiricist relies on the claim that all activities give rise to a separable, kindred quality of feeling over and above activities themselves. Dispositional theories, however, reject the possibility of separating pleasure from activities in this way. It sounds oddly implausible, they would argue, to suggest to someone who, for example, plays the piano for pleasure that she can get *that* pleasure in some other way without having to bother with the playing.[30] The dispositionalist argues that doing something for pleasure is doing it for itself; one cannot merely 'take pleasure,' one must take pleasure in *something* (cf. Aristotle, *EN* 1175a11, 1175a21–b1). Conceived of in this way, pleasure is not a feeling over and above an activity; it is some further description of the manner in which someone realizes a perceived good, engages in an activity, or perhaps attends to that activity.[31]

29. Cf. Aristotle *EN* 1154b4 for an example of this kind of strategy (*autoi goun autois dipsas tines paraskeuazousin*).

30. This example is adapted from Penelhum's discussion of Ryle in "The Logic of Pleasure," *Philosophy and Phenomenological Research* 17 (1956–57), 489.

31. For further discussion, see W. B. Gallie, "Pleasure," *Aristotelian Society Supplementary Volume* 28 (1954), 147–64; for important criticism, see U. T. Place, "The Concept of Heed," in *Essays in Philosophical Psychology*, ed. D. Gustafson (New York, 1964), pp. 206 ff.

It is important to notice, however, that the word 'pleasure' no longer seems to be strictly univocal in the context of this theory.[32] Accordingly, if we are urged to pursue pleasure as our final goal, it becomes difficult to see just how we are meant to follow such advice. Without a separable, measurable criterion, it becomes appreciably harder on the basis of hedonic criteria alone to rank our pleasures or satisfactions. On what purely hedonic grounds, for example, are we to compare the satisfactions of walking, or playing the piano, or reading Homer, or sipping coffee, once we have been deprived of the empiricist's handy yardstick? Not surprisingly, many philosophers who have held dispositional theories of pleasure have not been hedonists, since such theories make it difficult to explain our rational preferences solely on the basis of the hedonic quality of activities. Because we lack a common hedonic measure, they argue, we need to turn to other values and beliefs about the good in search of standards to explain and rationally to ground our actions.

One last distinction must be made before we can turn to Epicurus' theory. The claim that pleasure consists in the satisfaction of a desire or the realization of a good may conceal, as Aristotle noticed, three alternative conceptions of the good that is being realized:

(a) Pleasure is the attainment of what *seems* good to x.
(b) Pleasure is the attainment of what *is* good for x, though perhaps not for others.
(c) Pleasure is the attainment of what *is* good, *simpliciter*.[33]

Introspection, for the most part,[34] might determine whether we

---

32. Gosling, *Pleasure and Desire*, p. 55. Cf. Aristotle *EN* 1153a13–16.

33. Cf. Aristotle *EN* 1152b26–35 for these distinctions and a defense of his own view at 1175a21–22.

34. The Epicurean conception of 'natural and necessary desires' leads to further ambiguities in this context. It is not always clear that we are consciously aware of whether these 'desires' are satisfied. I may, for instance, be eating too much rich food without realizing it. In such a case, introspection will only tell me when an 'unnecessary' desire is satisfied. Epicurus' notion of individuals' having 'natural and necessary desires' that are not immediately open to introspection (at least for agents with corrupt beliefs) may seem to lead him in a Freudian direction. Thus, some have seen an appeal to unconscious desires and motivations in Lucretius' account of the fear of death. The extent to which Epicureans are prepared to extend such

have a particular desire and whether it is at present satisfied.[35] But we cannot decide solely from introspection whether we have desires that are good for us or, indeed, desires that are good *simpliciter*. These two objectivist claims clearly need a further defence not based solely on the evidence of our personal introspection. It is not always clear, however, which, if any, of these alternatives Epicurus' critics think he is committed to defending. We must therefore keep these three possibilities in the foreground to see the role that subjective and objective criteria are playing in Epicurus' arguments.[36]

With these preliminary distinctions in mind, we are now in a position to turn to Epicurus' discussion. I begin by examining a few key doctrines that have seemed to offer the most straightforward evidence that Epicurus treats pleasure as a uniform, introspectible feeling. A central feature of the empiricist account, for instance, is the possibility of determining a hedonic calculus that can rank pleasures on a measurable scale of feeling. It is often supposed that when Epicurus urges us to compare the outcomes of various activities and to choose the most pleasurable one overall, he must be relying on similar assumptions about pleasure and the possibility of a determinate hedonic calculus.

While it is no doubt true that Epicurus is committed to evaluating and ranking pleasures,[37] evidence for the actual mechanics of his particular calculus seems extraordinarily slim, even by Epicurean standards. We may be somewhat relieved that Epicurus avoids the obsessive categorization and classification of 'pleasure-making fea-

---

notions as desire, intention, or wish in a Freudian manner is problematic, however. Such desires may be 'unnoticed,' but it is misleading in an Epicurean context·to call them unconscious, if that is taken to imply that the unconscious corresponds to some special entity with its own explanatory principles. For purposes of the present discussion, I will try to clearly indicate when I am using 'desire' in a subjective or objective sense.

35. I may know by introspection whether my desire for tobacco is for the moment satisfied, but I do not know purely on the basis of introspective evidence whether it is, in principle, satisfiable.

36. For a general discussion of these alternatives, see R. Kraut, "Two Conceptions of Happiness," *Philosophical Review* 88 (1979), 167–97.

37. When we talk of ranking 'pleasures,' we may mean (a) sensations or (b) pleasurable activities. See chapter 3 for a discussion of the problems for Epicurus' account of friendship caused by conflating these two senses. I will argue that Epicurus thinks that ranking pleasures primarily involves (b), whereas British hedonists appeal to (a).

tures' that characterize a theory like Bentham's. At the same time, however, Epicurus tends to pass over, or at least downplay in very odd ways, what we might reasonably think are obvious and important candidates for ranking pleasures. Both duration and intensity, for instance, receive treatments that are hard to square with standard empiricist accounts. Epicurus asserts that the duration of pleasure is not ultimately important in any rational assessment of the overall pleasantness of our lives.[38] At *Kuriai doxai* 19, he claims that "Infinite time and finite time contain equal pleasure [*isēn hēdonēn*], if one measures its limits by reasoning" (cf. *De fin.* I.63). If we understand and achieve the rational limits of pleasure, he argues further, there is no reason to suppose that death subtracts anything at all from the best life (*ti tou aristou biou;* cf. *KD* 20).

Cicero takes Epicurus in these passages to be manifestly, though wrongly, denying that pleasure is increased by duration (*voluptatem crescere longinquitate*) or rendered more valuable by its continuance (*De fin.* II.88). He complains that nothing, in fact, could be more at odds with hedonism than the claim that death involves no loss or deprivation of hedonic goods. If pleasurable states make us happy, he argues, surely we will be happier if we can maintain these states longer. Epicurus' remark about duration at *KD* 19 certainly has a paradoxical quality, and we might think it merely a weak and ad hoc attempt to defend his rather extreme claim about death's

38. Cf. *De fin.* II.87–88. Gosling and Taylor find this claim about duration puzzling (p. 358) and attempt a solution based on the *Philebus* doctrine of mixed and unmixed pleasures. In their view, Epicurus can maintain his claim about duration if he means that we cannot compare the pleasantness of "two periods of unmixed pleasure," whatever their differences in length. They conclude that it is only in the "fanciful utopian conditions" of unmixed pleasure that we will not be concerned with duration. "In actual practice," they argue, "it will surely still be true that a wise man will always be concerned with increasing the proportion of pleasure in his life." It seems to me, however, that not only is there no evidence that Epicurus restricts his denial of the value of duration to "fanciful utopian conditions," but also it begs the question to claim that the wise man will always be concerned with increasing his proportion of pleasure, if by increase we merely mean duration. Conceptions of what an 'increase' in pleasure means depend on a whole range of theoretical commitments, not all of which must take duration as the primary element in increasing pleasure. Moreover, Epicurus' claim about duration is a crucial prop for his argument against the fear of death, which must be eliminated "in actual practice," not just in "utopian conditions."

inability to harm a pleasant life.[39] We may be tempted to conclude, therefore, that theoretical pressures external to his theory of pleasure are responsible for this odd remark, a remark apparently inconsistent with standard empiricist views of the hedonic calculus.

Another way of resisting Cicero's interpretation might be to take Epicurus' claim about equal pleasure (*isēn hēdonēn*) as a reference not to equal quantities but to equal levels of pleasure.[40] In this view, Epicurus does not say that duration has no bearing at all in assessments of pleasure; rather, he might be asserting merely that we can experience the same level of pleasure in a finite as in an infinite time. No particular complete experience of pleasure, he argues, can ever be intensified beyond certain limits (*KD* 18), even if it were to be repeated an infinite number of times. No matter how many times we enjoy a particular pleasure, each of our individual experiences will never exceed a certain level of intensity. Nonetheless, on such a reading, calculations of duration within a lifetime will still be important for Epicureans in rationally measuring and assessing pleasures; for example, they will want to maximize their pleasurable experiences and enjoy them for longer rather than for shorter periods of time.

There are two difficulties, however, with this attempt to soften the contradictions that Cicero finds in Epicurus' claims about duration. First and most important, it leaves the Epicurean without a leg to stand on in claiming that death in no way diminishes the complete happiness of mortals (*KD* 20, *DRN* III.830). If the duration of pleasure matters within a lifetime,[41] death obviously can harm us by cutting short our pleasures or by robbing us of them entirely; as a consequence, we would have a rational justification

---

39. For this view, see D. Furley, "Nothing to Us?" in *The Norms of Nature*, ed. M. Schofield and G. Striker (Cambridge, 1986), p. 81.

40. I am indebted to D. Sedley for suggesting this possible interpretation to me. For further defense see now A. A. Long and D. Sedley, *The Hellenistic Philosophers*, vol. 1 (Cambridge, 1987).

41. Epicurus tends to treat individual pleasures as well in terms of their completeness, hence giving a qualitative as opposed to a quantitative account of pleasures. By way of comparison, it is interesting to note that Aristotle too, in his discussion of completeness in the *Metaphysics*, tends to downplay duration in favor of a qualitative account (*Meta.* 1021b13–14).

for fearing it.[42] But this conclusion is something that the Epicurean can in no way allow. Second, if in pursuing pleasures we are attempting to maximize a particular uniform feeling, it is hard to see the point of Epicurus' comparison at *KD* 19, if he is asserting merely that a comparable quality of feeling arises in a finite or infinite time. If pleasure always consists of the same feeling or phenomenological condition, an individual experience of pleasure will consist of the same feeling whenever it happens to occur. Nor on such a view would it make sense for Epicurus to claim that our experiences of pleasure will feel the same only if we "measure the limits of pleasure by reasoning." If he is just comparing our pleasures in terms of their quality of tone or sensation, there would be no justification for adding this further qualification.

There seem to be no very strong reasons, therefore, for doubting Cicero's interpretation of Epicurus' claims about duration. Cicero registers another complaint, moreover, that seems to be justified by the surviving evidence. He objects to an asymmetry in Epicurus' treatment of pleasure and pain (*De fin.* II.88), since the Epicurean panacea against pain—namely, that acute pains last only for a short time (*KD* 4)—must rely on duration as an important criterion in assessing pains (*Ad Men.* 129: *polun chronon hupomeinasi*). If Epicurus, in the manner of an empiricist, were committed to treating pleasure and pain as contrary ends of a uniform scale, this would indeed be

---

42. See Lucretius, *DRN* III. 830–977, for some attempts to show that duration does not affect the overall pleasure of a life. Perhaps the most interesting is the so-called asymmetry argument at 972–77, where Lucretius raises the problem of the apparent asymmetry in our attitudes toward our death and our prenatal nonexistence. Most of us find it painful to think about our death and its deprivations, but we seem completely unconcerned about our previous nonexistence and its deprivations. Lucretius connects these asymmetrical attitudes to the past and future with our views about the duration of our lives in general, his argument being that if we are indifferent to the possibility of our life extending temporally in the past, it seems irrational to have any special concern about the possibility of persisting into the future. Thus our common attitudes seem to indicate that we have no specific rational attachment to our duration per se; otherwise, we would care just as strongly about our prenatal losses and deprivations. But if we have no concern about duration for its own sake, the Epicurean has an important supporting argument for showing that duration is of no special importance in assessing the overall pleasantness of lives. There are problems with Lucretius' argument, but it demonstrates that Epicureans are concerned with defending the stronger claim about duration that Cicero ascribes to them.

a serious objection. Epicurus' account of the intensity of pleasure seems to harbor a corresponding difficulty. Epicurus denies that pleasures vary, in one crucial respect, with regard to their intensity.[43] If I am thirsty and may satisfy my thirst either with brackish water or with some more appetizing drink, neither alternative, according to Epicurus, can be more intensely pleasurable, because whenever a pain is removed or a desire is satisfied, the pleasure of the resultant state cannot vary in intensity. We might argue, of course, that Epicurus' account of the alleviation of pain or distress will require some notion of variable intensity.[44]

If Epicurus holds that decreasing pain is equivalent to increasing pleasure, we would expect him to distinguish increasing and decreasing levels of intensity. As in the case of duration, however, it is hard to find any explicit evidence for this important canon of the empiricist's view of pleasure. Epicurus mentions that the removal of pain is followed by a state of pleasure (KD 3, 18; De fin. I.37), but he conspicuously fails to describe this change in terms of increasing and decreasing levels of intensity.[45] Rather, he describes pleasure and pain as two successive, contradictory states, without explicitly claiming that transitions between these two states will consist of variable intensities of a particular feeling. We might think that any plausible conception of a hedonic calculus will require discriminations of intensity and duration, but given such ambiguous indications in the surviving evidence, we should refrain from ascribing these empiricist assumptions to Epicurus without stronger justification.

If we look for evidence about the actual operations of the Epicurean calculus, we again are confronted with difficulties. Cicero's

43. At *Ad Men.* 131 Epicurus says that bread and water give *akrotatēn hēdonēn*. This is often translated as the "highest or most intense pleasure," and talk about intensity might ostensibly commit Epicurus to an empiricist view. Epicurus is concerned with the limits of pleasure (*Ad Men.* 133), however, and *akrotatēn* is better rendered with this in mind. Epicurus is claiming that by satisfying our hunger with bread and water, we reach the limit of pleasure, that is, complete satisfaction (D. L. X.121; cf. Bailey, *Incert. Ep. Frag.* 37, *KD* 3, 18).

44. Again, I owe this objection to D. Sedley.

45. Cf. Hossenfelder, "Epicurus," p. 255, for a different interpretation. He cites *KD* 18 for evidence that Epicurus conceives of "one and the same emotion that only varies occasionally in intensity"; this seems to me to go beyond the evidence, however.

various accounts of Epicurean criteria for ranking pleasures (*De fin.* I.32–33, 48) are all as disappointingly vague as Epicurus' own statement at *Ad Menoeceum* 130 ff.[46] There Epicurus merely suggests that it is "by means of a comparison [*summetrēsi*] and survey [*blepsei*] of advantages and disadvantages that we must judge [*krinein*]" matters of pleasure. The very generality of this passage's procedural recommendations, however, not only fails to commit him to anything so specific as the empiricist's theory of pleasure's measurable uniformity[47] but perhaps should also alert us to the possibility that Epicurus may be operating with an alternative conception of pleasure. His talk about comparing advantages against disadvantages might fit a dispositionalist view of pleasure just as well, if we take him to be arguing only that we should weigh the advantages of certain desires, pursuits, and activities.

The dispositionalist can deny that we are able to measure pleasure as a uniform feeling, yet still think it important to weigh the advantages and disadvantages of cultivating various desires. If, for example, I know that by cultivating a desire for cocaine I will be developing an addictive desire that will grow stronger, I can decide that it would be advantageous for me not to do so. That is, I can compare—without recourse to the empiricists' particular conception of pleasure—the hedonic advantages of having satisfiable desires with the disadvantages of having unsatisfiable desires.[48]

The empiricist might claim at this point that such a view still would leave unresolved the problem of ranking various satisfiable

46. This holds true for other doxographic reports as well. Cf. U. 440–45; also, Diogenes of Oenoanda 38.1.8 on the difficulty of comparing mental and bodily pleasures, and his vague statement about how the wise are able to manage such a comparison.

47. Nor does *KD* 9 give evidence for the uniformity of pleasure in this required sense. The present unfulfilled conditional is often used by Epicurus to deny the possibility of what is being asserted. And in any case, this claim would not commit him to an empiricist account; it might easily be taken as a reference to the equal value of katastematic pleasures, not their measurable uniformity on a common scale of feeling (cf. Gosling and Taylor, pp. 378–82, for an opposing view).

48. It perhaps should be noted that someone may have two satisfiable desires that taken together will conflict; or perhaps we might have a desire whose strength varies over time. The hedonic art will consist not just in evaluating particular desires but in ordering one's desires into a coherent whole, taking into account individual relative importance and their mutual relations.

desires in order to insure that we foster only those that have the greatest hedonic rewards. Even if we can roughly divide satisfiable from unsatisfiable desires without relying on the empiricist's measure, however, it might be argued that there still would be important hedonic differences among the remaining satisfiable desires. Would we not therefore require a more sensitive and fine-grained calculus to make these sorts of rankings? Whatever the plausibility of this empiricist objection, it does not seem to be one that would move Epicurus, and the reasons for his indifference again suggest that he may be approaching the calculus with a different conception of pleasure.

Epicurus broadly characterizes our natural and necessary desires as those which are easily satisfiable. Moreover, he claims that our proper attitude toward the various means or processes of satisfying these desires is one of complete indifference. If either white bread or brown bread will satisfy our hunger and both are readily available, Epicurus thinks that we have no hedonic justification[49] for choosing one over the other. Empiricists might insist, of course, that it is precisely when we are faced with these kinds of detailed choices that we need the precision of their calculus to help us maximize our pleasure. But, again, that Epicurus does not seem to be interested in such fine-grained and discriminating calculations suggests that his interests in the calculus as well as his view of pleasure may be very different.

Gosling and Taylor offer another reason for Epicurus' apparent lack of interest in more intricate hedonic calculation.[50] They claim that he is influenced by what has come to be a perennial objection

49. For this claim, Epicurus relies on his distinction between kinetic and katastematic pleasures. If neither of two choices jeopardizes my katastematic state, it does not matter which I choose, since they are equally good choices. One factor that cannot help rationally to guide my choice, however, is a preference for the different kinetic pleasures of eating white and brown bread. If I become attached to the pleasures of white bread and slowly learn to despise brown bread, I will be in danger of forgetting that the most complete pleasure consists in not being hungry. If Epicurus allowed kinetic pleasures to be of any rational concern whatsoever, someone might choose a katastematically harmful activity if it were accompanied by great amounts of the requisite kinetic pleasure. But Epicurus denies that we ever could have reason to do so. I take up these issues in more detail below, in "Kinetic and Kastatematic Pleasures."

50. Gosling and Taylor, pp. 359–60.

against utilitarianism: that constant attention to the details of hedonic reckoning will become a source of painful anxiety. That is,
if we continually concentrate on maximizing our pleasures in all
the minute dealings of our daily lives, we will quickly acquire the
habits and dispositions of somewhat obsessive, anxious, and myopic
accountants; our pleasures will slip through our fingers unenjoyed
as we nervously busy ourselves over our calculations.

The problem with their attempted solution, however, is that Epicurus insists that we must scrutinize every choice (*Ad Men.* 132)
and every desire (*SV* 71) at all times (*KD* 25) to make sure that
every one (*Ad Men.* 128) leads to our final goal, pleasure.[51] Epicurus
manifestly recommends the kind of continual attention to our choices
and desires that Gosling and Taylor find objectionable. He thinks
that paying meticulous attention to our desires not only fails to
cause anxiety but will actually reward us with a heightened sense
of self-sufficiency and a quiet confidence in our immunity from
fortune (*Ad Men.* 132). Similarly, only by properly monitoring our
desires will we make our pleasures complete (U. 417–22). Thus,
giving careful attention to our desires not only helps to insure that
they will be satisfied but apparently aids us in meeting the formal
conditions of happiness as well.

At the same time, however, Epicurus' interests in the calculus
seem to extend only to a few key criteria. Two of these might be
derived from or, perhaps, might be compatible with a dispositionalist theory of pleasure. Like the dispositionalist, Epicurus asks
whether a particular desire is satisfied and whether it will remain
satisfiable. On the other hand, although not strictly incompatible
with a dispositionalist theory, his other central questions about pleasures—"Will they expose me to fortune?" "Will they maintain or
threaten my self-sufficiency?" "Are they complete with respect to
their satisfactions?"—all would appear to be derived independently
from the formal requirements for happiness.[52] Epicurus thus avoids

51. It might be argued that Epicurus means only that we should evaluate every
action type, not every individual token in passages such as *Ad Men.* 132 and *SV* 71.
However, *KD* 25 and especially *Ad Men.* 128 suggest a strong concern with every
individual choice.

52. Similarly, whereas contemporary critics of hedonism might dispute the possibility of discovering and coherently using such a calculus, the criticisms offered

an intricate empiricist calculus, not because he views it as a source of possible anxiety, but because it relies on the wrong criteria to evaluate pleasures. For him, the proper criteria must be derived from these general eudaemonist conditions. Consequently, the Epicurean calculus does not give rise to detailed Benthamite calculations based on intensity, duration, and so forth, although it still will obviously require constant and careful application at this more general level.

The empiricist might complain at this point that the Epicurean calculus is not exacting enough to ensure that we will maximize our individual experiences of pleasure. But the Epicurean can answer that any pleasures[53] that register and are measurable on the empiricist's calculus alone will not meet the formal requirements for happiness; therefore, such pleasures are a matter of indifference.

Given these diverging approaches to the problems of the calculus, I think we now have at least some initial reasons to suspect that Epicurus' theory of pleasure has its own distinctive theoretical preoccupations that can cut across standard empiricist and dispositional theories in important ways. His appeal to formal requirements for happiness, for instance, would appear equally foreign to contemporary empiricists and dispositionalists alike. At the same time, comparisons of his theory to British hedonism clearly seem misguided, since Epicurus has, if anything, much more in common with certain forms of dispositionalism. Like the dispositionalist, he regularly equates pleasure with the satisfaction of desire and pain with the frustration of desires (*Ad Men.* 128, 130b; *SV* 33; see also *KD* 18 and *Ad Men.* 130–31 for the expression *to kat' endeian algoun*; Scholion, *KD* 29; *De fin.* II.9). Similarly, in assessing pleasures he focuses on activities and desires rather than on accompanying sensations (*Ad Men.* 132a; *SV* 78; *De fin.* I.55; *De abstin.* I.51)[54]. He also

---

by Epicurus' opponents reflect a concern with formal eudaemonist requirements. Cicero, for instance, argues that if pleasure is our final good our happiness will not be invulnerable (*De fin.* II.86), complete (*De fin.* II.38–44, 86, 87), or self-sufficient (*De fin.* II.86). Cf. Seneca, *De benef.* III.4.1. In the last section of this chapter, I take up the question of whether these formal requirements are in any sense hedonic, that is, whether they can be derived solely from an account of pleasure.

53. That is, kinetic pleasures.

54. Here it should be remembered that for Epicurus mental pleasures and pains

claims that all the pleasures that a rational agent should pursue presuppose an existing lack or want (*Ad Men.* 128; *KD* 18, 33).[55] From this, he concludes that someone with easily satisfiable desires will lead the most pleasant life, and he denies, moreover, that we can gain more pleasure by cultivating more demanding desires.[56] All these doctrines suggest a theory that is incompatible with the view that pleasure is a separable, episodic feeling that admits of varying degrees of intensity and duration.

One might object at this point that Epicurus unwittingly vacillates between differing conceptions of pleasure or, perhaps, thinks that they are somehow compatible. Other philosophers have similarly focused on the satisfaction of desires and yet have supposed that such satisfactions are "necessarily accompanied by [a] particular type of sensation of phenomenological condition."[57] Given the popularity of this conflation, why should we think that Epicurus is any more clearheaded about these problems? Could he not, regardless of his views about the calculus, still treat pleasure as a separable, measurable feeling in spite of his many affinities with a dispositionalist account?

It might be helpful to turn to a related doctrine that seems to give evidence for this kind of conflation. Notoriously, Epicurus claims that there is no middle state between pleasure and pain.[58] When all of our desires have been satisfied and we can expect them to remain satisfied, then, he argues, we are in a state of the highest pleasure (*SV* 33). It is widely believed that Epicurus is claiming here

---

fit this same model. The mind may be afflicted with unnecessary desires such as avarice or ambition; they are painful because they are impossible to satisfy. Nor does introspective access have any special role to play in evaluations of these mental pleasures and pains.

55. See below, note 67, for some difficulties.

56. For these connections between pleasure and the satisfaction of desires, see *Ad Men.* 127, 128, 130; *KD* 10, 11, 12, 15; *SV* 68, 69, 71, 80, 81; *De fin.* I.39; *DRN* II.14–36.

57. D. Lyons, *In The Interest of the Governed* (Oxford, 1973), p. 22. See Sidgwick, pp. 43–56, for a discussion of the source of this confusion. See *De fin.* I.37 and *Ad Men.* 131 for the way that Epicureans regularly use the satisfaction and frustration of natural and necessary desires (hunger and thirst) as paradigm examples of pleasure and pain. Cf. *KD* 30.

58. *to de ponou kai hēdonēs mēden einai meson,* Plutarch, *Adv. Colot.* 1123a (U. 420).

that the satisfaction of our desires is accompanied by a special, separable feeling. His particular description and assessment of this accompanying feeling have often been taken to be merely perverse or perhaps just nonsensical. Indeed, many have objected that it seems hardly conceivable that anyone could have made the elementary error of treating a neutral state of sensation as the most pleasant state possible. Not surprisingly, it has been suggested that Epicurus very easily could have refuted for himself this denial of a neutral state by a simple test of introspection. Others have argued that Epicurus did resort to introspection, but because of his innate optimism, mistook what most people[59] find neutral or indifferent for not only a pleasurable feeling but indeed the most pleasurable feeling we can experience.[60] If this is the highest state of pleasure Epicurus has to offer us, however, many have wondered why anyone would ever want it. Indeed we might wonder what could have possibly induced Epicureans to structure their whole lives around the so-called pleasures of such desiccated states of feeling and sensation.

Amid all this criticism, however, it has not been suspected that Epicurus is referring to anything other than a particular sensation or quality of feeling. We need to look more carefully at the kinds of questions Epicurus is asking and the theoretical commitments that are motivating his questions. Clearly, the denial of a neutral state between pleasure and pain would be somewhat implausible for anyone holding an empiricist view that treats pleasure as a separable feeling. But it is important to recognize that this particular view of our states of consciousness is hardly theoretically neutral.

Sidgwick, for instance, argues that if we think of pleasure and

---

59. Cicero, *De fin.* II.77: "quam praeter vos nemo appellat voluptatem."

60. Cf. Merlan, p. 10: "This, then, Anaxagorean pessimism (and Plato's 'neutralism') is the appropriate contrasting background to the Epicurean doctrine of the katastematic *hēdonē*. An organism left to itself alone, an organism just performing its vital functions in an unimpeded way experiences *hēdonē*, to be sure, a *hēdonē* sui generis. But according to the 'physiological' theory reported by Aristotle this organism experiences *lupē*. . . . Radical optimism and radical pessimism clash. And it seems that the choice between them will always be rooted in some personal factor." Merlan goes on to speculate that Epicurus' optimism about the pleasantness of the neutral state stemmed from a heroic defiance and, perhaps, overcompensation in the face of continual sickness.

pain as being opposite ends of a uniform scale, "we must therefore conceive, *as at least ideally possible*, a point of transition in consciousness at which we pass from positive to negative. It is not absolutely necessary to assume that this strictly indifferent or neutral feeling ever actually occurs" (my emphasis).[61] Sidgwick goes on to claim in this passage that we may sometimes experience states that approximate to neutrality, but he holds open to doubt the view that we can ever experience this theoretical 'point of transition' by means of introspection. Few of Epicurus' critics have been willing to show a similar caution.[62]

Moreover, arguments for a neutral state of feeling, at least as formulated by Epicurus' critics, are themselves susceptible to troubling regress arguments. The quarrel between Epicurus and his opponents is usually presented as arising from their different evaluations of a neutral sensation or state of consciousness. Epicurus, the argument goes, finds these neutral sensations pleasant and enjoys them, whereas his critics find them merely indifferent.[63] For the empiricist, however, this notion of finding sensations pleasant or indifferent leads to the following regress: If I ask you whether you find a particular sensation or state of consciousness pleasant, and you answer "Yes, very," on the empiricist view of pleasure this must mean that this sensation or state of consciousness is accompanied by another pleasurable feeling. The same question could then be asked about this further feeling, which would give rise in turn to a third-order feeling of pleasure, and so on ad infinitum.[64]

61. Sidgwick, p. 124.

62. An exception is A. A. Long (*Hellenistic Philosophy* [Berkeley, Calif., 1974], p. 64), who, although accepting the notion of neutral states of consciousness, thinks that it would be much rarer during our waking hours to describe ourselves as neither happy nor unhappy. Long's observation about happiness is central to Epicurus' denial of a neutral state. I doubt, however, that Epicurus is appealing to introspective experience to defend his claim. I will argue that he is asking the objective question of whether someone is happy, that is, meeting formal conditions; and that question admits of only a positive or negative answer.

63. See Long, *Hellenistic Philosophy*, p. 63.

64. For this regress argument, see Ryle, "Pleasure," p. 195, and Penelhum, pp. 489–92, who gives a succinct account of another regress described by Ryle in *Dilemmas*, p. 58:"We can say of any sensation that it is pleasant or unpleasant or neutral. The same sensation might be found pleasant one time, unpleasant at another, and

At the very least, such difficulties show that we should be more cautious before dismissing Epicurus' position as riddled with outright absurdities. Neither the logical status of claims about a neutral state nor the verdict of introspection suggests that empiricist objections to Epicurus are themselves unassailable. I would argue, moreover, that these kinds of objections to Epicurus' theory are misguided in a more fundamental way. To see why, we must remember the formal eudaemonist framework that motivates his questions about pleasure.

At *De finibus* I.38, Cicero gives the following account of Epicurus' denial of an intermediate condition between pleasure and pain:

Itaque non placuit Epicuro medium esse quiddam inter dolorem et voluptatem; illud enim ipsum quod quibusdam medium videtur, cum omni dolore careret, non modo voluptatem esse, verum etiam summam voluptatem. Quisquis enim sentit, quem ad modum sit affectus, eum necesse est aut in voluptate esse aut in dolore.

Thus, Epicurus did not accept anything intermediate between pleasure and pain; what some took to be intermediate—a complete lack of pain—was not only pleasure, but also the highest pleasure. For whoever is aware of his condition, must either be in pleasure or in pain.

Epicurus thinks that when we have satisfied our necessary and natural desires or needs, we will be in the most pleasant psychological (*ataraxia*) and bodily (*aponia*) conditions. Moreover, we also will have attained a condition that satisfies the formal eudaemonist requirements of completeness, invulnerability, and self-sufficiency. Given these particular theoretical interests, it would be very odd to take his denial of a midpoint as referring to states of a particular

---

be neither enjoyed or disliked on a third occasion. If enjoying something consisted in having a sensation at the same time, then it presumably would make sense to ask whether this sensation itself were pleasant or unpleasant or neutral. To answer that it was unpleasant or neutral would produce a contradiction, to answer that it was pleasant would lead to 'a redundancy or worse.' "

homogeneous 'feeling.'[65] In assessing pleasures, Epicurus examines individual desires to see whether they satisfy his formal requirements. Similarly, he wants to know whether we are in a state in which our natural bodily and psychological needs are satisfied overall and whether this state meets the formal conditions of happiness. If pleasure can be equated with the satisfaction of our natural needs and desires, he can claim that we are in a state of pleasure if and only if we meet his formal requirements, and that otherwise, we are in an unpleasant state. It clearly is not necessary that there be some third intervening possibility.

In this light, we can see why Epicurus' interests are not in contrary states of a special 'feeling' but in contradictory states that either pass or fail his objective, natural tests. He can argue that certain states of satisfaction meet his requirements, however, without assuming that all satisfactions give rise to a uniform sensation. If by pleasure he means the satisfaction of certain natural needs, moreover, then it is plausible for him to claim that there is no neutral state between pleasure and pain. A natural need is either satisfied or not, just as our natural needs overall are either satisfied or not. Consequently, the notion of neutrality or indifference has no legitimate role to play in his dichotomy.[66]

So far, I have used the terms 'natural needs' and 'natural desires' interchangeably, in part mirroring Epicurus' own procedures.[67]

65. Here is one place where decisions about translation are crucial. Rackham, for instance, translates *medium* as "a neutral state of feeling," which immediately decides the issue. A more neutral translation, however, carries no such commitments. It might be claimed that the clause ("Quisquis sentit . . .") surely implies an introspective test of one's feelings. Rackham's translation strongly suggests this: "A man who is conscious of his condition at all must necessarily feel either pleasure or pain." Again, however, it seems to me that a more neutral translation does not necessarily carry a reference to 'feelings' or introspective sensations in the required sense. The Epicurean text that Cicero's account is perhaps modeled on (Stob. *Flor.* 17.35; U. 422), as well as a further report by Diogenes of Oenoanda, mention *pathē* and *aisthēsis*, but there is no reason to see in this a reference to pleasure as a uniform feeling (see above, note 9).

66. Similarly, when applying the formal tests of completeness, invulnerability, and self-sufficiency, Epicurus, however plausibly, avoids allowing gradations in the happiness of sages. One is happy or one is not; there is no intermediate state.

67. For instance, see *Ad Men.* 127–28 for the way that Epicurus' arguments move easily among *epithumian, endeon, deometha, agathon, phusis,* and so on. This Epicurean move between 'needs' and 'desires' may account in part for another

Cicero complains (*De fin.* II.27), however, that equating a 'natural need' (*desiderium naturae*) with a 'desire' (*cupiditatem*) begs a number of important questions. To see why, it is useful to invoke Aristotle's tripartite division of objective and subjective goods, mentioned early in this section. We might, for instance, concede to Epicurus the plausibility of linking pleasure with the satisfaction of desires, if he is using 'desire' in the sense required by (a).[68] But his attempt to give his theory a further objective, naturalistic defence by grounding it in 'natural' needs and desires is more problematic. The association of pleasure with the satisfaction of objective, natural needs—either in sense (b) or sense (c)—is far less plausible if it bypasses any reference to our subjective states, intentions, and wants.[69]

Take the case of force-feeding a prisoner who is fasting in order to further a political belief. We might agree that an objective 'need' of the prisoner is being met when he is fed forcibly. It seems

---

difficulty in Epicurus' account. Epicurus, at times, identifies *hēdonē* with the absence of pain and also of fear. There is evidence that he tends to identify the removal of pain with the satisfaction of a natural need, hence natural desire (see *Ad Men.* 130–31, *KD* 18 for the expression *to kat' endeian algoun*). It is harder to see, however, how the removal of fear can be viewed as the satisfaction of a desire, even if it is true that having all of one's desires satisfied is a sufficient condition for the absence of fear. If Epicurus is moving between 'needs' and 'desires' in the way that Cicero suggests, it is somewhat easier to see the grounds for this conflation. We can view fear as the disruption of a natural psychological need—that is, *ataraxia*—hence also as the frustration of a natural and necessary desire. Similarly, it is plausible to view fear as a second order attitude focused on first-order desires. In chapter 4, I give some reasons for thinking that Epicurus tends to assimilate cases of second order attitudes and second order desires. See B. Inwood, *Ethics and Human Action in Early Stoicism* (Oxford, 1985) pp. 297–98, for other Hellenistic difficulties with characterizing fear.

68. To go back to an earlier example, the dispositionalist argues that the pleasure one takes from playing the piano is not separable from playing the piano. But this position admits of a subjective or objective interpretation: (a) My pleasure requires a *belief* that I am playing the piano; (b) My pleasure requires a *true belief* that I am playing the piano. By itself, (a) might allow me to lead a completely pleasurable life, even though I am continually deceived about the nature of my pursuits, my life, and the world as a whole. Epicurus is committed to defending (b) (*SV* 54; *KD* 11, 12).

69. D. Glidden ("Epicurus and the Pleasure Principle," *The Greeks and The Good Life*, ed. D. Depew [Fullerton, Calif., 1980], pp. 177–97), for instance, argues that Epicurus' theory attempts to bypass the need for intentional explanations altogether by assessing pleasures solely on the basis of their atomic configurations.

considerably more difficult, however, to agree that we can say the prisoner's 'desire' for food is being satisfied. To do so involves an equivocation between objective and subjective senses of 'desire,' since it is no longer clear that the requisite desire is still *his* in sense (a). Similarly, an equivocation between senses (a) and (c) accounts for the oddity of claiming that the prisoner is in a state of 'pleasure' after having his hunger forcibly satisfied. As Aristotle notices, pleasure seems to be strongly associated with voluntary actions. Just as a desire for food no longer seems to be strictly ascribable to the prisoner, in much the same way the 'pleasure' of satisfaction, in this important sense, no longer seems to be his.

Epicurus agrees with dispositional theorists in associating pleasure with the satisfaction of desires. But in moving from (a) to (c) and attempting to give his account this further objective, naturalistic grounding, he might seem to be denying one important feature of dispositionalism, or indeed any plausible account of pleasure: the necessary link between pleasures and our conscious intentions or attitudes toward our satisfactions.[70] Epicurus thinks that, in assessments of our overall pleasure, a central question is whether our objective needs are being met. But this position raises further difficult problems about the role that objective and subjective perspectives play in his evaluation of needs and goods. Consequently, we will have to raise some additional questions for Epicurus' theory. If Epicurus thinks that pleasure satisfies the formal conditions of happiness, are his accounts of both *eudaimonia* and pleasure excessively objective? That is, can Epicurus show that for individuals to be happy, they must be "in the same state of mind we say people are in when we call them happy"?[71] If he cannot, and if pleasure is associated solely with the satisfaction of our objective needs, will not agents have cause to be anxious if they wrongly assess their present states, even if all their objective needs are being fulfilled? Or, as in the case of the prisoner who is force-fed, may they not

70. If pleasure is a mode of attending to an activity or a further description of the manner in which we are engaging in an activity, Epicurus would claim that these are merely kinetic pleasures for which we can have no rational concern. He is not interested in whether someone eats with great animation or with rapt attention, since these are mere kinetic variations. What matters for him is whether someone is meeting the objective needs of his constitution.

71. Kraut, p. 168.

fail to find their states of natural satisfaction pleasant? In short, can Epicurus give a naturalistic, objective grounding for pleasure without undercutting the central role that our own judgments must play in evaluating our own pleasures?[72]

Epicurus attempts to meet such objections, curiously enough, by relying on his formal criteria for happiness. If our happiness must be in our own power, for instance, then clearly our attitudes toward the satisfaction of our natural needs will play an important role in assessing our *eudaimonia* overall. Moreover, if we feel content but are deceived about our condition, our feeling of contentment will be insufficient evidence that we are happy. Our pleasures must be veridically grounded or else they will not be up to us. Unless we correctly assess the sources and doxastic status of our pleasures (*De fin.* I.55; *KD* 8), therefore, we will not really be in full control of our happiness.

It is another question, of course, whether an account of pleasure can plausibly meet such formal conditions. At the same time, however, we will need to withhold judgment on what is often taken to be a knockdown objection to Epicurus' view. Long, for example, argues that Epicurus fails to notice in his account of pleasure that "one man's meat is another man's poison."[73] If we ascribe to Epicurus either an empiricist view of pleasure or the view that pleasure is merely the satisfaction of whatever desires people may happen to have, then Long's objection would be telling. But Epicurus is keenly aware that people have different desires. He does not have to conclude immediately, however, that *eudaimonia* consists in whatever states or activities people pursue. We may clearly demand a defense from Epicurus of the desires he thinks we should cultivate, but this sort of objection assumes only the impossibility of an objective defense of happiness and of pleasure.[74]

---

72. The problem here is strictly parallel to the one posed by Kraut, p. 192. Cf. Kraut's discussion and emendation of von Wright's claim that "Whether someone is happy or not depends on *his own* attitude to his circumstances in life. . . . To think that it could be otherwise is false objectivism" (*The Varieties of Goodness* [New York, 1963], pp. 100–101).

73. Long, *Hellenistic Philosophy*, p. 73. See J. Austin, "Pleasure and Happiness," *Philosophy* 43 (1968), 51–62.

74. Cf. J. Annas, "Aristotle on Pleasure and Goodness," in *Essays on Aristotle's Ethics*, ed. A. O. Rorty (Berkeley, Calif., 1980), p. 296, for some suggestive comments

Pleasure and Belief

We can reformulate Long's objection to raise another serious difficulty for Epicurus' account. We might reasonably claim that our pleasures are causally dependent on our beliefs or prior evaluations. The differing pleasures that the sensualist finds in indulgence and the Epicurean takes in temperance are equally dependent on their other beliefs about the good. Epicureans take pleasure in temperance because they believe it to be good; otherwise they would not find it pleasant. Yet if our beliefs about the good were irreducibly subjective, then it would be misguided to attempt to give an objective account of pleasure. Individuals will take pleasure in whatever they happen to believe is good (cf. *Laws* 658e-659a.) If the dispute between Epicurus and the sensualist is over beliefs, therefore, it is no longer clear that it could ever be resolved on the basis of hedonic criteria alone. Our beliefs about the good, not the evaluation of our pleasures themselves, will be the more fundamental area of dispute.

It is sometimes argued that Epicurus tries to bypass completely the role that our beliefs play in our pleasures. For instance, Cicero[75] attributes to Epicurus an argument, reminiscent of Eudoxus,[76] that every living being as soon as it is born pursues pleasure as the good and shuns pain as evil (cf. *EN* 1172b9-15). Diogenes Laertius further explains that this common desire for pleasure, shared by rational and irrational creatures alike, is taken by Epicureans[77] to be natural

---

about the possibility of an objectivist account of pleasure and the ways in which claims about pleasure and the good are mutually related.

75. "Omne animal simul atque natum sit voluptatem appetere eaque gaudere ut summo bono, dolorem aspernari ut summum malum et quantum possit a se repellere; idque facere nondum depravatum ipsa natura incorrupte atque integre iudicante" (*De fin.* I.30, II.31–32). Cf. Sextus, *PH* III.194, *M* V.96 (U. 398), and M. Giusta, ed., *I dossografi di etica* (Turin, 1964), 1:124 for the importance of Epicurean vocabulary in other formulations of the cradle argument; cf. also Brunschwig, pp. 113–14.

76. Cf. Gosling and Taylor, pp. 157 ff., 346–48, for the different status of this claim in Eudoxus and Epicurus.

77. The cradle argument is not found in any surviving text of Epicurus himself. However, Brunschwig (pp. 116–22) shows why Epicureans might feel the need for this kind of further naturalistic defense of what we as adults have come to recognize (*egnōmen; Ad Men.* 129) as our *prōton kai suggenikon agathon.*

and without *logos* (*phusikōs kai chōris logou*; X.137). Just as we perceive that fire is hot or honey sweet, so we perceive that pleasure is to be sought after (*expetenda; De fin.* I.30). If we take this analogy seriously, pleasure would seem to be an immediately felt sensation just like the sensations of touch or taste.

Such a view of pleasure might seem to put in jeopardy many of the claims that I have been making so far about Epicurean hedonism. If the truths of hedonism are immediately given in experience, why would Epicurus care whether pleasure can satisfy any further formal conditions? Furthermore, why should formal tests govern our use of the calculus and our assessments of *aponia* and *ataraxia*, if we have such a readily available shortcut to psychological and ethical truths?

For Epicureans, moreover, these connections between our sensations and our pursuit of pleasure might provide an additional valuable point of mutual support for their epistemology and their ethics. Epicurus argues that if we fail to take into account the evidence of our senses, everything (*panta*) will be full of confusion (*tarachēs; KD* 22). It is hard to decide from this passage whether Epicurus thinks that the kinds of confusions created by these failures are strictly epistemological, but if we keep in mind the strong ethical connotations of *tarachēs, panta* may also include a reference to our psychological states.[78] If this inference is justified, it suggests that Epicurus thinks that an important reason for relying on our senses is a hedonistic one. If we do not rely on our senses, we will be thrown into painful states of *tarachē*.[79] Thus our desire for pleasure offers support for our reliance on perception. The cradle argument,[80] in turn, would seem to suggest that our senses immediately perceive that pleasure is to be sought after. By relying

---

78. Epicurus elsewhere offers a hedonistic justification of our pursuit of knowledge (e.g., *KD* 11). *KD* 22, however, may imply a stronger immediate connection between pleasure and our reliance on our senses.

79. Lucretius is no more forthcoming about the possibility of this kind of hedonistic defense of perception. It is perhaps possible, however, to see the discomfiture of the radical sceptic of *DRN* IV in this light. On the passage in general, see M. F. Burnyeat, "The Upside-Down-Back-to-Front Sceptic of Lucretius iv 472," *Philologus* 122 (1978), 197–206.

80. Aptly named by Brunschwig, p. 113 (see *De fin.* V.55: "tamen omnes veteres philosophi, maxime nostri, ad incunabula accedunt").

on our senses we perceive the truth of hedonism, whereas the truth of hedonism gives support to our reliance on our senses.[81] Epicurus' argument here would be circular, of course; but for present purposes, it is more important to understand what this relation between pleasure and perception is supposed to show about the nature of pleasure. Does Epicurus think the cradle argument demonstrates that we are genetically programmed to pursue a particular 'feeling' that, independently of any of our beliefs, can serve as an inner meter to gauge the hedonic value we derive from various activities?

The cradle argument and *Ad Menoeceum* 129[82] are widely believed to show that each of us has an infallible sensory meter that registers the strength of our pleasures and serves to initiate our actions and choices. Beliefs and deliberation, it is claimed, play the merely negative role of corrupting and confusing our feelings. At *Ad Menoeceum* 132a, for example, Epicurus recommends the use of reason to drive out those opinions that most trouble our soul. Elsewhere, we find the claim that desires that are neither natural nor necessary arise from vain beliefs, and that vain beliefs are able to distort and lead astray even our necessary desires. It might seem that for Epicurus, and so he is often read, our inner feelings of pleasure and pain could lead us through life unthinkingly, if we could only free ourselves from acquiring opinions. We therefore would be happiest returning to the state of a small child or animal. In support of such a view, Rist argues that the "feelings of pleasure and pain are the criteria of how we should act. . . . Pleasure, which is appropriate to us, is appropriate in the sense that it indicates courses of action which will maintain us in an untroubled state. . . ."[83]

If all beliefs should be eliminated and feelings alone should guide our actions, however, it is not clear why, for instance, we need to know about the true nature of the physical world in order to achieve *eudaimonia*.[84] Furthermore, Epicurus does not urge us to eliminate

81. I am thankful to C. Shields for suggesting these possible links between Epicurus' ethical and his epistemological doctrines.

82. Cf. J. Rist, *Epicurus: An Introduction* (Cambridge, 1972), p. 31. However, Brunschwig, p. 115, convincingly shows that *Ad Men.* 129 is talking about the intellectual recognition (*egnōmen*) of the truths of hedonism; it is the conclusion of rational adults reflecting on their own beliefs and experiences.

83. Rist, p. 31.

84. M. C. Nussbaum, "Therapeutic Arguments: Epicurus and Aristotle," in *The*

all our beliefs, only those that are harmful.[85] For Epicurus, the *pathē* provide a standard of truth and a criterion by which to judge actions.[86] They therefore have the same kind of foundational role to play in our moral life that sensation does in grounding the pursuit of knowledge. Both serve to give us infallible, causal contact with the world. Yet both are *alogos* (*ad Hdt.* 38, 82.5) in the sense that they are merely the raw data of our perceptual and moral judgments. They must be sorted out and fitted together by further judgments, or *prolēpseis*, if they are to guide our epistemological or moral judgments reliably. Thus, at *Ad Menoeceum* 132a, Epicurus argues that reason should drive out troubling opinions, but he does not claim that all opinions are troubling. On the contrary, at *Ad Menoeceum* 133, we find a list of true beliefs necessary for the pleasant life.[87]

Consider the following example: If I find myself before an altar of Zeus, I will experience certain sensory and affective states. If I have mistaken beliefs about Zeus and suppose that he punishes the wicked or rewards the virtuous, I may have feelings of fear, dread, hope, awe, and so on. If I have a correct Epicurean *prolēpsis* of Zeus

---

Norms of Nature, ed. M. Schofield and G. Striker (Cambridge, 1986), pp. 33–34, similarly argues that the Epicurean does not wish to live the life of an untutored child. She stresses perhaps more strongly than I would, however, that the child "is taken to be a reliable and sufficient witness to the end" since it grasps everything that is instrinsically good. However, other claims about the end—the mutual entailment of virtue and pleasure, the attempt to show how pleasure, properly understood, meets the formal requirements of happiness, friendship as an intrinsically valuable part of happiness—suggest that Epicurus sometimes characterizes *eudaimonia* in ways that would conflict with a child's grasp of the *telos*; a child's grasp of the end may be uncorrupted, but it is not self-sufficient, autonomous, or defended by knowledge. (Cf. the last section of this chapter.)

85. For negative views about beliefs, see *Ad Men.* 132a; *SV* 16, 59; *KD* 16, 29, 30.

86. Here I follow E. Asmis, *Epicurus' Scientific Method* (Ithaca, N.Y., 1984), who argues that *pathē* are standards of truth and of action for Epicurus. For differing views, see Glidden, "Epicurus on Self-Perception," *American Philosophical Quarterly* 16 (1979), 297–306, who argues that *pathē* serve as criteria only for action, not for truth; G. Striker (*Kritērion tēs Alētheias*, Nachrichten der Akademie der Wissenschaften in Göttingen, Philologisch-Historische Klasse, 2 [Göttingen, 1974], p. 60) suggests that Epicurus perhaps treated the *pathē* as a subset of sensation only in the *Kanōn*.

87. He argues that we need (a) true beliefs about death based on a grasp of atomic theory; (b) a reasoned account of the *telos* of life; (c) true beliefs about necessity, chance, and human agency; (d) the right sort of *prolēpseis* about the gods.

and know that the gods have no concern for human affairs, I will be in a calm and pious state. My *pathē*, in and of themselves, do not indicate anything about Zeus except that I have come into contact with his altar and it has causally affected me. We can explain my *pathē* only by ascribing further beliefs to me. Thus the *pathē* secure infallible causal contact with the world, since every *pathos*, like every sensation,[88] consists in a real causal event. By itself, however, a *pathos* can serve only as a sign or as a basis of inference that must be confirmed or disconfirmed by subsequent affective evidence, by *prolēpseis*, and by our knowledge in general.

Brunschwig argues that the Epicurean use of the cradle argument sets up "a delicate balance between a summons to intuition and a return to reasoning."[89] The Epicurean insists that pleasure is to be sought after (*expetenda*), but this normative claim is not directly derived from the evidence of animals and children, since that evidence is, in and of itself, *alogon*, irrational and needing further confirmation. Rather, as Brunschwig maintains, the cradle argument serves the more negative role of "authenticating the origins" of the Epicurean's normative claim by showing how an adult's beliefs about pleasure are not invalidated when we examine the unadulterated *pathē* of children. The observation of children is not sufficient, however, to justify the value of pleasure as a criterion. As Epicurus argues (*Ad Men.* 129), we, as adults, come to recognize pleasure as the end.

I would like to postpone further discussion of the relation between pleasures and belief until we have had a chance to examine Epicurus' account of katastematic and kinetic pleasures. A clearer understanding of this distinction will enable us to see some further connections between pleasure and the formal conditions of hap-

88. See C. C. W. Taylor, " 'All Perceptions Are True,' " in *Doubt and Dogmatism*, ed. M. Schofield, J. Barnes, and M. Burnyeat (Oxford, 1980), p. 105, for a discussion of Epicurus' causal account of perception; I take Epicurus' account of *pathē* to be strictly parallel, in the sense that every *pathos* consists of a real atomic event.

89. Brunschwig, p. 122. It is interesting that, as in the case of friendship, later Epicureans tend to emphasize different strands of an argument that Epicurus tries to hold in balance. In this case, some Epicureans emphasize the intuitionist element in this argument, while others rely exclusively on discursive argument to show that pleasure is the *telos* (cf. *De fin.* I.31).

piness and, as a consequence, the nature and scope of the ties between pleasure and our beliefs about the good.

Kinetic and Katastematic Pleasures

Epicurus distinguishes two varieties of pleasure: the kinetic pleasures of motion (satisfying a desire) and the katastematic pleasures of stability (having a satisfied desire).[90] A brief example might help to clarify the chief features of this distinction. We know that Epicurus postulated certain natural and necessary desires. Suppose that I am an Epicurean with a proper conception of the natural limits of my desires and that at present I am faced with the need to satisfy my hunger. Suppose also that I have a good supply of various kinds of bread, all of which will equally satisfy my hunger without any harmful consequences to my constitution.

Epicurus suggests that the pleasure of eating, say, brown bread or white bread, and in the process, stilling my hunger is a kinetic pleasure. When my hunger has been satisfied and my natural constitution has been restored to a state of balance,[91] my occurrent state of satisfaction is a katastematic pleasure.

Scholars have construed the point of this distinction very differently, depending on whether they think Epicurus is appealing to psychological data or to facts about our constitutions at the atomic level.[92] The priority of atomic explanations in Epicurus' theory of

90. For the Aristotelian background of this distinction, see *EN* 1154b27–32 and the discussion of Merlan, pp. 19–20.

91. Gosling and Taylor, pp. 361–62, argue that because of Epicurus' physicalism, he construes the value of pleasures of restoration strictly in terms of their contribution to the general physical balance of an organism. One must be careful, however, of conflating atomic and intentional explanations. Gosling and Taylor tend to move between these two explanatory levels without comment and can give the (wrong) impression that Epicurus' interest in a balanced *katastēma* is limited solely to the material effects that certain activities have on our atomic constitutions. See the following two notes for criticism of more explicit defenses of such a view.

92. Rist argues that the distinction between katastematic and kinetic pleasures stems from their differing atomic properties. 'Katastematic' "must mean pleasure deriving from a well-balanced and steady state of the moving atoms in a sensitive organ. And perhaps kinetic pleasures are pleasures deriving from a steady, though

pleasure has been defended by David Glidden,[93] who argues that Epicureans attempt to bypass entirely the need for intentional explanations of pleasure by focusing strictly on the atomic configurations of our psychological states. This claim is misleading, since Epicurus embeds his account of kinetic and katastematic pleasures in macroscopic descriptions of desires, needs, rational preferences, and a knowledge of nature's dictates. Moreover, he derives these from our experience of pleasure and pain at a macroscopic level. Thus, although Epicurus may think that on one level of explanation pleasure is a mechanistic, atomic event, throughout his ethics he appeals to further features about pleasure, which, although ultimately rooted in atomic events, require their own explanatory level.

---

limited and temporary change, in the state of those atoms" (p. 102). He therefore finds Cicero's distinction at *De fin.* II.31 between *voluptas stans* and *voluptas movens* misleading, since the atoms of katastematic states will also be in motion. However, Rist's own appeal to atomic properties is misleading in this context. Like Aristotle, Epicureans surely might defend this distinction by appealing to the differences between states of stable satisfaction and the states involved in satisfying desires. Cicero's account of the distinction stays securely on a macroscopic explanatory level and appeals to features of our psychological states.

93. D. Glidden argues that Epicurus' "confidence in our ability to detect the feelings, or *pathē*, of pleasure and pain does not rest on the certainty of a Cartesian self-consciousness, but rather on the material identity of these *pathē* with atomic motions in our bodies, understanding these psychophysical experiences, with Freud, in mechanical terms" ("Epicurus and the Pleasure Principle," in *The Greeks and the Good Life*, ed. D. Depew, p. 184). Glidden is right, I think, to deny that ascriptions of pleasure ultimately rest for Epicurus on the certainty of reports based on introspection. Glidden's general view of Epicurus as an eliminative materialist is misleading, however (see chapter 4 for a more detailed discussion). He claims, for instance, that the distinction between kinetic and katastematic pleasures distinguishes not two kinds of intentional states but "two types of pleasurable atomic episodes" (p. 189). But even in attempting to formulate this distinction strictly in atomic terms, Glidden must continually rely on descriptions of macroscopic properties and states (see especially p. 189). Epicurus, I think, appeals to supposedly natural facts about our desires, intentions, and psychological states at the macroscopic level to justify this distinction. Even if he thinks that material explanations of pleasurable states can be given in principle, he does not need to eliminate all reference to intentional states to give objective natural criteria for distinguishing among pleasures, as Glidden supposes; he can rely on his defense of natural and necessary desires to show which satisfactions give rise to *ataraxia*. A word of caution: Glidden's idiosyncratic use of 'psychological' to refer to atomic explanations and 'moral' to refer to macroscopic or intentional explanations makes his argument sometimes unduly obscure. In discussing his views I use 'psychological' to refer to intentional explanations at the macroscopic level.

To see the force of Epicurus' distinction between types of pleasure at the level of our psychologies, we can return to our example. On the empiricist account of pleasure, it is possible for someone to fail to get any pleasure from stilling a desire or satisfying a need. If I am hungry and faced with another dull meal of brown or white bread, I may gain no pleasure from satisfying my hunger, if pleasure is construed as a separable feeling over and above the activity of eating. Perhaps while eating, my mind was elsewhere, or perhaps I was really in the mood for steak and lobster. For the empiricist, the mere stilling of a desire is not enough to qualify as a pleasure; an activity must give rise to the proper accompanying subjective sensation. Similarly, on this view, it is possible to satisfy a desire or need, but then continue to derive further pleasure from an activity: although no longer hungry, I might continue to take pleasure in eating a rich dessert.

Such assumptions about pleasure, however, appear to be exactly what Epicurus means to combat with his distinction between katastematic and kinetic pleasures. He focuses on the question of whether the natural needs of our bodily and psychic constitution are being fulfilled by the things that we desire. Consequently, he argues, desires for goods that satisfy these natural needs are natural and necessary. When the needs of our constitution have been met, we will have achieved a pleasurable state of katastematic balance. Epicurus denies, however, that we could ever satisfy a natural need and fail to gain pleasure. Unlike the empiricist, Epicurus argues that the various kinetic states[94] that occur in satisfying genuine needs do not affect our overall satisfaction; they are mere variants[95] that can give us no rational grounds for preference.

94. It is perhaps worth asking whether Epicurus must treat painful kinetic states with similar indifference. For instance, given that we want to be in a katastematic state of good dental health, do we have any rational preference for having our teeth extracted with or without anesthetic? By parity of argument, Epicurus must hold that we can try the kinetic variations of Novocaine on a whim, if it is readily available; but our overall experience in the dental office, with or without Novocaine, will be no more or no less pleasant.

95. The view that kinetic pleasures are mere variants has been defended by Rist (pp. 170ff.) on the basis of *KD* 18 and *De fin.* II.9. Long argues that some kinetic pleasures are a necessary means to katastematic pleasure (*Hellenistic Philosophy*, p. 65). For present purposes, however, on either view kinetic pleasures cannot add to

The empiricist might argue that this highly unintuitive doctrine can easily be embarrassed by introspection. Even if we grant Epicurus his claim about the importance of satisfying natural needs, still, surely someone who prefers white to brown bread, and satisfies her hunger with white bread, will have a more pleasant meal overall than if she had to make do with brown bread. Should we not agree with the empiricist that Epicurus' story about the satisfaction of natural needs cannot capture all we need to say about pleasure? Dispositionalists will also object to this element in Epicurus' theory, since an important feature of their view is the claim that pleasure is linked in crucial ways to our manner of engaging in or attending to an activity.

Epicurus admittedly does not seem particularly interested in whether someone eats with great animation or with rapt attention, carefully savoring every mouthful.[96] Clearly, Damoxenus (Kock, frag. 2) is merely wrong to suggest that Epicurus thought we should squeeze out the maximum of pleasure by "chewing carefully." If anything, Epicurus' continual focus on the satisfaction of natural needs can give the impression that he is completely indifferent to subjective states of conscious awareness.[97] We might think, then, that for the Epicurean, it merely will be a matter of kinetic indifference whether someone eats with great animation or bored re-

---

the completeness of an overall state of katastematic pleasure. Epicurus apparently feels little pressure to include kinetic pleasures as parts of our final good. The sage will undoubtedly have kinetic experiences but cannot assign them any rational value. I will argue that he feels considerable pressure from his own demand for the completeness of *eudaimonia* to include both the virtues and friendship as parts of our *telos*.

96. Such a view is suggested by Diano's interpretation of *DRN* IV.627–29: "Deinde voluptas est e suco fine palati; / cum vero deorsum per fauces praecipitavit, / nulla voluptas est, dum diditur omnis in artus." (See "Note Epicuree," *Studi italiani di filologia classica* 12 (1935), 253, and "La psicologia d'Epicuro e la teoria delle passioni," *Giornale critico della filosofia italiana* 20 (1939, 1940, 1941, 1942). Diano takes this passage as evidence for his general claim that kinetic pleasures supervene on prior katastematic states. In this case, the kinetic pleasures of taste cease (*nulla voluptas est*) once food passes from the mouth to the rest of the body. But katastematic equilibrium is presupposed throughout this passage, and, consequently, these kinetic pleasures are a matter of indifference. For a differing view of this passage, see Gosling and Taylor, p. 376.

97. For instance, in the Epicurean definition of pleasure as the stable condition of the flesh (*sarkos eustathes katastēma*), healthy function seems to be stressed as opposed to subjective sensation (cf. Gellius IX.5.2; U. 68).

luctance, or, indeed, has to be force-fed.[98] What will matter most are the objective questions of whether one's natural needs are being met and whether one's katastematic equilibrium has been achieved.

To see the precise force of Epicurus' claims, however, we need to recall his reliance on the formal conditions of happiness. He argues that our final good must be entirely in our own control; therefore, since pleasure is our final good, our pleasures must be completely in our own control as well. Accordingly, by claiming that kinetic pleasures are mere variants and readily substitutable for one another, Epicurus greatly decreases the vulnerability of our pleasures.[99] If I can achieve the same katastematic satisfaction from a wide range of goods, then I greatly increase my ability of avoiding the frustration of my desires. Since some goods may be hard to secure and dependent on chance features of the world, my preferences for the kinetic pleasures associated with such goods would make me more vulnerable.

Yet if Epicurus thinks that our pleasures must be in our own power (*par' hēmas*), he must also allow that our rational assessments, beliefs, and conscious attitudes play a crucial role in our happiness. My knowledge that I can be just as happy eating brown bread or

98. We might think that in the latter example the links between katastematic states and psychological explanations of pleasure in terms of desire, wants, and so on have been completely broken. If Epicurus can claim that the force-fed prisoner is in a pleasurable condition of satisfaction, we might suspect that he is describing only an underlying atomic configuration and bypassing the prisoner's intentional states. This sort of extreme case, however, is merely an instance of the general difficulties Epicurus must face in linking pleasure to the satisfaction of natural, objective needs. This example also raises further questions about choice, responsibility, and the importance of autonomy, which I take up in the last chapter.

99. Gosling and Taylor, pp. 373–96, claim that Epicurus has no theoretical motivation for distinguishing katastematic from kinetic pleasures in the way that Cicero suggests. It seems to me, however, that one very clear motivation for making kinetic pleasures mere variants (Diano, Rist) or substitutable means (Long) is Epicurus' attempt to ensure the invulnerability of pleasure. Gosling and Taylor argue that Cicero's account of the distinction between kinetic and katastematic pleasures is unsympathetic and confused, and shows little understanding of his Epicurean sources. I strongly disagree, but I doubt that it would be worthwhile to attempt to meet their many detailed objections here (I try to do so in a forthcoming commentary on *De finibus* I-II; cf. *ad loc.* I.37, 39, II.9, 10, 16). For present purposes, either Long's or Diano's account is compatible with my view that kinetic pleasures and katastematic pleasures are incommensurable and that kinetic pleasures are a matter of rational indifference to our overall happiness.

white bread is important to my overall happiness and allows me to react to the incursions of chance with minimal risks of pain and frustration. It gives me confidence that my desires will continue to be satisfied.[100] Epicurus thinks, therefore, that when we are eating bread, it is wrong to focus on our subjective awareness of kinetic pleasures, since by concentrating on these we do not give expression to our autonomy and self-sufficiency. Rather, by being aware of our ability to substitute or eliminate such pleasures, we gain a stronger sense of our autonomy and self-sufficiency in the face of the world's sometimes threatening randomness. Thus, Epicurus thinks that his attention to this requirement of happiness will sufficiently account for the role that subjective states play in *eudaimonia*. We must display the proper rational attitudes and exert the right sort of control over the satisfaction of our objective needs. Otherwise, we will be subject to *tuchē*.

Although we can see how this distinction between katastematic and kinetic pleasures meets the demands for the voluntariness of our happiness, it would appear to fail Epicurus' further condition that our happiness be complete. We might reasonably object that our satisfactions will be more complete if, in addition to satisfying our natural and necessary needs, we can also include a wider range of kinetic pleasures in our lives. Similarly, wouldn't our happiness be greater if we could experience a fuller array of goods and their consequent kinetic pleasures? Epicurus' attempt at an answer to this question shows how he must subordinate his requirements for completeness to the demand that our happiness be under our control. He suggests that we can try various kinetic variants as long as we can do so without running risks or developing inflexible attachments to the goods that give rise to them. He denies, however, that richer kinetic experiences can add to our happiness or make it more complete.

Epicurus' account of the relations between these two requirements reverses Aristotle's priorities and gives rise to a contrasting evaluation of external goods, the value of practical reasoning, the range of natural capacities, and death. Aristotle subordinates voluntariness to completeness because he thinks that some goods nec-

100. Cf. Orig. *Contra Celsum* III.80: *to peri tautēs piston . . . elpisma*; cf. U. 68.

essary for happiness may be vulnerable to loss. Epicurus maintains the invulnerability of happiness, but he lets the scope of satisfactions expand and contract to adjust to individual circumstances. He argues that in such a way we can still achieve complete happiness; but it is difficult to see how he can plausibly defend this claim without in some way reducing the strength of his commitments to invulnerability.

Pleasure, *Ataraxia*, and *Aponia*

Epicurus thinks that there are certain desires whose satisfaction is necessary for happiness (*pros eudaimonian; Ad Men.* 127). He further claims that someone who satisfies these desires will be in a state of *aponia* and *ataraxia*. In identifying these states with *eudaimonia*, Epicurus relies on the assertion that a necessary condition for happiness is the satisfaction of our natural and necessary desires. It will be useful, however, to raise some objections to his account to see how he can defend this identification of *eudaimonia* with both *aponia* and *ataraxia*.

(1) Why should someone impressed with Epicurus' arguments about happiness and pleasure not cultivate a very narrow range of easily satisfiable desires and thereby avoid the dangers of frustration? It is difficult to see how Epicurus can avoid the inference that we should select our desires solely on the basis of how easily they can be satisfied. In the *Philebus*, Plato argues that the hedonist will have to admit that the life of a contented jellyfish is a happy one (20c), if pleasure or the satisfaction of desire is the sole good and nothing else can be added to it to make our lives more complete. Can Epicurus give a robust enough account of hedonism to make it more attractive than Plato claims? In other words, can an Epicurean's happiness really be complete?

(2) Cicero, on behalf of the Cyrenaics, argues that *ataraxia* is the summum bonum of a corpse (*De fin.* II.22). If we think that pleasure arises from the satisfaction of our desires, should we not try to satisfy as many as possible and as often as we can? If I have satisfied one desire, that will just give rise to another, which also will require

satisfaction. Instead of imitating corpses, should we not live a life of restless desire, moving eagerly from satisfaction to satisfaction?

(3) Finally, one might raise a Cyrenaic objection. Why should we care at all about the satisfaction of our future desires? If I develop second-order attitudes and desires about future satisfactions, is it really possible to achieve the *ataraxia* that Epicurus recommends? Will I not rather be continually worrying about my future states and consequently spoiling my present pleasures?

It might be helpful to deal with the last two objections first, since Epicurus thinks that (2) will collapse into a version of (3). The view of desires endorsed in (2), familiar from Plato's *Gorgias* and often attributed to Hobbes,[101] holds that happiness consists in the continual movement from desire to desire and from satisfaction to satisfaction. As soon as we have satisfied one desire, we will immediately feel new urges that we must satisfy. In this view of happiness, if all of an agent's desires were ever satisfied, the resulting state, by definition, could not be a happy one. States of *ataraxia* and *aponia*, in this view, would be conditions in which our desires have lost their motive force. Consequently, there could be no future satisfactions or pleasures awaiting us.[102] As Hobbes argues, "The Felicity of this life, consisteth not in the repose of a mind satisfied. For there is no such *Finis Ultimus*, (utmost ayme,) nor *Summum Bonum*, (greatest Good,) as is spoken of in the Books of the old Morall Philosophers. Nor can a man anymore live, whose Desires are at an end, than he, whose Senses and Imagination are at a stand. Felicity is a continuall progresse of the desire, from one object to another; the attaining of the former, being still but the way to the later" (*Leviathan*, pt. I, ch. 11).

101. This conception of desire is explored by T. Irwin in "The Pursuit of Happiness" (unpublished) and in "Coercion and Objectivity in Plato's Dialectic," *Revue Internationale de Philosophie* 156–57 (1986), 65–74. In the following section, I am greatly indebted to his discussions and to conversations with J. Whiting and M. Neuburg. Contrasts between Epicurus and Hobbes are taken up in a rather different manner by J. Nichols, *Epicurean Political Philosophy: The "De Rerum Natura" of Lucretius* (Ithaca, 1972), p. 183.

102. It is not always clear whether Epicurus thinks of *ataraxia* as a desireless state, in the sense of a total removal or lack of desire, or as a state in which desires are continually satisfied. Sometimes this ambiguity creates a related confusion about the range of our desires (see *Ad Men.* 128), since Epicurus is ambiguous about whether he requires a broad range of desires or just the fewest possible for happiness.

Epicurus takes the proponents of this view of pleasure and desire to be 'sensualists' who claim that one should abandon all restraint and continually develop stronger appetites. In Epicurean terms, they wrongly value kinetic as opposed to katastematic pleasures. Epicurus tries to counter this extreme claim with his arguments about the virtues. Anyone interested in living a life of pleasure will have to be temperate, courageous, wise, and just (*Ad Men.* 132; *De fin.* I.42–54). If we value our future states of satisfaction, we may have to restrain some present desires in order to satisfy future ones, or we may have to restrain or eliminate desires whose present satisfaction may have disastrous future results. At the same time, we must be careful about attaching the right value to our future states. Too strong a desire for security or survival, for example, might lead one to develop derivative desires for power, money, or wealth (*DRN* V.1120–35; *KD* 7).

Epicurus thinks that those who are interested either in maximizing future satisfactions or in acquiring power and wealth must agree with him that concern about future satisfaction is important. Consequently, they should not cultivate desires that are not amenable to restraint. Although sensualists may disagree with him about the best means to future satisfaction, they too will begin from this point of agreement; they will reject the radical Cyrenaic claim that we should not worry about our future states at all. Therefore, they will be just as concerned as the Epicurean with rationally ordering desires to insure future satisfactions.

Epicurus portrays his differences with the sensualists as over the means to an agreed-upon determinate end: pleasure (*KD* 8, 10–13). He suggests that the sensualists agree with him about the contents of happiness and its formal requirements but disagree about how best to achieve this end. He argues that if the sensualists were able to attain *ataraxia* and *aponia*, even without a knowledge of *phusis*, death, and the limits of desire, they would be happy. He denies, however, that this could ever happen and outlines what he takes to be the necessary means for achieving both *aponia* and *ataraxia*.

Here we need to ask whether the sensualists agree that they really want *aponia* and *ataraxia* or whether they disagree with Epicurus about the contents of happiness as well. The sensualist can endorse

Epicurus' view of the value of future states without agreeing that his is the only plausible conception of happiness linked to this requirement. To justify his identification of *eudaimonia* with his conception of pleasure, Epicurus must invoke the further formal requirement that our happiness must be entirely in our own control. We should care, he argues, only about those future states that are *par' hēmas*. And the most plausible candidates for satisfying this condition are inner states that are invulnerable to chance and frustration.

The controversy between Epicurus and the sensualists is thus over a formal requirement of happiness, not a particular type of feeling. Here again, a comparison with Sidgwick's view of the dispute between philosopher and sensualist might be instructive. Sidgwick claims that their disagreement arises from different assessments of subjective feelings. He further argues that no one can tell whether "the philosopher's constitution is not such as to render the enjoyments of the senses, in his case, comparatively feeble; while on the other hand the sensualist's mind may not be able to attain more than a shadow of the philosopher's delight."[103] Epicurus does not think that his dispute with the sensualists is over their respective capacities for enjoying particular qualities of feeling. Rather, he challenges the sensualists' ability to satisfy the formal requirements of happiness. The sensualist's pleasures, he argues, will be vulnerable to chance and frustration, and they will be incomplete.[104] However, Sidgwick's remarks show why it is unclear that these formal conditions can be justified on the basis of hedonic criteria alone.

Epicurus' difficulties over an adequate justification of *hēdonē* as our final goal will emerge more clearly if we briefly examine some

103. Sidgwick, p. 148.

104. We might think that the sensualists' pleasures are more complete in that they cover a greater range of satisfactions. Both Mill and Epicurus claim that the sensualist's pleasures will in some way be incomplete. It is important, however, to distinguish Mill's conception of completeness from Epicurus'. Mill thinks that certain capacities and accomplishments are necessary ingredients in complete happiness. For pleasure to be complete, it must encompass a sufficiently rich range of activity. Epicurus regularly takes the completeness of pleasure in a different sense. He does not argue that an unsatisfied Metrodorus is better than a pig satisfied; rather, he takes completeness to be a feature linked to the limits of individual pleasures and desires. I have complete pleasure when I have reached these limits, not when I have satisfied a large range of desires and capacities.

of the objections raised in (3). The Cyrenaics claim that one should not take the trouble of rationally modifying one's desires in order to secure future states of satisfaction. They similarly deny the possibility of coherently ordering desires for some more ultimate goal. In the context of Greek ethics, this claim is radical, since most Greek moralists assume that without an ultimate structure to relate and adjust our various aims and desires, our individual satisfactions, goals, and so forth will form a disordered heap. Since *eudaimonia* consists in this correct structuring of desires, the structure as a whole becomes more ultimate and choiceworthy than any of its individual parts. Similarly, prudential calculation to secure future fulfillment becomes a central element in this overall structure.

In replying to the Cyrenaic who claims to dissociate himself from his future states and desires, Epicurus again must rely on the formal conditions for happiness. Although this reliance may give him a more compelling view of happiness, it also shows why his account cannot be defended on the basis of his hedonism alone.

Epicurus argues against the Cyrenaic that mental pleasures are greater than bodily pleasures (*De fin.* I.55). The chief reason for the priority of mental pleasures is that they are temporally extended in a way that pleasures of the body are not. To show that this kind of temporal extension is valuable, Epicurus appeals to a conception of our personal identity, which is similarly extended in time. Rational agents must abstract themselves from their present situations and give equal weight to their future interests and desires.[105] Prudence and practical reasoning are therefore not eliminable if we are concerned about *our* satisfactions (*KD* 11, 12). Nagel, for instance, argues that it would "be wildly peculiar for someone to be unmoved by the possibility of avertable future harm or accessible future benefits."[106] Although Epicurus might disagree with Nagel's

---

105. Two other Epicurean claims seem to conflict with this demand for prudential calculation of future interests. Epicurus denies that death can harm us by cutting short any of our extended projects, and he denies that duration will increase pleasure. Both these claims are influenced by his strong emphasis on the voluntariness of happiness. Epicurus tries to show how we can take future states seriously by limiting our concern to those that are immune to chance and not enhanced by duration.

106. T. Nagel, *The Possibility of Altruism* (Oxford, 1970), pp. 37–38. Cf. N. P. White, "Rational Prudence in Plato's *Gorgias*," in *Platonic Investigations*, ed. D. J. O'Meara (Washington, D.C., 1985).

conception of harm and benefit, he can agree about the need for prudence and a concern for future states of an extended self. But can he do so entirely on hedonistic grounds? He and the Cyrenaics disagree about the hedonic benefit of showing concern for future states of ourselves.[107] The Cyrenaic argues that we will gain more pleasure by viewing ourselves as discrete, momentary selves enjoying momentary episodes of pleasure. Epicurus, however, thinks that we will gain more pleasure by regarding ourselves as self-sufficient sages rationally planning for our future. Epicurus can argue that he is explaining more plausibly the ordinary belief that *eudaimonia* is not just a momentary episode but a stable, persisting condition; similarly, he can claim to be offering a more plausible conception of personal identity, that is, one that requires more than a series of discrete, unrelated, episodic 'selves.' But to make this counterargument, he must appeal to nonhedonic criteria derived from the independent formal conditions of *eudaimonia*.

In much the same way, these considerations will affect our views about the value of developing second-order desires focused on our first-order desires. The Cyrenaic claims that developing second-order attitudes to our satisfactions is misguided, since we will not be worried about satisfactions that are really ours; our plans will really be for 'other selves' for whom we have no rational concern. Epicurus disagrees, but in some ways his difficulties in justifying concern for our future selves anticipate the problems he faces in justifying concern for others' interests, something he attempts to do in his account of friendship.[108] In each case, he must show how hedonic criteria can give us reasons to take a more expansive view of our present interests. But at the same time, he insists that this more expansive conception must be compatible with the demand

---

107. We need to distinguish two questions:
  (a) I get more pleasure from the belief that I am a discrete, momentary self with no concern for the future.
  (b) I get more pleasure from the true belief that I am a discrete, momentary self with no concern for the future.
For present purposes, I am only ascribing (a) to the Cyrenaics.

108. Chapter 3 takes up Epicurus' problems with justifying concern for friends' interests. This analogy between friends and future selves is explored with great subtlety by J. Whiting, "Friends and Future Selves," *Philosophical Review* 95 (1986), 547–80.

for invulnerability. We might object that similar inconsistencies are inherent in his defences of prudence and of friendship. Just as he cannot justify a sufficiently rich account of friendship without modifying his demand for invulnerability, so this same formal demand will keep him from justifying a sufficiently wide range of future interests. Epicurus urges us to show concern for our future states only if they are *par' hēmas*. But can he defend plausible conceptions of *phronēsis* and *eudaimonia* without modifying this demand?

At this point, we can return to our initial question (1). If we are convinced that happiness must be entirely *par' hēmas*, why should we not reduce our chances of frustration by cultivating the barest minimum of desires? Or, if we can be completely happy on the rack, as Epicurus maintains, can the Epicurean give us any rational justification for desiring a life without torture?

Epicurus argues that in order to be happy we must be virtuous. We might think that here would be a promising place to look for a justification of a more expansive view of individual development. On this score, however, his conception of virtue will leave us disappointed. Epicurus, as we shall see, attempts to redescribe the virtues so that they will be compatible with the virtuous agent's invulnerability. Epicurean justice consists of a strong noninterference claim: we are just if we can restrain our desires and avoid interfering with others. We might think that, given such a view, we will have even more incentive to pare away our desires to the barest minimum. Surely we will be able to avoid provoking conflicts and thereby increase our chances of being just if we reduce and eliminate as many of our desires as possible.

Epicurus' account of courage and temperance initially seem more promising. He argues that we should display our courage by facing up to strong desires that will have harmful future consequences; similarly, we need to know how to moderate our desires to insure that they are satisfied more advantageously. This argument seems to suggest that we may choose to undergo a fair amount of frustration in pursuit of wider goals. Thus we might think that Epicurus' defense of these virtues would enable him to defend our acquisition of a broader range of desires. Epicurus thinks, however, that he can derive his account of courage and temperance from his account of pleasure. But if he conceives of pleasure as the satisfaction of desires, a justification of virtues that allow or enjoin the frustration of desires would be problematic. He would need a further evaluative criterion, independent of pleasure, to justify frustration for the sake of the further development of desires.[109] Given his commitment to the voluntariness condition, moreover, it becomes difficult for Epicurus to justify any frustration of desire whatsoever. Thus he seems constrained by this formal requirement to give a somewhat anemic and unattractive account of happiness, but if he attempts to weaken his commitment to this *par' hēmas* condition, he can no longer defend his particular conception of happiness or his account of *hēdonē*; if he grants that we should develop desires for activities outside of our control, other conceptions of happiness will pass this more relaxed requirement. The sensualists, for instance, can claim that the added risk of pain and frustration from external sources is necessary for pursuing greater hedonistic rewards. The Peripatetic can similarly claim that our final good is composed of several activities, capacities, and goods that are subject to *tuchē*.

Epicurus, then, is caught in a dilemma, yet one that poses interesting challenges for the rest of his ethical theory. He relies on a plausible conception of happiness as the satisfaction of our 'natural' aims and desires and outlines a strategy for rationally structuring and satisfying them. If we want to satisfy our desires in certain circumstances, it seems reasonable to adjust and limit them to insure their satisfaction. It is also reasonable, however, to risk the possibility of some frustration in achieving our goals and developing our capacities. Epicurus finds the anxiety of possible loss more painful than the promise of potential, though perhaps vulnerable, pleasures. Consequently, his inability to justify the latter alternative, combined with his unwillingness to modify his *par' hēmas* claim, generates widespread difficulties in his ethical theory. To understand the further effects of his commitment to invulnerability on his ethical theory, it is now time to turn in more detail to his arguments about the virtues and friendship.

109. Nor would his account of responsibility offer opportunities for a wider conception of development. Epicurus derives his theory of responsibility from his account of pleasure and concludes that we are responsible only for an inner condition that is invulnerable to chance. (See chapter 4.)

2

Justice and the Virtues

We often are reminded that in making moral evaluations we must take into account not only the things that people do but also the intentions, motives, and desires governing their actions. Indeed, many contemporary ethical theorists have argued that until we develop an adequately grounded moral psychology capable of explaining the psychological and motivational background of our actions, we cannot begin to approach moral questions with any reasonable assurance or prospects of success.[1] This concern with moral psychology has led, on the whole, to a renewed appreciation of the methods and conclusions of Greek ethical thought. Greek ethics commonly placed great emphasis on the role played by our states of character and our inner attitudes in explaining and justifying moral action. The carefully developed moral psychologies of Plato and Aristotle are particularly striking cases in point, as are their detailed analyses of our states of character or virtues and vices.[2] For Greek moralists, moreover, an analysis of virtuous states of character must remain part of a wider inquiry into the nature and conditions of human happiness. Plato and Aristotle argue, for

1. See G. E. M. Anscombe, "Modern Moral Philosophy," *Philosophy* 33 (1958), 1–19, for a vigorous statement of this view.

2. For a defense of the claim that all states of character are virtues or vices, see N. J. H. Dent, *The Moral Psychology of the Virtues* (Cambridge, 1984), p. 10. While Aristotle would agree that all virtues and vices are states of character, he does not directly claim that all states of character are virtues or vices. Dent shows, however, how the stronger claim might be attributed to Aristotle.

example, that to understand the virtues properly, we must not only examine the internal states of those who are virtuous but also assess the contribution these virtuous states of character make to our happiness.

Epicurean investigations of these particular questions of moral psychology, virtue, and happiness have met with little detailed comment and even less enthusiasm. For the most part, the Epicurean is portrayed as giving at best a kind of grudging lip service to the necessary role that virtue plays in the life of pleasure. Moreover, Epicureans have little patience with the intricacies of Platonic and Aristotelian systems of moral education and their supporting psychological apparatus. When faced with such seemingly barren moral vistas, it becomes all too easy to overlook Epicurus' remarks on the psychic underpinnings of virtue and, consequently, to lose sight of their overall significance for his ethical thought. This is a mistake, however, since Epicurus' psychology of virtue not only has a crucial function within his own ethical theory but is of considerable philosophical interest in its own right.

What makes this neglect of his moral psychology all the more puzzling is that there are obvious reasons for thinking that Epicurus, at least in principle, might show a high degree of sensitivity to psychological elements of morality. A characteristic feature of his ethical thought, in contrast with that of even, say, Plato or Aristotle, is the attempt to show that our happiness consists entirely of internal states such as *ataraxia*, *aponia*, *aphobia*, and *hēdonē*. Coupled with this marked emphasis on the inner psychology of happiness is his claim that virtuous states of character are connected to happiness by the strongest possible causal links.[3] We might therefore think it likely that Epicurus would call attention to the inward aspect of these connections and offer a psychological analysis of the virtues. On the whole, such expectations can be borne out by a thorough examination of Epicurus' remarks on the virtues. Moreover, only when a better understanding of his account of the psychological foundations of virtue emerges can we begin to situate such indi-

---

3. The virtues are naturally united (*sumpephukasi*) with a life of pleasure (*Ad Men.* 132), while virtue alone (*monēn*) is inseparable (*achōriston*) from pleasure (D. L. X.138.4); cf. Seneca, *Dial.* VII.6.3; Cicero, *Tusc. disp.* III.49.

vidual virtues as courage, temperance, and especially justice in his overall ethical framework.

Looking briefly at a few more general features of Epicurus' discussion of virtue should provide enough context for his specifically psychological claims. Epicurus insists (*Ad Men.* 132)[4] that living pleasantly is inseparable (*achōriston*) from living virtuously; conversely, he denies that it is possible to live virtuously without living pleasantly. Pleasure and the virtues, therefore, are mutually entailing.[5] The virtuous modes of living that Epicurus singles out in this passage, living well (*kalōs*) and justly (*dikaiōs*), are naturally united to prudence (*phronēsis*), which itself can be identified with *nēphōn logismos*, sober reasoning (*Ad Men.* 132). Analogous links can be found for courage (D.L. X.120b.2–3),[6] which, he thinks, also arises from reasoning about pleasure and personal advantage (*logismōi tou sumpherontos*). Temperance,[7] as well, can perform the same function in this taxonomy of the virtues.

In addition, Epicurus, like Socrates and the Stoics, thinks that the virtues can be best explained by reference to their cognitive components, and hence he views them primarily as cognitive states

4. The full text: *ouk estin hēdeōs zēn aneu tou phronimōs kai kalōs kai dikaiōs [oude phronimōs kai kalōs kai dikaiōs] aneu tou hēdeōs.* Bollack does not accept Stephanus' addition of the bracketed words, but throughout the doxography the mutual entailment of virtue and pleasure is almost formulaic (see Cicero, *De fin.* I.57; Seneca, *Epist.* 85.18).

5. They are interentailing, though of course not identical, for reasons clearly brought out by Seneca, *Ep. Mor.* 85.18: "Epicurus quoque iudicat, cum virtutem habeat, beatum esse, sed ipsam virtutem non satis esse ad beatam vitam, quia beatam efficiat voluptas, quae ex virtute est, non ipsa virtus. . . . idem negat umquam virtutem esse sine voluptate" (U. 508). See Diogenes of Oenoanda 26.1.2 (Chilton). Cicero (*De fin.* II.50), however, complains that statements such as *KD* 5 should commit Epicurus to an identity statement, since he must allow for the substitution of terms (that is, it is impossible to live *kalōs* [*honeste*] without living *kalōs* [*honeste*]). But if virtue is a necessary means to an end (happiness), Epicurus can claim that happiness and virtue are mutually entailing without being identical. See *Gorgias* 507b8–c7 for a similar problem and *Topics* 103a6 for Aristotle's discussion.

6. See Origen, *Contra Celsum* V.47 (U. 516).

7. Cicero maintains that temperance figures prominently in Epicurean discussions of the virtues (*multa multis locis; De off.* III.117), but no mention of it remains in Epicurus' surviving works (although it presumably might play some role in what Epicurus calls *kalōs zēn*). Cicero connects Epicurean temperance with *logismos* both at *De off.* III.117 and at *De fin.* I.47.

or types of knowledge.[8] However plausible we find this rationalistic strategy, it allows Epicurus to give a simple and powerful argument for cultivating virtuous states. Wisdom, courage, temperance, justice, and all the virtues bound up with living *kalōs* are closely related traits that aid us in our pursuit of pleasure[9] and happiness. Virtue, in short, is the only indispensable and reliable means to happiness,[10]

8. See below, "Justice, Psychic States, and the Unity of Virtue."

9. Alexander Aphrod., *De anima* II.22 (U. 515): [*Hē aretē*] *peri tēn eklogēn esti tōn hēdonōn kat' Epikouron*.

10. It is easy to underestimate the strength of Epicurus' claim that virtue alone is inseparable from happiness. A weaker connection between virtue and happiness might allow the following propositions: (a) Some other means besides virtue can produce happiness; or (b) Virtue can produce some other end besides happiness. Epicurus denies both, however. Some have thought that *KD* 10 supports (a). There Epicurus claims that he would not censure even the sensual pleasures of the profligate if such pleasures secured happiness. But the counterfactual implies that such activities cannot lead to happiness because of their ensuing painful consequences (see *KD* 9, 11, and *SV* 51 for similar conditionals). *KD* 11 is answered by *KD* 12, and *KD* 10 is answered by Ad Men. 131 (*ou tas tōn asōtōn hēdonas*). Cicero (*De fin.* II.21.70) takes Epicurus to be either uttering a pointless tautology ("non reprehenderem asotos si non esset asoti") or arguing for the inclusion of sensual pleasures in the happy life. But compare the admonitory "I wouldn't mind your smoking if it were good for your health." Moreover, at D.L. X.138 we find the claim that virtue alone (*monēn*) is inseparable from happiness. Other goods, even food (*ta d'alla chōrizesthai hoion brōta*) are separable from the happy life. C.B. Bailey (*Epicurus: The Extant Remains* [Oxford, 1926], p. 422) argues that *brōta* refers only to "this particular food"; but he neglects the force of the contrast with *monēn*. Such a strong claim seems difficult to square with passages such as *Ad Men.* 127, which suggest that happiness requires some minimum of nonmoral goods for sustaining life itself. Epicurus is reluctant to specify what minimum levels of nonmoral goods are necessary for happiness, since to do so would jeopardize his claim that the happiness of the *sapiens* is invulnerable. At D.L. X.130, however, Epicurus argues that nonmoral goods, unless they are controlled by *phronēsis* and the virtues, cannot reliably benefit us (in this context it is useful to compare *Euthydemus* 281d ff. and G. Vlastos's discussion "Happiness and Virtue in Socrates' Moral Theory," *PCPS* 30 [1984], 182–213). Epicurus refrains from making the Stoic inference that virtue alone is sufficient for happiness. Individual nonmoral goods such as food may be separable from happiness in a way that virtue is not (i.e., I may go without food for three days and still be happy), but at least some minimal range of necessary desires must be fulfilled in order to sustain life (cf. *auto to zēn*; *Ad Men.* 127). Thus, while virtue is the dominant and inseparable component in any search for Epicurean happiness, it is not sufficient for happiness. It remains open to further question, however, whether Epicurus can maintain that the sage's happiness is invulnerable without the Stoic inference.

By denying (a), Epicurus maintains that no one will be forced to choose a nonvirtuous over a virtuous path to happiness. Similarly, if Epicurus were to allow (b), virtue might sometimes fail to produce happiness, and hence be unreliable. In the

our only infallible guide (*certissimam ducem*; *De fin.* I.43) in seeking out pleasure.[11]

Scattered among Epicurus' remarks on the virtues are diverse observations about not only their utility but also about the various psychological states associated with a virtuous life.[12] Since we benefit so greatly by developing virtuous states of character, Epicurus reasonably attempts to give some account of the inner aspect of these states. At this point, it will be helpful to focus primarily on justice,[13] since it is the virtue that brings into sharpest relief a difficult problem facing Epicurus' theory. A key text occurs at *Kuria doxa* 17: *Ho dikaios ataraktotatos, ho d' adikos pleistēs tarachēs gemōn* ("The just [life]

Peri telous (U. 70), Epicurus says that virtues should be valued only if they produce pleasure, otherwise they should be cast off. Elsewhere, he says that he spits on virtues not productive of pleasure (Athen. XII.547a), and Torquatus accuses the Stoics of practicing an irrational, shadowy type of virtue (*De fin.* I.61) that does not secure pleasure. This position would seem to commit Epicurus to (b). At *De fin.* I.42, however, Torquatus claims that no one would pursue virtue if it did not produce pleasure. We can resolve this seeming contradiction by noting that although someone might be able to practice an irrational kind of virtue that does not contribute to one's own good, Epicurean virtues are imbued with reason and are focused on an agent's good; they are inseparable from the pleasant life and produce no other end.

11. Epicurus believes that our virtue is entirely up to us and not vulnerable to outside intrusion or manipulation; hence, it is the surest path to happiness. At the end of his panegyric to the life of wisdom (*Ad Men.* 135) Epicurus claims, *kreitton einai nomizei eulogistōs atuchein ē alogistōs eutuchein*. The virtuous, even when unlucky, will be better off than those who are lucky but not virtuous. Those without wisdom, even when lucky, cannot reliably benefit themselves, nor is their happiness under their control. The less one relies on chance, then, the greater possibility one has of achieving happiness. The wise man, no matter how unlucky, prefers no other way of life to a virtuous one, since such a life is best in either success or failure (*KD* 16: *sophia de oudamōs tuchēi koinōnei*; cf. Bailey, *Epicurus*, frags. 76–77); similarly, Torquatus (*De fin.* I.62) claims that the wise man is always happy, presumably by cultivating the virtues, though his actions may not always be successful. Epicurus, therefore, is committed to the claim that no desirable outcome can be specified independently of the process that achieves it. Like Sidgwick, he must rely on a distinction between the 'right' and the 'rational,' that is, he must distinguish 'what is most rational' from 'what has the best consequences.' For a discussion of the necessity of such a distinction in consequentialist theories, see J. J. C. Smart, "Extreme and Restricted Utilitarianism," *Philosophical Quarterly* 6 (1956), 344–54.

12. This feature is especially prominent in panegyrics to the Epicurean *sapiens*. For instance, Torquatus (*De fin.* I.58–62) moves easily from an account of wise men's virtue to a detailed description of their interior states. (See *Ad Men.* 133.)

13. D.L. X.28 reports that Epicurus wrote a work titled *On Justice and the Rest of the Virtues*, and so perhaps gave a similar emphasis to questions of justice in his discussion of the virtues.

is most free from disturbance, but the unjust is full of the greatest disturbance").[14]

Here Epicurus makes an important connection between justice and *ataraxia* at the level of our inner psychology. Our being just benefits us by allowing us to achieve the highest state of inner calm, *ataraxia*, and hence the happiest possible condition. Given that happiness and virtue are mutually entailing, it is not surprising that Epicurus finds essential links between justice and *ataraxia* at a psychic level.[15] The rest of the virtues have similar psychic ties to happiness, ties that we can reveal by comparing the inner condition and psychological states of the virtuous[16] with those of the happy. In the case of justice, however, the nature and scope of these psychological connections are extremely problematic.[17]

If we had only the evidence of *Kuria doxa* 17, the *Epistola ad Menoeceum*, the *Gnomologium vaticanum*, and Cicero's various ac-

---

14. D. Clay ("Epicurus' *Kuria Doxa* xvii," *Greek, Roman and Byzantine Studies* 13 [1972], 59–66) shows how, in adapting and modifying an ethical precept of Solon (Plut., *Vita Sol.* 3 = fr. 9 West), Epicurus emphasizes the effect of justice and injustice on the individual and not, as in the case of Solon, on the polis.

15. There is, perhaps, an initial oddity in viewing a virtuous state of character as a means to another psychic condition (*ataraxia*). M. F. Burnyeat ("Virtues in Action," in *The Philosophy of Socrates*, ed. G. Vlastos [New York, 1971], p. 234) argues that claims about the instrumentality of virtue make little sense in an ethics, like that of Socrates, that favors 'being' over 'doing.' We may think that a similar problem would arise for Epicurus. On such a view, *KD* 17 might suggest an identity between the psychic condition someone is in when just and when untroubled. This issue is complicated, moreover, because Epicurus sometimes makes statements that seem to equate the virtuous life with the happy life (e.g., *KD* 5). We can resolve the difficulty posed by Burnyeat, however, by keeping in mind that Epicurus views the virtues as cognitive states. Further reflection shows how little difficulty there is in conceiving of various cognitive states as productive of other psychic conditions (*pace* J. C. B. Gosling and C. C. W. Taylor, *The Greeks on Pleasure* [Oxford, 1982], p. 363)—for example, "Smith's knowledge of counterpoint gives him pleasure" or "Jones's knowledge that Smith is terminally ill has put him in a state of distraction." For the instrumentality of virtue in general, see *De fin.* I.42–54; D. L. X.138; Diogenes of Oenoanda 26.1.2 (Chilton). For justice as a productive means to *ataraxia*, see Bailey, *Epicurus*, frag. 80: *Dikaiosunēs megistos karpos ataraxia*.

16. See *Ad Men.* 133 for the psychic condition associated with wisdom and the other virtues.

17. In an intriguing though badly mangled passage, Origen contrasts Epicurean, Stoic, and Platonic conceptions of justice on the basis of their accounts of *psuchē* (*Contra Celsum* V.47; U. 518). This discussion reflects the importance of the psychic components of Epicurean justice.

counts of Epicurean virtue, we might well think that Epicurus'
defense of justice, however successful, is taken up primarily with
questions of individual psychology and the psychic benefits of justice. However, we need to look at another body of evidence as well,
especially since scholars have concentrated on it almost exclusively
and have thereby located questions about Epicurean justice quite
differently. Elsewhere[18] in Epicurus' writings and in the doxography, a contractual theory of justice is given greater prominence.
This emphasis is curious, since contractual theorists generally have
been unmoved by the sorts of questions about our psychic states
and inner calm that Epicurus finds important. We might feel frustrated, resentful, disdainful, or greatly agitated when acquiescing
to the terms of the contract, or, perhaps, we may harbor a secret
wish to violate a contract, even as we go through the motions of
honoring it. The contract theorist, though, maintains that if we
meet our contractual obligations, we have fulfilled the requirements
of justice, regardless of—or perhaps, in spite of—our inner attitudes and motivations. Such theorists generally are interested in
formulating rules for coordinating societal interests and thereby
preventing potentially harmful conflicts. But this preoccupation
with following rules generally is accompanied by a corresponding
lack of interest in the accompanying psychological states of the
individuals who are party to a contract.

18. A brief note about sources. It is important to remember that a contractual
theory of justice is not nearly so prominent in Epicurean sources as recent scholarship
may imply. Not only do contracts fail to appear in the *Epistola ad Menoeceum* or the
Gnomologium Vaticanum, they are missing from Cicero's *De finibus* and, as I argue
below ("Epicurean Contracts"), from key places in Lucretius' account where we
clearly might expect to find them. Our primary source for a contractual theory is
the *Kuriai doxai*. Some have argued (among them W. Crönert and H. Usener) that
many passages in the *KD* have been lifted from their immediate context and should
be used with caution (but cf. Bailey, Giussani, and Bignone for a defense of the *KD*
as a practical handbook for the convinced Epicurean or what V. Goldschmidt calls
in a nice phrase "une pharmacie portative" ["La théorie épicurienne du droit," in
Science and Speculation, ed. J. Barnes et al. (Cambridge, 1982), p. 310]). We might
want to disregard evidence from the *Kuriai doxai* in order to avoid these apparent
inconsistencies in Epicurus' account, or it might be tempting to conclude that he
held different theories of justice at different times in his philosophical career. I
think, however, we should entertain either of these measures only as a last resort.
I will argue that our evidence about contracts is explicable in the light of Epicurus'
general theoretical commitments.

We can see these features more clearly if we remember Plato's and Aristotle's reasons for rejecting the contractual theories developed by the Sophists. In the *Politics*, Aristotle mentions the contract theory only by way of a rather brusque dismissal of Lycophron (*Pol.* 1280b10)[19] and complains that it inadequately explains and defends our pursuit of justice.[20] His objection is that contractual theories fail to show how justice makes us better. In other words, contracts have no necessary connection with our overall interest; they are merely convenient ways of solving conflicts among the interests we already may happen to have, without showing us why we should have such interests. Two thieves may form a contract to share stolen goods; but such a contract reflects neither their true interests nor their final good. Or they may honor a contract for reasons that have nothing to do with a just concern for each other's interests; they may indeed do the right action, but for the wrong reason. Read in the light of Aristotle's worries in the *Nicomachean Ethics* about states of character and their relation to happiness, we can see that his objections to contractual theories mirror those found in *Republic* II. Plato argues that a contract theory cannot adequately demonstrate why justice is a virtue that we should cultivate. Without a reference to our psychic condition, our intentions, and our overall interests, Plato thinks that a contractual theory cannot even explain why justice should be called a virtue.[21]

From this perspective, Epicurus' espousal of a contractual theory of justice initially seems at odds with his worries about the relation of justice to individual psychic tranquillity. We can tease out deeper conflicts, moreover, by focusing on his attitude toward the fear of death. Freeing us from the fear of death is a chief goal of Epicurean ethics. This fear is a primary cause of our unhappiness, since it can impel us into self-defeating competitions for power, honor, and

19. See D.-K. 83 for Lycophron. N. Denyer rather misleadingly suggests that Aristotle's most fundamental objection to the contract theory is that it restricts laws to enforcing only justice and not the rest of the virtues ("The Origins of Justice," in *Syzētēsis: Studi sull' epicureismo greco e romano offerti a Marcello Gigante* [Naples, 1983], p. 143).

20. For an opposing view of Aristotle's attitude toward contracts, see Goldschmidt, "La théorie épicurienne du droit," p. 305.

21. For a fuller discussion of these issues in Plato see T. H. Irwin, *Plato's Moral Theory* (Oxford, 1977), p. 204.

wealth. Contractual theorists, however, have no program for de-livering us from the fear of death. On the contrary, many of them would argue that it is an important, if not primary, motivation for not only forming but also maintaining contracts. Hobbes, for in-stance, includes the fear of death among "the Passions that incline men to Peace."[22] Epicurus would object that the fear of death does not incline men to inner peace, and inner peace is our more fun-damental goal.[23] Hobbes, on the other hand, wants to formulate rules to insure civic peace and he therefore finds the fear of death extremely useful. What motivates a Hobbesian contractual partner to honor a contracted obligation is ultimately the fear of death, since self-preservation, not inner peace, is, in his view, our most fundamental goal. Thus our most basic fear not only effects great social good, since it helps to create necessary social bonds, but also is an important personal good, to the extent that it makes us more careful about our lives. The fear of death and hence inner psychic disturbance make us less inclined to a wide variety of aggressive behaviors, with all their consequent dangers.

We have, then, several *prima facie* indications of a tension between central aims of Epicurus' ethics and a contractual theory of justice. Scholars have been quick to ascribe to Epicurus a purely contractual theory that derives both its impetus and its solutions from the psychological and political doctrines of the Sophists. One imme-diately can see how problematic such parallels become, though, when we pay closer attention to Epicurus' moral psychology and the whole of his theory of virtue. Faced with such conflicting signals,

22. Hobbes, *Leviathan*, pt. I, ch. 13.

23. Clearly, these opposing attitudes toward the fear of death are bound up with Epicurus' and Hobbes's different conceptions of happiness. The Hobbesian is more ready to risk possible frustration and inner disturbance in order to achieve greater hedonic rewards. The Epicurean's primary goal of inner peace precludes this Hobbesian strategy. Given these different conceptions of happiness, it is also possible to see why the Hobbesian is more interested in formulating rules for outward behavior than in examining our inner condition. Epicurus thinks that the inner condition of those who are happy is relatively stable and uniform, and therefore amenable to analysis. The Hobbesian agent can find pleasure even in various states of inner turmoil, which can lead to outward conflicts. For the Hobbesian, rules must be formulated for controlling external conflicts, and it is important that agents learn to follow these rules. For the Epicurean, it is more important to learn to recognize the inner states that are conducive to happiness and *ataraxia*.

it might be tempting to think that Epicurus has perhaps unwittingly conflated two powerful, though clearly incompatible, theories of justice.[24] We have good reasons for doubt on this score, however, because there are signs that Epicurus attempts to adjust and harmonize the demands of a contractual theory with his view of justice as a virtuous psychic state. The final conception of justice that emerges from this intermingling of theories is complicated and not, I think, entirely successful. But with Epicurus' attempt to find room for moral rules within a tradition of ethical thought that takes virtue to be a state of character, something new enters the history of Greek ethics.[25] Moreover, by demonstrating how dangerous it is to fashion moral·rules independently of our accompanying psychic states,[26] Epicurus has something of importance to say to many contemporary theorists.

In any case, we clearly do Epicurus no favors by simplifying his theory or by smoothing over the tensions in his account. In attributing a sophistic contractual theory to Epicurus, scholars have

24. For an extreme statement of this type of interpretative strategy, see G. Bonelli, *Aporie etiche in Epicuro* (Brussels, 1979), who argues that there are widespread contradictions throughout Epicurus' ethics because of unresolved allegiances to Aristippean hedonism and Socratic asceticism.

25. A similar attempt to make room for moral rules in a morality essentially rooted in character traits appears among the Stoics. See I. Kidd ("Moral Actions and Moral Rules in Stoic Ethics," in *The Stoics*, ed. J. Rist [Berkeley, Calif., 1979], pp. 247–58) for Stoic views on the relation of *decreta* and *praecepta*. B. Inwood ("Goal and Target in Stoicism," *Journal of Philosophy* 83 [1986], 547–56) underestimates the role that moral rules perform in Stoic ethics and thinks that the sage in some circumstances will break moral rules. Gisela Striker convincingly argues, however, that the problem for the sage is to apply the right rule in each particular case according to proper priority principles ("Origins of the Concept of Natural Law," in *Proceedings of the Boston Area Colloquium in Ancient Philosophy*, ed. J. J. Cleary [Lanham and London, 1986] 2:79–94).

26. The psychological assumptions of most contractual theorists make some accompanying dissatisfaction and personal frustration inevitable. For the Hobbesian or Humean, no matter how much I am benefited overall by entering into contracts, I must suffer some loss of personal advantage in particular instances. If self-preservation is my primary aim, though, I clearly should be willing to undergo some frustration of desire and discontent. Different conceptions of happiness, however, might allow different levels of frustration and dissatisfaction. Epicurus' emphasis on personal contentment as opposed to self-preservation leads him to pay more attention to the occurrent psychological states of those entering into contracts. This preoccupation also helps to explain why he links contractual adherence to the inner states and intentions of contracting agents.

wrongly extracted his theory of justice from its proper place in his general theory of virtue. They have also glossed over important elements of Epicurean moral psychology that clearly must affect any final verdict on his conception of justice. In redressing these errors, a more complex picture of Epicurean justice will emerge, and one that, I hope, holds more historical and philosophical interest.

Our most comprehensive and detailed evidence for Epicurus' theory of the virtues appears in Torquatus' account in Cicero's *De finibus* (I.42–55) and in his extended criticism (II.45–78).[27] The evidence of the *De finibus*, however, presents serious exegetical difficulties. First of all, the virtues singled out for discussion by Cicero seem to correspond narrowly, and somewhat suspiciously, to a standard Stoic list.[28] Similarly, instead of articulating a positive theory of his own, the Epicurean Torquatus seems at times somewhat too eager to redescribe this standard list in Epicurean terms, as if he were trying to convince a Roman audience that Epicurus' theory really can accommodate commonly recognized features of morality. Perhaps an even greater obstacle in the way of recovering Epicurus' doctrine arises from the potential distortions of Cicero's political and moral vocabulary. For instance, Torquatus rather casually lists *iniustitia* (injustice) with such strong terms of moral disaproval as *improbitas* (depravity), *libido* (violent desire), and *ignavia* (cowardice) (*De fin.* I.50). Many have argued, though, that this kind of moral censoriousness is uncharacteristic of the Epicurean contract.[29] Again, in denying that there is any need to commit unjust acts, Torquatus claims that there is no reason for transgressing (*nulla sit causa peccandi*), since desires that arise naturally are easily satisfied without any wrongdoing (*sine ulla iniuria*) (*De fin.* I.52–53). Here *peccandi* (transgressing) and *inuria* (wrongdoing) might suggest to a Roman ear moral or religious reasons for not breaking contracts, reasons that are independent of an Epicurean's enlightened self-interest.

---

27. At the end of *De off.* III Cicero gives a brief summary of this fuller account.

28. For instance, Cicero leaves unexplained what virtues Epicurus takes to be involved in living *kalōs* at *Ad Men.* 132; nor does he mention piety.

29. Cf. A. A. Long, *Hellenistic Philosophy* (London, 1974), p. 71, who argues that the contractual element in Epicurus' concept of justice "is not advanced as a basis of moral or social obligation."

Moreover, Cicero's moral vocabulary is heavily weighted toward societal attitudes and obligations in a way foreign to Epicurus. Torquatus' arguments are generously sprinkled with such common terms of Roman public approval as *liberalitas* (liberality), *caritas* (esteem), and *benevolentia* (kindness) (*De fin.* I.52). He thereby injects into his account of Epicurean justice strong overtones of social class and social obligation that are absent from Epicurus's own account.

Nonetheless, when used with proper caution, important elements come to light in Cicero's discussion that enable us, with considerable plausibility, to fill in important gaps in the fragmentary remains of Epicurus' writings.

Justice, Psychic States, and the Unity of Virtue

In *De finibus* I, Torquatus argues that virtue is our only reliable means to pleasure. In further characterizing the individual virtues, he claims that the same explanation (*eadem ratione*; *De fin.* I.47, 49) can be given for wisdom, temperance, and courage, while practically the same (*similia fere*) can be given for justice (*De fin.* I.50). Wisdom, temperance, and courage are, in his view, strictly self-regarding,[30] since their defining characteristic is their ability to obtain personal pleasure. This ability to acquire pleasure is further equated with the knowledge of good and evil (*De fin.* I.43). Thus Torquatus, by strongly emphasizing the cognitive elements of virtue, attributes to Epicurus a theory that has suggestive parallels to the doctrines of Socrates and the Stoics. In addition, by arguing that all the virtues are susceptible of nearly the same explanation, Torquatus might appear to register agreement with Socratic and Stoic claims about the unity of the virtues. Given the thoroughgoing rationalism of Epicurus' account of action, it is not difficult to see why he might be attracted to a cognitivist theory of the virtues and, hence, to a theory that unifies the virtues and equates them with species of knowledge. We need to be fairly precise, though, about the nature

---

30. For the Epicurean, piety is purely cognitive and self-regarding. It consists in knowing the nature of the gods and their indifference to our world, and thereby benefiting ourselves by approximating their state of *ataraxia* (*Ad Men.* 123, 133).

and extent of Epicurus' commitment to identifying the virtues with cognitive states.

At *Nicomachean Ethics* 1144b19–21, Aristotle distinguishes his account of the relation of *phronēsis* and virtue from that of Socrates. In Socrates' view, all the virtues are instances of *phronēsis* (*phronēseis einai pasas tas aretas*), whereas for Aristotle, although all the virtues require *phronēsis* (*pasas tas aretas, ouk aneu phronēseos*), each has different noncognitive roots.[31] Epicurus' statement of the relation of the virtues to reason is unfortunately ambiguous between these two alternatives.[32] Neither his own works nor the doxography indicates, though, that he describes the virtues in anything other than cognitive terms.[33] On the other hand, both contain important general indications that he holds doctrines that support a strongly rationalistic theory of virtue. As we turn to his account of the individual virtues, moreover, Epicurus' agreements with Socrates and the Stoics about the cognitive underpinnings of virtue become all the more striking.

Courage, for Epicurus, arises simply from the calculation of personal advantage (D.L. X.120b2–3) and would seem to serve the same function as *phronēsis*. In Torquatus' more detailed account, we find that courage also frees us from the fear of death and enables us to endure present pains for the sake of greater future pleasures (*De fin.* I.49). Fearlessness and endurance are features readily associated with common intuitions about courage, and we might initially conclude that they are purely affective conditions. If this is indeed the case, Torquatus would appear to be augmenting, perhaps illegitimately, the rather austere rationalism of Diogenes Laertius X.120b by including additional important affective com-

---

31. Cf. R. R. K. Sorabji, "Aristotle on the Rôle of Intellect in Virtue," *PAS* n.s. 74 (1973–74), 107–29.

32. Cf. *Ad Men.* 132: *phronēsis, ex hēs hai loipai pasai pephukasin aretai.* Epicurus' use of *ek* is compatible with either an Aristotelian or a Socratic view.

33. There are, of course, passages in Epicurean texts that describe the passions and relate them to our individual genetic make-up (e.g. *DRN* III.258–322). For instance, Lucretius connects a tendency to become angry with the inherited mixture of our soul atoms. Thus, we might think that a prior dispostion for, say, courage might have similar affective roots. Lucretius avoids making such a connection, however, and concludes his discussion by saying that reason can expunge any prior nonrational tendencies to the extent that we all can live a life worthy of the gods.

ponents in courage. Furthermore, if fearlessness and endurance are affective conditions, they might come into conflict with the prudent calculation of rational self-interest. In criticizing the Epicurean account, for example, Cicero repeatedly praises the courage of Torquatus' ancestors for these very traits; but he suggests, not without considerable irony, that the courage practiced by these hardy Roman warriors is incompatible with the prudent calculation of self-interest, not to mention Epicurean *ataraxia* (*De fin.* II.60).[34] Epicurus, on the other hand, ensures that courage can never conflict with self-interest by closely linking it with *logismos*, his favored term for prudential reasoning. It might appear, therefore, that Torquatus, by including fearlessness and endurance as components of courage, makes a concession to ordinary intuitions that undermines Epicurus' attempt to reduce courage purely to a rational technique for acquiring pleasure.

These differences between Torquatus and Epicurus become far less pronounced, however, if we view fearlessness and endurance not merely as independent affective conditions but as states that are thoroughly dependent on our beliefs. For example, Epicurus argues that to rid ourselves of the fear of death we must have a proper knowledge of the nature and composition of the human soul, the indifference of the gods, and so on. It ultimately will do us no good to practice nonrational techniques for expelling our incorrect beliefs, since without a knowledge of nature as a whole our pleasures will never be unmixed with pain (*KD* 12). The primary causal origin of fearlessness, then, is knowledge or *logismos*. Given Epicurus' predilection for rationalist explanations, Torquatus' inclusion of fearlessness as a component of courage might augment Epicurus' remarks plausibly, when viewed in this strongly intellectualist context. Similarly, if courage is primarily a matter of *logismos*, we might think of endurance not only as an affective condition but

---

34. *De fin.* II.60: "fortes viri voluptatemne calculis subductis proelium ineunt, sanguinem pro patria profundunt, an quodam animi ardore atque impetu concitati?" We might think that someone who is imprudent, reckless, or ignorant of tactics is more courageous than someone prudently calculating the outcome of an action; or we might think that courage, in order to be distinguished from mere recklessness, requires prudence. Common intuitions seem to hold both the Epicurean and Ciceronian conception in an uneasy balance (see *Laches* 192b–94a; Irwin, *Plato's Moral Theory*, p. 47).

also as a state with cognitive features. For instance, we could attribute our ability to stick to our beliefs not to some independent nonrational emotion or desire but to the strength of our beliefs themselves. The more our beliefs begin to coincide with true doctrine and knowledge, the more stable and less changeable they become. Our ability to endure in a beneficial course of action would depend, therefore, directly on the strength and fixity of our beliefs.

If we focus on the causal roots of our endurance, we will find that the most salient explanatory feature is actually the strength of our beliefs. Given the possibility of this rationalistic redescription of endurance and fearlessness in terms of cognitive characteristics, we can see how Torquatus' account of courage can be defended in an Epicurean framework. It is by no means clear, then, that Torquatus is either misrepresenting or illegitimately extending Epicurus' account of courage.

We might object that even if beliefs are the primary causes of our courage, reason must still be supplemented by affective elements in order to issue in an action. But to defend his procedure of singling out cognitive elements in explanations of virtuous action, Epicurus need not follow the Stoics to the point of arguing that cognitive and affective states are identical, nor must he affirm that there are no noncognitive elements in the soul. Epicurus merely can rely on some fairly obvious and familiar connections between our beliefs and our affective states. For example, if I believe that death is a great evil and find out that I am about to die, I will be greatly disturbed. If my beliefs about death are corrected by Epicurean doctrines, however, I no longer will be disturbed, assuming that my affective states are completely dependent on my beliefs.[35] My beliefs about death, therefore, are necessary and sufficient for

35. This claim is, of course, open to debate, but it is central to the whole Epicurean project. He denies that one could ever master Epicurean physics, no longer believe death to be an evil, and yet still fear death because of an irrational emotion or fear. Similarly, Epicurus denies the possibility of incontinence (cf. SV 16) or the necessity of noncognitive training. A central motivation for Epicurus' rationalism is that it increases our invulnerability to factors out of our control. If my desires are thoroughly dependent on my beliefs, they will be flexible and readily adaptable to individual circumstances. Problems raised by an adaptive conception of happiness are discussed by Irwin, "Socrates the Epicurean?" Illinois Classical Studies (forthcoming).

my corresponding affective states. In stressing the cognitive element in endurance and fearlessness, Epicureans are interested in picking out those aspects that have the greatest explanatory power and are most thoroughly under our own control, hence most susceptible of rational correction. They do not need to deny, however, that courage may include further affective conditions, or *pathē*; they only need to argue that courage has no separate affective origins or elements that are independent of our own rational control. Thus, in explanations of virtuous actions, the most informative causal features are an agent's beliefs; and it is these that concern the Epicurean.

The same general considerations hold for temperance. Although no mention of temperance survives in the remaining fragments, *sōphrosunē* is a natural candidate for the same kind of rationalistic reduction. First of all, *(sō)phronein* is readily equated with *(eu)phronein* (Cicero, *De off.* III.117; cf. *Protagoras* 333d5), hence it is easy to see how Epicureans might come to identify temperance closely with *phronēsis*, given their emphasis on the cognitive elements of virtue. It is not surprising, therefore, that Torquatus equates temperance with reason. But he further suggests that temperance causes us to abide by our hedonic judgments and enables us to resist succumbing to the attractions of momentary pleasures whose consequences are harmful overall.

As in the case of courage, we ordinarily might think of these further components of temperance as affective impulses or restraints that are necessary to enforce the dictates of reason. But the problems generated by these apparently noncognitive aspects of temperance admit of the same solution as we found for the seemingly noncognitive components of courage. When viewed in a rationalist light, these further attributes of temperance described by Torquatus are traits that stem from the tenacity and strength of our beliefs.

It perhaps is worth noting at this point how difficult it is to distinguish courage from temperance in Torquatus' account. Both appear to have extremely similar functions; nor are they individuated by any specific affective features of their own. It might therefore be tempting to attribute to Epicurus a belief in the unity of the virtues. One clear benefit of such a claim would be that it removes the possibility of conflicts between individual virtues. If, for example, our pursuit of courage somehow interfered with our pursuit of the other virtues, it would be unclear how we always would benefit by cultivating all the virtues. Or, perhaps, we might wrongly temper our pursuit of wisdom or of courage, unless we had a proper understanding of our overall good. By focusing on the cognitive elements of temperance and courage, Epicurus removes the possibility of these sorts of conflicts with prudential reasoning, *phronēsis*. Consequently, Epicurus has strong initial motives for unifying the virtues.

In Torquatus' account, moreover, it is difficult not only to distinguish courage from temperance but also to differentiate both courage and temperance from wisdom. Unlike Aristotle, Epicurus isolates no prior, natural affective components for these virtues; they all equally spring from *phronēsis* and arise from the calculation of one's own good (*Ad Men.* 132). We may fail to achieve happiness because of failures in knowledge (*inscientia; De fin.* I.46), but we will not fail because of any prior affective barriers or incorrigible emotional traits.[36]

If Epicurus believes that the most fundamental element in all the virtues is the knowledge of good and evil, it is quite plausible for him to view them as forming a unity. We have no evidence, however, that he ever explicitly endorses such a claim, even though the separability of the various virtues clearly might pose difficult problems for his general ethical strategy. If courage, temperance, and wisdom had their causal roots in noncognitive tendencies, they either might come into conflict or be unresponsive to rational control. Epicurus, though, strongly denies the possibility of incontinence (*SV* 16) and affirms that all our desires can be focused on our own good by *phronēsis*. Thus we have good reason for supposing that he would deny that the virtues have affective elements that are not entirely amenable to rational control.

In addition, Epicurus fails to map out separate spheres of activity

---

36. Cf. Lucretius, *DRN* III.319–22:

> illud in his rebus videor firmare potesse,
> usque adeo naturarum vestigia linqui
> parvola quae nequeat ratio depellere nobis,
> ut nil inpediat dignam dis degere vitam.

for different virtues; they all share the same goal of rationally securing our pleasure. Accordingly, his remarks about the connections between courage and pleasure suggest that we can display courage not only on the battlefield[37] but also in turning down any tempting pleasure whose overall hedonic benefits are dubious. Therefore, in denying that the virtues have either separate causal roots or specific fields of activity, he removes two important grounds for distinguishing them.

Given that Epicurus has so many compelling reasons for adopting such a claim, we might reasonably wonder why he never endorses or even explicitly mentions the unity of the virtues. There are, I think, two likely explanations. First, Epicurus, like the Stoics, usually is careful to adjust the demands of his ethical theory to his epistemology and philosophy of language. The Stoics concluded, probably not without some reluctance, that the unity of the virtues fit very awkwardly with their theory of sayables (*lekta*). For the Stoics, each virtue has a different corresponding *lekton* and hence a separable identity. Therefore, they had difficulty treating the virtues as strictly identical entities. Epicurus has to reckon with some similar pressures from his epistemology. For Epicurus, each virtue has its own corresponding *prolēpsis* (preconception); thus, it also would be awkward for him to treat individual virtues as if they were not discrete or separable entities.[38]

A second reason for his reticence about the unity of the virtues arguably derives from his account of justice. Torquatus claims that of the virtues, only justice does not admit of the same treatment as the others. Epicureans think that our courage, temperance, and wisdom will invariably benefit us. Yet, although these virtues might plausibly be characterized as self-regarding traits, justice presents more severe difficulties. First, Epicurus needs to show that a virtue which ordinarily is perceived as benefiting others can also infallibly

37. See Cicero's criticism at *De fin.* II.60, which reflects an Aristotelian concern with mapping out the proper domains of activity for the various virtues.

38. Surviving evidence mentions only a *prolēpsis* of justice. Given Epicurus' general theory of *prolēpseis* and the role that they play in language and thought, however, it is safe to assume that each virtue has its own *prolēpsis*. For further defense of this claim, see A. Manuwald, *Die Prolepsislehre Epikurs* (Bonn, 1972). It might be the case, however, that Epicurus just failed to concern himself with the logical niceties of this particular problem about the virtues.

benefit rational agents aiming at their own pleasure. He does not merely attempt to redescribe justice as a self-regarding virtue, however; he also attempts to account for this common belief in the other-regarding focus of justice (*KD* 36, 37). Consequently, it becomes extremely difficult for him to maintain that justice and the rest of the virtues have the exact same function or explanation.

At *De finibus* I.50, Torquatus takes up these issues and argues that being just not only never harms anyone, it actually is always of some (personal) benefit ("non modo numquam nocet cuiquam, sed contra semper [impertit][39] aliquid cum sua vi atque natura"). He further claims that one important benefit of justice is psychic tranquillity (*quod tranquillet animos*), which closely mirrors Epicurus' assertion about the relation of justice and *ataraxia* (*KD* 17). Injustice, on the other hand, when it takes root in the mind ("in mente consedit"; *De fin.* I.50) or is continually present in someone's mind ("cuius in animo versatur"; I.53) violently disturbs psychic tranquillity by its mere presence ("hoc ipso quod adest"; I.50). In Torquatus' account, therefore, justice and injustice are treated as types of psychic conditions or characteristics that can either benefit or harm us.[40]

We might object at this point that it is merely Cicero's loose way of describing justice and injustice that allows us to attribute to them this kind of reified psychological status as virtues and vices. After all, Epicurus, in one of his most notorious maxims (*KD* 34), asserts that by itself injustice is not an evil (*hē adikia ou kath' heautēn kakon*). It is an evil only because we cannot be confident that we can escape detection (cf. *KD* 35) and, hence, must be disturbed by nagging fears.[41] Thus we might take Epicurus' claim that injustice is not an

---

39. Madvig marks a lacuna and various emendations have been suggested (*addit aliquid* [Martha], *affert aliquid* [Bentley], *impertit aliquid* [Muller]); the sense that justice is always of benefit is clear, however, because of the contrast with the preceding clause. This claim is further explained at *De fin.* I.53.

40. In addition to *KD* 17, cf. *SV* 79–81. It is interesting to compare the undefended Democritean claim that justice is a kind of inner cheerfulness (*euthumia*). Goldschmidt, I think, would describe such passages as part of what he calls "l'intériorisation de la sanction" ("La théorie épicurienne du droit," p. 322). Although this process may be part of the story, it is by no means the whole story.

41. For opposing views of *KD* 34, see R. Philippson, "Die Rechtsphilosophie der Epikureer," *Archiv für Geschichte der Philosophie* 23 (1910), 302, and Clay, "Epicurus'

evil *kath' heautēn* to be a denial of any independent psychological status to injustice. But in this passage, Epicurus' target is most likely the Platonic notion of an ontologically separate universal that is capable of independent existence.[42] In refusing this status to justice and injustice, Epicurus is not denying that they are psychic conditions or traits of our individual *psuchai* that strongly affect our *ataraxia*.[43]

Given Epicurus' general theoretical treatment of the virtues, we should expect an account of justice that concentrates on the psychological condition of those who are just. Furthermore, since courage, temperance, and wisdom can plausibly be described as psychic states or characteristics, we can see why Epicurus might think that the same holds true for the virtue of justice. Since Epicurus believes that virtue is the infallible craft of securing happiness, then, it is by no means a very large step to Torquatus' claim that being just is always good for an individual soul, whereas being unjust is always an evil.[44]

Such a claim is more difficult to defend within the framework of a contractual theory. Contract theorists generally argue that one has reasons for being just only if others comply with the terms of a contractual obligation. Justice, in this view, is strictly a relational concept inasmuch as it arises only within a structure of mutual obligations. Hobbes, for instance, claims that "Justice and Injustice are none of the Faculties neither of the Body, nor Mind. If they were, they might be in a man that were alone in the world" (*Leviathan*, pt. I, ch. 13). He appends (ch. 15) this important warning: "he that should be modest, and tractable, and performe all he promises, in such time, and place, where no man els should do so,

---

Kuria Doxa xvii," pp. 65–66. Clay is right, I think, to read *KD* 34 together with *KD* 17.

42. Epicurus makes a corresponding attack on the notion of justice as a Platonic universal at *KD* 33 (*ouk ēn ti kath' heauto dikaiosunē*), which still clearly allows justice to be *ti*; in fact, it is always instantiated in the dealings of men. I take up the relation of *KD* 32–33 to problems of psychic justice in "Epicurean Contracts" in this chapter.

43. "Itaque non ab ea solum incommoda quae eveniunt improbis fugiendum improbitatem putamus, sed multo magis quod, cuius in animo versatur, numquam sinit eum respirare, numquam acquiescere" (*De fin.* I.53).

44. It is interesting in this context to compare Socrates' mode of expression at *Crito* 47d4.

should but make himselfe a prey to others, and pursue his certain ruine." If, however, as Epicurus believes, my just state of character always benefits me and contributes to my psychic tranquillity, it appears that I may have compelling reasons for being just[45] that derive solely from my inner states. And these reasons clearly may be independent of or, in fact, prior to any other reasons I might have for joining in contracts with others.

Contract theorists, moreover, make our pursuit of justice contingent on the beliefs and actions of others. In part, no doubt, it is to avoid this troubling ethical and epistemological result that Plato treats justice not as a compact between rational egoists but as a beneficial psychic state. By showing that justice, like temperance, wisdom, and courage, involves psychological states that always benefit us, Torquatus thus seems to be undermining the contractualist view of justice as mere convention or watchful compromise. Clearly, the actions or opinions of others notwithstanding, we may have good hedonic reasons for being wise, temperate, or courageous. Since Epicurus attempts to make our happiness entirely up to us, moreover, he has strong reasons for espousing a theory that places our virtue entirely in our own power instead of making it vulnerable to the beliefs or whims of others. Thus, given that a defense of justice as a beneficial psychic state seems more compatible with such a large range of Epicurean ethical concerns, we must ask why Epicurus also feels the need for a further contractualist account of justice.

Epicurean Contracts

Since a contractual theory initially seems to present so many difficulties for his ethics, it is necessary to be precise about Epicurus' particular version of the theory. First of all, his account needs to be distinguished from contractual theories like Locke's or Rous-

---

45. Just as we need not the appearance of health but real health (*SV* 54), so (in contrast to Glaucon's account) we have reasons for being just and not merely appearing to be just. Contract theories also tend to engender tensions between various virtues—courage and prudence, or courage and justice—whereas Epicurus attempts to remove the basis for such conflicts among the virtues.

seau's. Epicurus does not appeal to the contract for moral certification;[46] rather, Epicurean contracts explain why being just is in an individual's own interest. For Locke and Rousseau, however, the idea of contracting itself (or an appeal to the procedural fairness of the formation of a contract) is sufficient to justify an individual's obligation and continued adherence to a contract.[47] In contrast, at *Kuriai doxai* 37 and 38, Epicurus argues that a law is just (i.e. that it has *tēn tou dikaiou phusin*)[48] only so long as it continues to reflect agents' mutual advantage.[49] For him, it is not the agreement itself or the contract that justifies our adherence. A contract, for instance, may be made in ignorance of one's true advantage or through a miscalculation of expected pleasure. Epicurus argues that such contracts are not in accord with the *prolēpsis* of justice (*enarmottonta eis tēn prolēpsin; KD* 38). But by claiming that such contracts are not

46. See David Lyons, "The Nature of the Contract Argument," *Cornell Law Review* 59 (1974), 1019. Instead of giving a generalized theory of our moral convictions or "moral certification," the Epicurean contract "confers independent rational force." Epicurus grounds his theory not on the beliefs of agents entering into a contract but on an independent theory of rational self-interested action (cf. R. Dworkin, "The Original Position," *University of Chicago Law Review* 40 [1973], 507). Nor are his contracts meant to give a moral justification for compliance; rather, they are meant to explain why contracts are in our interest. Here it is useful to compare Hobbes, who argues that compliance to contracts ultimately depends on the continued protection of a subject's life, not on contractual bonds or promises (*Leviathan*, pt. II, ch. 21).

47. See J. W. Gough, *The Social Contract* (Oxford, 1957), passim, for an account of contracts based on consent.

48. For a discussion of this use of *phusis*, see R. Müller, "Sur le concept de physis dans la philosophie épicurienne du droit," in *ACGB* 1968 (Paris, 1969), pp. 305–18, and more recently, "Konstituierung und Verbindlichkeit der Rechtsnormen bei Epikur," in *Syzētēsis: Studi sull' epicureismo greco e romano offerti a Marcello Gigante* (Naples, 1983), pp. 153–83. For a compelling discussion of the ways Epicurus gives a naturalistic foundation to the notion of law as contract, see Goldschmidt, "La théorie épicurienne du droit," p. 317. He finds further nonconventionalist grounding in Hermarchus' account of man's natural aversion to homicide (Porphyry, *De abstinentia* I.7–12); see P. A. Vander Waerdt, "Hermarchus and the Epicurean Genealogy of Morals," forthcoming in *TAPA* 118 (1988).

49. This requirement shows why it is mistaken to call the Epicurean contract utilitarian or protoutilitarian, since the utilitarian contract attempts to maximize total well-being or utility; it may not take into account each person's interests. Epicurus considers the interest of each individual a necessary condition for the contract. For a general discussion see D. P. Gauthier, "Morality and Advantage," *Philosophical Review* 76 (1967), 460–75.

just, he denies the justificatory power of the contract itself.[50] Thus, in making *to sumpheron* (advantage/self-interest/pleasure) an independent, prior standard by which contracts themselves are justified, Epicurus must offer a further defence of his criteria for distinguishing among contracts. He must appeal, that is, to his conception of our *telos* or happiness.[51]

Epicurus' reliance on this prior theory of the good perhaps might provide us with an initial point of contact between his account of justice as a virtue and his use of a contractual theory, especially since his controlling psychological assumptions clearly are tailored to a conception of the good as *ataraxia*. To bring these connections into better focus, though, we should look more carefully at Epicurus' psychological claims.

Cyril Bailey[52] compares the Epicurean theory of the contract to

---

50. T. Nagel, "Rawls on Justice," *Philosophical Review* 82 (1973), 220–34. This distinction suggests as well that Epicureans will contrast justice with mere contractual adherence. One plausible way for them to maintain this distinction is to distinguish justice as a virtuous state of soul from mere conformity to the terms of a contract, as I argue below.

51. Epicurus answers the moral sceptic, who claims that there is no rational basis for ranking different conceptions of justice, by appealing to a prior argument about the good:

(a) Justice always benefits me more than injustice.
(b) What benefits me is more pleasant, or less painful overall.
(c) Justice is always more pleasant, overall, than injustice.
(d) It is rational for me to pursue what is pleasant.
(e) It is rational for me to be just.

If pleasure is a state identifiable independently of moral beliefs, Epicurus has an objective, interpersonal standard of good that allows him to rank differing conceptions of justice. It is objective in that "pleasure acts as a common denominator among a plurality of persons with different preferences and aims" (J. Rawls, *A Theory of Justice* [Cambridge, Mass., 1971], p. 556). Notice, however, that if pleasure is merely a subjective feeling, the problem of ordering a plurality of conflicting ends merely reappears. Epicurus further defends his claim by arguing that justice, so conceived, is a *prolēpsis*. Thus it is not a subjective criterion; rather, it describes an objective state of affairs; see *De fin.* I.31 for the attempts by later Epicureans to justify the pursuit of pleasure as the *telos* by appealing to a *prolēpsis*.

52. Followed, among many, by J. Rist, *Epicurus: An Introduction* (Cambridge, 1972), and, most recently N. Denyer. P. A. Vander Waerdt provides a welcome note of dissent to this common consensus. He supports some of the conclusions that I argue for in this section (i.e., that the Epicurean wise man will not commit injustice even if undetected, that laws are for protecting the wise, not for restraining them

Republic II and assumes that Epicurus shares a similar view of human nature and of the necessity of contracts. *Republic* II broadly sums up the chief assumptions and goals of sophistic contractual theories. Glaucon (358e–6oe) begins by presenting an extremely harsh picture of man's basic psychology: what is most desirable is to have the maximum power of hurting others, combined with minimum risks to oneself. What everyone most wishes, however, is to avoid being injured by others without being able to retaliate. Individuals form contracts by compromising; they give up what is best in order to avoid what is worst. Assimilating Epicurus' theory to this sophistic model, Bailey[53] argues that the Epicurean must give up the "pleasures of aggression" when entering into a contract. In his view, Epicureans would be happiest acting with utter disregard for the lives and interests of others, and their ideal would be a life of unrequited injustice and violence. They might even indulge in the dubious "Lucretian pleasure" of schadenfreude.[54]

---

from injustice), though from a somewhat different perspective. He follows Goldschmidt, however, in reducing questions of justice to questions of obedience to laws, and it is not clear to me how he can reconcile his attribution of a legal positivism to Epicureans with the teleological claim that their theory of justice is grounded in an independent conception of the good. Justice as a virtue, I will argue, is not identical with mere conformity to law (Vander Waerdt, "The Justice of the Epicurean Wise Man," *Classical Quarterly* 37 [1987], 402–22.) Cf., for adumbrations of this position, D. Konstan, *Some Aspects of Epicurean Psychology* (Leiden, 1973), pp. 54–58, and A. H. Chroust, "The Philosophy of Law of the Epicureans," *Thomist* 16 (1953), 82–117, 217–67.

53. Bailey's view has recently been reaffirmed by Denyer, p. 145. Using the game-theory matrices of the 'Prisoners' Dilemma,' he relies on the same undefended assumptions about Epicurean psychology made by Bailey. See also *De fin.* II.51–59, *De leg.* I.40–43. For a sensitive discussion of some general features of Epicurean psychology, see Konstan. Denyer wrongly attributes to Epicurus the psychological theories of the Sophists and *Republic* II, since without such assumptions the Prisoners' Dilemma cannot be generated. In the context of Epicurus' account of our natural desires, however, the Prisoners' Dilemma is lacking in force.

54. C. B. Bailey, *The Greek Atomists and Epicurus* (Oxford, 1928), p. 511. These Lucretian pleasures, however, are given a rather benign twist at D.L. X.121b: "the sage will rejoice at another's misfortune, but only for his correction." Nor does the famous "Suave, mari magno" passage at the beginning of *DRN* II suggest malicious or intrinsic pleasure in the sufferings of others; it suggests only that we can derive pleasure and an increased sense of security from perceiving the kinds of ills we ourselves lack. We may come to this realization through a comparison of our condition with that of others and we may derive pleasure from the *comparison*, but we do not delight in the suffering of others for its own sake.

But this account is surely misleading and glosses over important differences between the psychologies that support Epicurean and sophistic versions of the contract. For Epicurus, there is no basic, natural desire to harm others. One may come to have desires to harm others in order to protect one's life, psychological calm, or even friends. Epicurus agrees that in such cases, one may use any device whatsoever to secure protection (*KD* 6); but such desires are clearly derivative. Our primary and natural concern is with personal security and peace of mind (*KD* 8, 40); moreover, we would prefer neither to harm others nor to engage in any sorts of troubling pursuits. A wise man, like the gods (*KD* 1), is not disturbed; nor does he disturb others (*SV* 79), since the necessities of life are easily obtained and there is no need for a life of struggle (*KD* 21; *De fin.* II.28). Accordingly, individuals have no natural need to engage in troubling competitive pursuits and have no reason for harming others. Desires for harming others arise only from a mistaken estimate of the nature and limits of human desire (*KD* 15; *SV* 68).

Lucretius' anthropological account (*DRN* V.925–1457) corroborates this rather benign story. In the earliest stages of human development, Lucretius argues (925–1010), individuals were unable to look to the common good (955) or to govern their actions by law. He does not claim, however, that at this primitive stage individuals desire to harm one another. Inasmuch as their desires are extremely limited, they find their satisfactions easily. Nor do conflicts arise from a scarcity of desired goods (*pabula dura tulit, miseris mortalibus ampla;* 944). Individuals make do with whatever goods they chance upon, but there is no suggestion of widespread or persistent violence.[55]

In the next stage of development (1011–27), Lucretius presents the beginnings of organized social life. Families are formed and familial groups begin to enter into contracts. Neighbors join in these

---

55. The sole exception is the possibility of sexual violence between men and women (*DRN* V.962). There are rapes, but they are apparently more a matter of unchecked desire than assertions of power. Moreover, the general tone and context of the passage is somewhat lighthearted and deflationary; there is no suggestion of domination, humiliation, or victimization. Given Lucretian preoccupations, it is difficult to see whether this faithfully reflects Epicurus' views on the nature of untutored sexual desires. Unlike the unjust man of *Republic* II, the Epicurean *sapiens* presumably would avoid sexual attachments or conflicts even if given Gyges' ring.

agreements eagerly (*aventes*), wishing neither to do harm nor to suffer it. Again, the contrast with Glaucon's account is marked. Glaucon claims that the weak, being more numerous, band together to coerce the few strong into contracts that are not in their best interest. In Lucretius' account, strong individuals urge one another to take pity on the weaker members of their respective families, since such a course is reasonable and fair (*aecum;* 1023).[56] He never hints that by joining in compacts they are compromising or giving up what they most of all want. These early covenants serve more to coordinate common familial interests and to facilitate the creation of offspring than to solve conflicts of interest.[57] Consequently, at this stage contracts are not viewed as compromises or as giving up what is best in order to avoid what is worst. Individuals benefit by these early contracts, which, although not always entirely successful,

56. Denyer, p. 150, notices that the Prisoners' Dilemma arises only in situtations where individuals are equal in strength. In the Lucretian account, the strong pity the weak in entering contracts with them, hence the Prisoners' Dilemma does not arise. Also, the dilemma must rely on a Rawlsian veil of ignorance, that is, agents must not be apprised of one anothers' intentions or of their own situations; but this is clearly not the case in Lucretius' account. Some have argued that in this passage Lucretius is misrepresenting Epicurus' harsher view of the contract (especially since Lucretius seems to appeal to moral sentiments that exist prior to the formation of contracts). But Epicurus never suggests that agents must sacrifice their best interests in entering contracts and settle for what is second best. Since these early contracts appeal to sentiment and a sense of right, however, they are imperfectly grounded, inasmuch as reason, not sentiment, justifies any Epicurean course of action. These initial contracts are natural, but not yet perfected by reason (for the Epicurean distinction between actions *kata phusin* and *kata logismon*, see *Ad Hdt.* 75 and the discussion of E. G. Asmis, *Epicurus" Scientific Method* [Ithaca, N.Y., 1984], p. 56). Lucretius, though, gives a plausible account of Epicurus' views on the state of man's untutored natural desires and the kinds of contracts that might arise in such a setting.

57. It is often overlooked in discussions of the Epicurean contract that contracts can serve to *coordinate* interests, not just solve conflicts of interests. In Epicurus' description of contracts there is never any sense that contracts are second best or that agents enter into them reluctantly; they are always portrayed as mutually advantageous (*sumpheron*). See C. Kahn for a discussion of the differences between contracts that found communities and those that are put to political and rhetorical use in resolving conflicts of interest ("The Origins of the Social Contract Theory," in *The Sophists and Their Legacy*, ed. G. B. Kerferd [Wiesbaden 1981], pp. 92–108). But Kahn conflates the differences between contracts that are meant to give moral certification and those that are meant to offer independent rational grounds for obeying laws (cf. note 46 above), and this confusion tends to vitiate his account of the "political neutrality" of the contract.

are essential to human survival ("nec potuisset adhuc perducere saecla propago;" 1027)[58]. Unlike sophistic contracts, though, these contracts do not put an end to a war of all against all; a widepread competition for goods and power has not even made an appearance at this early stage of development.[59]

These new communities not only help ensure human survival but also offer security and a buffer against fortune. At the same time, however, the growth of language and of communal living contribute to the development of technology; consequently, more sophisticated and more demanding desires arise. Individuals begin to acquire huts and skins, and with the promise of novelty and the threat of scarcity come possibilities for violence. Later in his account (*DRN* V.1420), Lucretius confirms these hints: the first man to wear skins was probably killed for them by his fellows. Thus men begin to desire goods that no longer are easily obtainable, and the types of goods now possible in a social setting become a source of contention. At their earliest stage of development men were unacquainted with goods that could be a source of conflict.[60]

Next, kings begin to found cities.[61] But when individuals' natural

58. These first contracts are imperfect inasmuch as the contracting parties still have an imperfect view of their own good. For Hume (*Essays*, pt. II, no. 12, "Of the Original Contract"), the first "precarious acquiescence is produced by habit." This habit of compliance gives one reasons to comply because of the expectation that others will do so as well. Habit, then, gives reasons for trustworthiness, but habit alone is not enough to rationally justify any pursuit. For Epicurus, this imperfect view of the grounds for compliance must be replaced by a more articulated version. Reason, not habit, justifies contractual compliance. Thus there is no suggestion that Lucretius thinks we would be better off returning to this more primitive stage of society.

59. Given that agents' interests at this stage seem to be relatively uniform, the major hurdle in achieving cooperative goals is what Sen has called the "assurance problem" ("Choice, Ordering, and Morality" in *Practical Reason*, ed. S. Korner [Oxford, 1974], p. 59, and "Isolation, Assurance, and the Social Rate of Discount," *Quarterly Journal of Economics* 81 [1967], 112–24), that is, one's own assurance about the actions of others when embarking on potentially cooperative goals. Only when desires, preferences, and interests become much less uniform do agents become far less willing to contribute to cooperative goals even if everyone else is doing so; as N. Cooper observes, "they may be unwilling *because* everybody else is doing so" (*The Diversity of Moral Thinking* [Oxford, 1981], p. 265).

60. Cf. *DRN* V.953–54:"necdum resigni scibant tractare neque uti, / pellibus et spoliis corpus vestire ferarum."

61. It is useful in this context to compare *De off*. II.41–42.

desires have been distorted by the belief that power and wealth will give them security, kings are overthrown and a widespread competition for dominion begins ("imperium sibi cum ac summatum quisque petebat;" 1142), which degenerates into a war of all against all.[62] Later, individuals finally become weary of violence, and lawgivers teach them to submit to law (1143–44). There is no explicit mention of contracts at this stage, although Lucretius does allude to doctrines that may form part of the contract theorist's argument. He claims, for instance, that the war of all against all leads to utter confusion, that individuals long for some respite from violence, and that laws prevent the kind of excessive revenge that men would take if they had their own way. But it is not clear that Lucretius thinks that contracts[63] are capable of solving or putting an end to conflicts at this advanced stage.[64] His explicit account of the contract occurs before mankind's desires have been corrupted by the pursuit of power.

A parallel passage in Plutarch's *Adversus Colotem* affirms that lawgivers bring serenity to human life (1124): "If, moreover, the rule of law were ever removed, men would quickly return to living like brutes, and anyone who chanced upon another would all but devour him." Again, however, there is no explicit reference to contracts in this context. It also is clear that an advanced stage of development is being described in which individuals' desires already have been inflamed by their mistaken estimates about the good. Consequently, their present desires no longer reflect their natural needs.

---

62. Lucretius prefaces his account of the war of all against all with a solemn warning and reminder: "Quod siquis vera vitam ratione gubernet, / divitiae grandes homini sunt vivere parce / aeque animo, necque enim est umquam penuria parvi" (*DRN* V.1117–8).

63. Cf. Goldschmidt, "La théorie épicurienne," p. 315, for a contrasting account. He relies heavily on Lucretius' phrase *communia foedera pacis* (1155), which he thinks recalls the earlier phase of "sentimental" contracts. There are, however, no parallel formulations in Epicurus' account of contracts per se, nor is there any mention of persuasion, mutual advantage, or other key elements that we find in the earlier account of contracts for mutual noninterference.

64. Lucretius' expression "sponte sua cecidit sub leges atque iura" (*DRN* V. 1147) seems compatible with any number of noncontractual conceptions of law; moreover, *cecidit* contrasts rather sharply with such Epicurean expressions for entering into contracts as *sunthēkas poieisthai*.

Leaving aside for the moment the exact role that contracts[65] play at this stage, the important point for my argument is the difference between our natural desires and those that arise because of our mistaken beliefs about the necessity of acquiring power and wealth. The Epicurean cultivates only the desires that satisfy our natural psychological and bodily needs. Clearly, these do not include aggression or inflicting harm on others.[66]

Another comparison with Hobbes will help us see further the gulf separating Epicurus' and Glaucon's account of man's basic psychology. For Hobbes, our desire for power is a basic and natural desire. Individuals will come into conflict, because the scarcity of a desired good like power is inevitable. It is impossible for each person to continue increasing his power over everyone else. A basic desire for power will therefore lead to derivative desires for harming others and to widespread war. For Epicurus, though, the situation is very different, inasmuch as the desire for power is not basic. Rather, it is an unnatural and harmful desire that arises from a mistaken estimate of what produces security. For Epicurus, then, the scarcity of desired goods is not inevitable. Individuals can be completely happy with little and need not come into conflict. As Torquatus insists, there is no reason for transgressing, because desires that arise naturally are easily satisfied without any wrong-doing whatsoever (*De fin.* I.52–53).

We might reasonably protest that Epicurus' claim about the ready availability for one and all of enough goods for a happy life might be subject to embarrassment. Or we could object that conditions of extreme scarcity eventually might drive even a community of Epicurean sages into aggressive and stressful competitions for goods

65. Part of the confusion about the nature of contracts at this stage rests on differences between contracting parties. Those who, like Epicurean sages, attempt to fulfill only their basic desires do not view contracts as compromises. Those who want power and wealth may be caught in the Prisoners' Dilemma. Since, in Epicurus' view, both sorts of individuals will eventually enter into contracts, it is difficult to give a uniform account of the functions and aims of the contract at this advanced stage. This perhaps accounts for Lucretius' reticence about contracts at *DRN* V. 1136–60.

66. For this reason, Epicureans can be defended against the charge that they will try to exploit those who have not formed contracts with them. They may not show a Good Samaritan's positive concern for a stranger's interests, but they have no reason for exploiting others, whether they share contractual ties or not.

(however, see SV 44).[67] But it is important to see why Epicurus would remain unmoved by this kind of objection. For Epicurus, this optimistic claim about the convergence of all natural, rational interests is not just a matter of empirical verification. Rather, his argument depends on a radical inversion of the logic of Hobbes's argument. Epicurus considers it impossible for the genuine interests of individuals ever to conflict. For the Epicurean, no matter what kinds of constraints are placed on our desires and no matter how severely we restrict the range of our desires, we still can achieve happiness. Even in conditions of extreme scarcity, we can remain completely happy and need not come into conflict or resort to injustice.

Of course, problems still remain for Epicurus' account. If only a few individuals are convinced of their need for power over others, a war of all against all can get started.[68] Although the Epicurean has no desire to harm or to compete with others, the Hobbesian would argue that sometimes even the Epicurean may need to take up an aggressive posture of defence. But, given the Epicurean conception of happiness, it is hard to say what goods or interests Epicureans would find it necessary to defend. Even their own survival cannot be of overwhelming concern to them. Lacking an inflexible Hobbesian commitment to self-preservation, however, an Epicurean could not easily be coerced into taking part in a psych-

67. Epicurus regularly includes the health of the body in his conception of happiness (see SV 33), which would seem to present serious difficulties for his claims about the convergence of interests. We easily can imagine conditions of famine, for example, where even the minimal sustenance required by sages is not available to everyone. As Cicero complains (De fin. II.89), "Totum autem id externum est, et quod externum, id in casu est. Ita fit beatae vitae domina fortuna." But D.L. X.138 suggests that even food is separable from the pleasant life and that under normal conditions, virtuous individuals will be less prone to sickness because of their moderate desires. In any case, Epicurus thinks that diseases either will kill us or will not interfere with our happiness (Bailey, Epicurus, frags. 64, 65; D.L. X.120b: tēn hugieian tisi men agathon, tisi de adiaphoron). Because Epicurus never lists the desires whose satisfaction he believes necessary for happiness, he seems to leave himself open to Cicero's charge of a naive optimism about our ability always to find enough for the good life. Given his claim that a good life is not enhanced by duration (KD 19), however, the sage will presumably, when minimal resources are no longer available, leave life at no cost to his overall happiness.

68. See D. Lewis, Convention (Cambridge, 1969), p. 88, for an account of the instability of a state of peaceful anarchy.

ically troubling conflict.[69] Epicurus does claim that anything to secure protection is a great natural good (*KD* 6); but he does not
think that power or aggression will provide security. Rather, one's
retirement and refuge in the *doctrina sapientium* are one's greatest
protections (*DRN* V.1125–35). Thus, even in these more extreme
cases, Epicurus is far less inclined to see the need for conflict than
is Hobbes.

Accordingly, contracts for mutual noninterference save the Epicurean from any possible inconveniences. By entering into contracts, the Epicurean can gain security from those who are not
sagelike.[70] Therefore, *pace* Bailey, the Epicurean has much to gain
and nothing at all to lose by forming contracts.[71] He has no desire
or need to harm others, while the contract in turn protects him
from being harmed. It is within this wider perspective, then, that
we must read a problematic passage in Stobaeus (*Flor.* 43.139; U.
530), which reports Epicurus as saying that "the laws exist for the
wise, not that they may not do wrong, but that they may not suffer
it."[72]

69. See Plutarch, *An recte dictum sit latente esse vivendum* 1130c.

70. See *De abstin.* I.10.2. In a certain sense, the Epicurean remains a free rider
on the system. An aggressive non-Epicurean has no reason to enter into a contract
for mutual noninterference with an Epicurean, since the Epicurean presents no
real threat (again, this inequality shows why the Prisoners' Dilemma, which assumes
a uniformity among the aims and desires of agents, is inappropriate for an Epicurean
context). If, however, there is a large enough system with enough aggressive non-
Epicureans, the Epicurean can take advantage of the resulting contract as a free
rider. Among Epicureans, there might be contracts strictly for coordinating interests.
For instance, Cicero claims that some Epicureans form contractual friendships in
which they treat one another as themselves (*De fin.* I.70). Such contracts do not solve
conflicts of interest; rather, they maximize pleasure by coordinating and consoli-
dating mutual interests.

71. Carneades (*Resp.* III.13) gives an account of these options with admirable
brevity: (a) do harm and not suffer it; or (b) both do and suffer harm; or (c) neither.
Option (a) is the best, (b) is the worst, and (c) is second best. In contrast, Epicurus
would claim that (c) is the best, but it is unclear that he would immediately choose
(a) over a possibility not mentioned by Carneades, namely, the Socratic option: (d)
do no harm but suffer it. Given his emphasis on the psychic benefits of justice, being
unjust may cause more disturbance than does suffering an injustice. Also, given the
Epicurean emphasis on rationality and autonomy, the activity of being unjust may
be more disturbing than suffering an injustice, especially since the Epicurean will
not be disturbed if he wrongly suffers the loss of property, power, and other goods
whose loss is conventionally thought to be unjust. See *Republic* 591b.

72. Cf. Bailey, *The Greek Atomists*, p. 514, for a differing account (also Long,

Another contrast with sophistic views of the contract should be noted. One might compromise and obey a contract while secretly wishing to violate its terms. For Epicurus, such a person would be filled with the greatest turmoil (*KD* 17) and would lack peace of mind. If we are just only because of fear[73] or if we nurture frustrated desires, we will not be in a state of *ataraxia* or katastematic pleasure. Thus, although the majority of men may need to be restrained by the fear of punishment,[74] Epicureans understand the psychic harmfulness of injustice and fear; they have no reason to engage in injustice or, for that matter, to long secretly for the power to commit injustices.[75]

Hellenistic Philosophy, pp. 69–71; Rist, p. 132; Goldschmidt, "La théorie épicurienne"; and Denyer).

73. A passage in Lucretius (*DRN* V.1151–160), often taken as evidence that the sage is restrained from injustice only by the fear of punishment, actually has a more specific target. Lucretius argues that the fear of punishment taints the *praemia vitae* for those who (*quemque* in 1152 is not all-inclusive) commit violence and injury. The sage has no desire to be violent or to injure anyone. He thus has no reason to be anxious about future detection and punishment (see *De fin.* I.44, II.71). At *De off.* III.9, the Epicureans refuse to believe in the possibility of the Gyges myth since they maintain that one cannot be sure that an injustice will never be detected (*KD* 35). But it is nowhere hinted that an Epicurean would find Gyges' life happy. One badly fragmented text further confirms this view about the sage: *ou parontos oudenos ho kektēmenos to tou genous telos paraplēsios estin agathos* (Bailey, *Epicurus*, frag. 93). See U. 533 and Konstan, pp. 56–57, for further defense of the claim that the fear of punishment is not the sage's motive in following commonly recognized requirements of morality.

74. Cf. Konstan, p. 45, for Epicurean attitudes toward punishment as an institutional and educative practice. Konstan argues that, just as he hopes to save mankind from religious fears, Epicurus also hopes to release the masses from the fear of punishment; but until such time as agents learn the psychic benefits of justice, the benefits of fear probably outweigh the harm caused by a war of all against all. Threats of punishment, however, are not addressed to sages (Porphyry, *De abstin.* I.7–12).

75. A passage in Plutarch (*Adv. Colot.* 1127d) that apparently quotes one of Epicurus' *Diaporiai* (*Puzzles*) is sometimes taken as support for the claim that the sage is restrained from injustice only by the fear of punishment. When asked whether the sage will break the law if undetected, Epicurus replied, "the unqualified predication [*epikatēgorēma*] is not free from difficulty." But as De Lacy notes (*ad loc.* p. 313), sages will break only laws that no longer reflect mutual advantage (*sumpheron*) and hence are no longer just; cf. *KD* 38. This position leaves open the possibility that the sage will break an unjust law even if detected. Imagine the case where in a particular society practicing Epicureanism is punishable by one day in prison.

Here we see another point of contact between Epicurus' conception of justice as a virtuous inner state and his account of the contract. Those who enter into contracts with the right conception of their own good also will have a just state of character and hence will enjoy *ataraxia*. They adhere to contracts not merely because of fear but because they understand why they should refrain from harming others and why psychic benefits will accrue to them by adhering to contracts. In this important sense, then, justice is a virtuous state and not mere conformity to the terms of a contract. The virtuous enter contracts for the right reasons and with the proper psychic dispositions. Yet, in so doing, they in no way sacrifice their self-interest.

For the Epicurean, moreover, there are further links between our happiness and our pursuit of justice. To guarantee that we achieve *ataraxia* and *aponia*, we must be capable of restricting our desires to those that are necessary and easily satisfied. Justice depends on this same ability to control and limit our desires rationally. It is not surprising, therefore, that Epicurus believes refraining from injustice will benefit us; we have compelling hedonic reasons for doing so.[76]

Clearly, the Epicurean would have overwhelming hedonic reasons for breaking such a law. The sage has no reason, however, to be dissatisfied with laws that are naturally just. E. Zeller, *The Stoics, Epicureans, and Skeptics* (London, 1880), p. 259, gets this right. For the opposing view see, most recently, Denyer. Vander Waerdt, "Justice of the Epicurean Wise Man," argues that "the content of justice is entirely derived from the compact of advantage embodied in the positive legal order." I doubt that *KD* 37 and 38 can support this claim. Moreover, it collapses distinctions between positive law and natural advantage in disturbing ways; for instance, it would restrict the Epicurean from pursuing great advantanges (say, practicing Epicureanism), at the price of blind and unreflective obedience to unjust and harmful laws. See Philodemus, *Rhet.* 24.26. Lucretius' comment at *DRN* V.1127 (*ut satius multo iam sit parere quietum*) is not necessarily unqualified.

76. A further difficulty arises here that is also troubling for Plato's defense of justice on the basis of its psychic benefits (cf. Irwin, *Plato's Moral Theory*, p. 205). Can Epicurus show that sages will have sufficient reason for refraining from isolated acts of injustice that do no irreparable harm to their overall psychic tranquillity? Epicurus is not necessarily vulnerable to these types of objections to teleological defenses of morality, which attempt to drive a wedge between justice and happiness. Relying on his account of katastematic pleasure, Epicurus can claim that no hedonic reward (presumably kinetic) would justify even an isolated or momentary disturbance in the sage's tranquillity, that is, happiness.

If everyone were pursuing happiness in the proper Epicurean manner, there would be no conflicts among individuals and consequently no need for contracts (see Porphyry, *De abstin.* I.8.4).[77] But since not everyone has a correct Epicurean understanding of the good, contracts protect the Epicurean from harm.[78] The Epicurean has ample reasons for cultivating both a just state of character and, until others also become Epicureans, contractual justice.[79]

Conclusion

In *Republic* IV, Plato argues that justice, along with courage, temperance, and wisdom, is an internal character trait that enables us to control and adjust our desires rationally in order to achieve psychic harmony and happiness. A somewhat analogous defense

77. Cf. H. Kelsen, "What Is Justice?" in *Essays in Legal and Moral Philosophy*, ed. O. Weinberger (Boston, 1973), p. 4, "where there are no conflicts, there is no need of justice"; also Hume's opening argument in the *Enquiry* that in conditions of 'superabundance' rules of property and justice are superfluous; see Democritus 68.B.245. A fragment of Diogenes of Oenoanda (Smith, *Thirteen New Fragments,* frag. 21) states that when men's lives are filled with justice and friendship, there will be no more need for city walls or laws. Diogenes does not claim that there will be no more need for justice, since we presumably will still derive psychic benefits from our being just; there will be no more need for contracts, however, since all will understand their proper *telos.*

78. Since injustice upsets the sage's *ataraxia*, the Epicurean has reasons independent of the contract for restraining his desires. But if a basic motivation for joining in contracts is the desire for *asphaleia*, there is a further problem. Epicurus claims that a sage cannot be harmed with respect to his happiness. This assertion, however, seems to allow for a number of different conceptions of harm. For instance, if physical harm does not significantly diminish a sage's happiness but psychic disruption does, Epicurus might allow:

(a) I may be physically harmed without upsetting my *ataraxia*.

(b) I may physically harm others without upsetting their *ataraxia*.

(c) I may physically harm others without upsetting my *ataraxia* (since I am not significantly harming them).

All three options seem to undercut reasons for worrying about the compliance of others to a contract. In general, Epicurus seems to be less concerned about problems of others' compliance, in part because he worries not only about following rules, but also about just states of character.

79. Thus the Epicurean is not in the position of G. R. Grice's 'Master Criminal' who finds it in his interest to make a contract to do X, without deeming it in his interest to actually do X (*The Grounds of Moral Judgment* [Cambridge, 1967], p. 101).

of justice has many attractions for Epicurus. As we have seen, Epicurus also thinks that being virtuous is the surest path to happiness. In pursuing *ataraxia* and *hēdonē*, therefore, we have compelling prudential reasons, independent of the attitudes and actions of others, for refraining from folly, cowardice, intemperance, injustice, and their resulting psychic disturbances. Epicurus thus agrees with Plato that if we are capable of being virtuous and of controlling and rationally ordering our desires, we will be better off than those who are at the mercy of their desires, regardless of the conduct of those around us.

Plato, though, argues that a contractual theory of justice is incompatible with a conception that treats justice as a virtuous psychic state. He argues that we will not understand why we should be just until we see that justice is a psychic condition that invariably benefits us and contributes to our happiness.[80] The Epicurean, however, would claim that Plato is being too hasty. Although agreeing with Plato about the psychic benefits of justice, Epicurus thinks that a contractual theory has important practical benefits, as well as a paedeutic function for those who are not yet just. Contracts can help protect those who already are just from those who are not. Thus, Epicurus thinks that we can reconcile and harmonize the demands of psychic[81] and contractual justice,[82] since the requirements of contractual justice do not interfere with our pursuit of

80. Here, of course, I refer only to Plato's views in the *Republic*. In the *Crito* and the *Laws*, for example, he has a different attitude toward contracts.

81. I use the expression 'psychic justice' guardedly, since it is liable to create confusions. I do not mean that Epicurus' view is in any sense identical to Plato's elaborate theory about the inner workings and harmony of different parts of the soul. At the same time, however, Epicurus' emphasis on contentment demonstrates a stronger concern with inner harmony than do other theories that treat justice as a virtue. One might, for instance, think that a virtuous state of character is compatible with, or is even enhanced by, a considerable amount of inner turmoil. Thus, it is too weak to claim merely that Epicurus views justice as a virtue; he associates it with a particular state of psychic calm.

82. In so doing, Epicurus makes a stronger attempt than Plato to account for and explain the connections between psychic and 'vulgar' justice. Plato might object, however, that the Epicurean contract not to harm or be harmed fails to capture many of the activities required by vulgar justice. If Epicurus must construe the demands of vulgar justice more widely and expand the requirements of the contract accordingly, it becomes harder for him to claim that this broader range of demands will never jeopardize our psychic calm.

psychic calm. Furthermore, if we enter into contracts with a just state of character and a proper conception of our good, we will understand that refraining from harming others does not diminish our self-interest. Indeed, by entering into contracts, many can come to learn the psychic benefits of refraining from injustice.

By the same token, Epicurus wants to maintain the invulnerability of the wise and to argue that their happiness is entirely under their own control. When coupled with his belief that the virtues are inextricably linked to happiness, we can readily understand why Epicurus would be attracted to a view of the virtues as psychic states that depend neither on chance features of the world nor on the actions of others. On the other hand, justice is a virtue predominantly associated with the actions and interests of others, and thus might seem to be subject to the vagaries of chance. A contractual theory is meant to explain, among other things, how benefiting others can for the most part be in one's own interest. Within such a perspective, the actions of others strongly influence one's own actions, since the compliance of others to a contract provides strong motivation for one's own compliance. Yet even the most sanguine contract theorist rarely claims that our compliance to a contract will invariably benefit us (see *KD* 38).[83]

It might seem that in attempting to harmonize the demands of contractual justice with justice as a virtuous psychic condition, Epicurus would be caught in an impossible dilemma: either he can attempt to show, within the framework of his contractual theory, how justice is a virtue that benefits others but does not always benefit the one who is just; or, relying on his theory of justice as a virtuous inner condition, he can show how justice invariably benefits one who is just, without, however, entirely explaining how being just also benefits others. It often is claimed that Plato's account of psychic justice in the *Republic* is marred for this very reason. Plato begins with the assumption that justice, since it is a virtue, must reliably benefit someone who is just. But only after he has shown how one benefits from psychic justice does he attempt to show, often with

83. The Epicurean does not agree with Hume that one has reasons to support a particular beneficial system that may diminish one's self-interest on some occasions (*KD* 37–38), although the non-Epicurean may be motivated by such reasons (*DRN* V.1142).

mixed results, how one's justice also benefits others and is consonant with the demands of 'vulgar' justice.

The Epicurean, similarly, is perhaps too eager to prove that someone will always benefit from being just (*De fin.* I.50). Those who practice Epicurean justice will refrain from injustice and will have reasons for acting in a conventionally just way,[84] and the Epicurean contract, neither to harm or be harmed, gives further grounds for refraining from injustice. But Epicurus' account of justice fails to show why we should have positive regard for others' interests. He only can claim to have accomplished the more negative task of showing that our refraining from injustice can be mutually beneficial.

Although Epicurus can argue with some plausibility that we have good reasons, derived from our pursuit of the untroubled life, to be psychically just and to refrain from injustice, it is much less clear that he can offer any reasons for showing positive regard for others. *Gnomologium vaticanum* 44 suggests that a sage, having accommodated himself to straits (*eis ta anagkaia sugkatheis*), knows better how to give than to receive. But it is not clear that Epicurus formulates any reliable guidelines for tapping the sage's fund of self-sufficiency (*thesauron autarkeias*). In any case, the sage's dispensations may not

84. In this context, it is helpful to remember Vlastos's claim that 'justice' for the most part in Greek ethics was used with a more specific sense of refraining from *pleonexia* (see "Justice and Happiness in the *Republic*," in *Platonic Studies* [Princeton, 1973], p. 111). It is by no means clear that this intuition is shared only by the Greeks. Mill makes a similar claim, and recently G. Harman (*The Nature of Morality* [Oxford, 1977], pp. 110 ff.) has suggested that another central moral intuition is captured by this more restricted sense of justice. Normally, he argues, we think it much worse to harm someone than to refrain from helping someone. (We should add to his account, however, the restriction that this holds in cases of equal harm—that is, Smith would suffer greater harm if I refrain from telling him that a truck is about to hit him than if I maliciously step on his toes.) Such a general principle might seem irrational or unmotivated unless we view it as a convention arising from a principle of noninjury and a much weaker principle of mutual aid among nonequals. Everyone would benefit equally from a conventional practice of trying not to harm one another, while not everyone would benefit equally from a strong helping principle. Otherwise, he argues, it would be hard to see why we should suppose that there is a moral difference between harming and not helping. Cf. T. M. Scanlon, "A Contractualist Alternative," in *New Directions in Ethics*, ed. J. P. De Marco (New York, 1985), p. 44, for a further account of the contractual theory's link to this principle on the basis of 'rejectability,' that is, what rational agents can reasonably accept and reject.

coincide with commonly recognized demands of justice; or in giving, perhaps, he may not be motivated by other-regarding considerations.

Thus Epicurus perhaps can show that injustice harms a rational agent's pursuit of the pleasant life, but he has not shown that a positive concern for others' expectations and interests will benefit a rational agent. Though the Epicurean contract prevents mutual harm, it requires no positive commitment to the interests of others. It is surely possible to frame contracts requiring stronger principles of mutual aid, but Epicurus suggests that such contracts do not conform to the *prolēpsis* of justice. Epicurus' rather hygenic *prolēpsis* of justice, therefore, seems to be cleansed of troubling features of ordinary beliefs and neatly fitted to his account of justice as a virtuous psychic condition. In one important sense, contractual justice is the outward expression of psychic justice: while both are fitted to Epicurean arguments about the achievement of *ataraxia* through the rational control of desires, neither shows why we should value the interests of others, especially in a way that might endanger our psychic invulnerability. If, in order to be just, we must value and have positive regard for others, Epicurus' account falls short.[85] Before we can conclude that there is something objectionably egoistic about his ethical theory as a whole, however, we must wait until we have examined his theory of friendship as well, especially since he argues that friendship is the proper locus for developing concerns for others' interests.

Cicero claims that the Epicureans' psychological assumptions make

---

85. A word of caution is in order. Epicurus can object that these arguments show only that his account of justice does not fall neatly into traditional categories of justice. They do not show that he has not captured the most important characteristic of justice, namely, that it restrains us from harming one another; nor do they show that one cannot best demonstrate positive regard for another's interests in another context, for example, friendship. Bailey praises Epicurus for the "ruthless consistency" with which he applies his egoistic theory, but laments the extent to which he is unable to account for moral intuitions and "the most natural impulses of most normal human beings" (*The Greek Atomists*, p. 528). Like many other teleological theorists, Epicurus may prefer the results of his own theory to the dictates of common beliefs (cf. H. J. McCloskey, *Meta-Ethics and Normative Ethics* [The Hague, 1969], p. 174, and H. Sidgwick, *The Methods of Ethics* [London, 1907], p. 467). See chapter 3 for further discussion of this general issue and some important qualifications.

for easy solutions to problems of justice and suggests that their conception of pleasure arises, in part, from a failure of nerve and a timid desire to avoid conflict. He argues that Epicureans mistake timidity for rationality and adds that taking risks for some goods may be more rational than merely shunning risks. In a certain sense, this Ciceronian claim is not wholly misleading, since the Epicurean defence of justice is clearly tailored to psychological claims rooted in a distinctive theory of pleasure. But to the extent that the Epicurean analysis of pleasure and of *eudaimonia* is plausible, Cicero's objection misses the mark. At the very least, we are faced with an original and subtle attempt to show that contractual and virtue-based theories of justice are not strictly incompatible.

3

Friendship and Altruism

Discussions of altruistic friendship figure prominently in Epicurean ethical theory. At first glance, this is rather surprising. In view of the strength of Epicurus' commitments to hedonism and egoism, we might expect the Epicurean to be a kind of Hobbesian egoist. Lucretius, for instance, adopts a harsh, almost neurotically bitter view of man's social condition. The world of *De rerum natura* V is populated by solitary and brutish individuals who, acting from purely selfish motives, inevitably collide and inflict mutual harm. Under the best of circumstances, it can be hoped that agents, schooled by their suffering, will grudgingly restrain their immediate appetites and realize the advantages of avoiding a self-destructive competition for goods and power. Indeed, only when individual interests have reached such an equilibrium can any semblance of stability or civil life emerge. One readily understands why it might be in the interest of rational agents to agree to a kind of wary cooperation, but it is extremely difficult to see why anyone in such a setting should be altruistic and care for others apart from their merely instrumental value.

Epicurus' ethical theory is commonly taken to be narrowly egoistic,[1] and many of his maxims on friendship reveal a correspondingly prudent and careful attention to self-interest. His emphasis on the

---

1. A common verdict of the doxography (and of most modern scholarship) is voiced by Lactantius: "dicit Epicurus neminem esse qui alterum diligat nisi sua causa" (*Institutiones Divinae* III.17.42).

security and utility afforded by friends, his continual effort to link friendship and pleasure, his description of friendship as a means to relieve anxiety—all give strong indications of a somewhat timid, but nonetheless inflexible egoism. Clearly, if personal pleasure is the ultimate goal of the Epicurean's actions, his hedonic calculations can include others only as a means to his own selfish gratification. Altruistic friendship requires, at the very least, an interest in others for their own sake.[2] Thus, given its general structure and principles, Epicurus' ethical theory would seem unable to allow for the varieties of motivation and concern for others' interests that we are inclined to think necessary for altruistic friendship.

It would be reasonable to suppose that, within such an ethical framework, Epicurus might endorse what Aristotle calls friendships of advantage or pleasure. It is quite easy to imagine him, with characteristic vehemence and disdain, deriding altruistic friendship either as a misguided illusion or the result of hedonic miscalcula- tions. Yet rather unexpectedly, he commends altruistic friendship so zealously that at times he seems almost a kind of pagan high priest of *agapē*.[3] In Diogenes Laertius, for example, we find that the Epicurean wise man sometimes will die for a friend, *kai huper philou pote tethnēksesthai* (D.L. X.121b). Elsewhere, it is reported that the *sapiens* will endure the greatest pains for his friends, *huper tōn philōn tas megistas algēdonas anadechesthai* (Plutarch, *Adv. Col.* 1111b). Initially, it is tempting to explain away these passages as merely apparent cases of altruism. After all, Epicurus parts company with egoists such as Hobbes, who, when reckoning with death, rank self-preservation even above pleasure as the ultimate goal of conduct. For Epicurus, death is nothing to us, nor should it be, since it in no way is able to diminish our pleasures (*KD* 19). On such a view, dying might easily be preferable to the anxious, vulnerable, and hence painful life one might face without friends. Instead of being the ultimate sign of altruism, sacrificing oneself for a friend might

2. "Aut quis [potest] amicus esse cuiquam quem non ipsum amet propter ipsum?" Cicero, *De fin.* II.78; see Aristotle, *Rhet.* 1380b36, *EN* 1156b7, 1156b31, and the classic discussion of G. Vlastos, "The Individual as an Object of Love in Plato," in *Platonic Studies* (Princeton, N.J., 1973), pp. 1–34.

3. See N. De Witt, *Epicurus and His Philosophy* (Minneapolis, Minn., 1954), p. 31 for the rather odd notion of altruistic hedonism and a view of Epicureanism as a species of *praeparatio evangelica*.

actually be an acceptable egoistic strategy for avoiding pain.[4] Similarly, although he has more reason to fear pain than to fear death, the Epicurean can expect to enhance his prospects for safety (*asphaleia*; *KD* 7, 13–14) and its consequent pleasures by enduring even very great pains for the sake of friendship.

Other evidence, however, resists translation into an egoistic calculus. At *De finibus* I.68, we find the requirement that a wise man feel exactly the same toward his friends as he does toward himself.[5] At *Gnomologium vaticanum* 23, Epicurus says that all friendship is choiceworthy for itself apart from its instrumental benefits, *pasa philia di' heautēn hairetē*.[6] These passages strongly suggest an un-

4. Epicurus grants, for example, that the *sapiens* should commit suicide if his overall prospects for pain outweigh his prospects for pleasure. Given the Epicurean view of death, an egoistic justification of self-sacrifice might be possible along the lines I have suggested. But it is important to note that Epicurus himself nowhere formulates such a defense; nor does the Epicurean Torquatus, who thinks that dying for a friend is the clearest indication of genuine altruism. At the beginning of his exposition of Epicurean friendship (*De fin.* I.65), Torquatus likens Epicurus to mythical figures willing to die for their friends. Similarly, Cicero contrasts this type of "Pyladic friendship" (see *Lael.* 24) with ordinary friendship (*De fin.* II.80). The evidence is too scanty to determine whether Epicurus thinks that dying for a friend ever can be consistent with egoism. But Cicero suggests that Epicureans are defending Pyladic friendships (II.84) which are not justifiable solely on the basis of self-interest. Thus, although we can perhaps give dying for a friend an egoistic justification by bringing together various elements in Epicurus' thought, we should be wary of artificially removing altruistic elements from D.L. X.121b.

5. "Quocirca eodem modo sapiens erit affectus erga amicum quo in se ipsum, quosque labores propter suam voluptatem susciperet, eosdem suscipiet propter amici voluptatem." Cf. *SV* 56.

6. See *KD* 27; *De fin.* I.65, II.83. *SV* 23 is a brief but fundamental text: *pasa philia di' heautēn hairetē; archēn eilēphen apo tēs ōpheleias. Hairetē* is Usener's correction. Jean Bollack ("Les maximes de l'amitié," in *ACGB 1968* [Paris, 1969], pp. 221–36) retains the manuscript reading, *aretē*, as does A. A. Long, "Pleasure and Social Utility—The Virtues of Being Epicurean," in *Aspects de la philosophie hellénistique*, Fondation Hardt, Entretiens sur l'antiquité classique 32 (Geneva, 1986) p. 305. J. Rist (*Epicurus: An Introduction* [Cambridge, 1972], p. 131), finding it strange to speak of friendship as an *aretē*, defends *hairetē* and tries to soften the conflict with egoism by drawing a parallel to Stoic usage. He suggests that *hairetē* is equivalent to the Stoic *proēgmenon*: "When Epicurus says that friendship is to be chosen for itself, perhaps he merely means not that it is ultimately valuable, but that it leads directly and without intermediaries to the acquisition of pleasure" (132); see also R. Müller, *Die Epikureische Gesellschaftstheorie* (Berlin, 1972), p. 118. This suggestion is interesting, given the Stoics' and Epicureans' many mutual borrowings of terminology.

selfish picture of friendship and seem to enjoin the positive, altruistic concern for others' interests rejected by the Hobbesian. Surely, though, any recommendation of unselfish friendship sharply conflicts with Epicurus' much-repeated claim that only one's own pleasure is the *telos* of action and desirable for itself. Herein lies the dilemma of Epicurean friendship.

Unhappy with these inconsistencies, scholars have attempted to explain the divergent elements in Epicurus' account of *philia* by means of either associationist or Hobbesian arguments. Associationism acknowledges the possibility of altruism but attempts, nonetheless, to set altruistic action on a firmly egoistic foundation. Like Mill's miser, who begins by valuing money for its use, then comes to regard it as an end in itself, individuals initially form friendships for mutual advantage, but in time come to value friends for their own sake, regardless of any instrumental benefit. Altruism, on this view, is entrusted by Epicurus to the effortless custody of habit; it is aroused by degrees and results unreflectively, and somewhat mechanically, from habit and continual association. In contrast, on the Hobbesian construal of Epicurus' theory, altruism is merely disguised egoism, an unintended result of hedonic miscalculation, or, perhaps, just simply irrational. If it is reasonable only to pursue pleasure, and if pleasure necessarily is an egoistic state, all actions, no matter how seemingly altruistic, are either self-regarding or irrational. If Epicurus recommends friendship, it is argued, it must therefore be as an egoistic ploy for maximizing personal pleasure.

Curiously, these recent characterizations of Epicurus' theory bear

---

On Rist's view, however, it is unclear why the virtues (especially prudence) would not be *hairetai* as well, since they lead directly (and with even fewer intermediaries) to the acquisition of pleasure; see *Ad Men.* 132 and A. W. H. Adkins, *From the Many to the One* (Ithaca, N.Y., 1970), p. 259. Rist's suggestion further neglects how in this particular context we can attribute a strictly instrumental sense to *di' heautēn*, since it clearly is being contrasted with *apo tēs ōpheleias*. Elsewhere, in the handful of surviving occurrences of *hairetos* and *hairesis*, Epicurus, unlike the Stoics and Aristotle, is quite fastidious about its noninstrumental sense (*Ad Men.* 129, *SV* 16). Similarly, although Long is right to claim that it might be perfectly intelligible for Epicurus to call friendship a virtue (as Aristotle does at *EN* 1152a2), it is far less clear what it would mean for Epicurus to call friendship an *intrinsic* virtue. Usener's emendation, although by no means certain, gains further support from Cicero's account in the *De finibus*.

a striking correspondence, according to Cicero, not to Epicurus' own doctrine but to theories formulated by his *diadochoi*. At *De finibus* I.65–70, Torquatus outlines three distinct theories of friendship held by Epicureans.[7] He briefly discusses associationism (I.69) and friendships based on self-seeking, Hobbesian contracts (I.70). Arguing that these were later developments in Epicureanism, not attributable to Epicurus himself,[8] he presses another view of friendship (I.66–69), which Cicero takes to be Epicurus' own.[9] From Torquatus we learn that Epicurus requires the wise man to love (I.67) and feel toward (I.68) his friends exactly as he loves and feels toward himself. Thus Torquatus' description of these altruistic elements in Epicurean friendship appears to fit coherently with Epicurus' contention that friendship is choiceworthy in itself, *di' heautēn hairetē* (*SV* 23), since by showing disinterested concern for friends, one treats friendship as a noninstrumental end. Taken together, these passages suggest a set of requirements consonant with the demands of altruistic friendship. Though Cicero clearly is at great pains to emphasize the essential links that Epicurus sees between friendship and pleasure (I.68, II.82), it is difficult to ascribe to Epicurus a consistent Hobbesian egoism, since the Hobbesian cannot advocate that anyone, let alone a wise man, regard a friend as another self. Cicero's testimony, in conjunction with *Gnomologium vaticanum* 23, should give us some grounds, then, for questioning recent attributions of either associationist or strictly self-seeking friendship to Epicurus. The *De finibus*, moreover, provides an extremely plausible theoretical and historical backdrop against which to examine and articulate Epicurus' sometimes disconnected pronouncements.

7. A fourth, discussed at *De fin.* II.80–81, suggests that Epicurus is a strict egoist in theory but a disinterested friend in practice ("facere melius quam dicere"). This view grows out of the testimony for Epicurus' lofty practice of friendship and the belief that he is committed to a strictly egoistic theory. I argue that there is also within Epicurus' theoretical framework a commitment to altruism, thereby removing the asymmetry between his theory and his practice of friendship.

8. "Numquam dictum ab ipso illo" (*De fin.* II.82).

9. Initially, these theories are presented as three more general Epicurean alternatives. However, at *De finibus* II.82, Cicero responds in turn to each of the three theories described at I.65–70. He contrasts the first theory with more recent ones and claims to find elements of Epicurus' view only in this first theory ("e quibus unum mihi videbar ab ipso Epicuro dictum cognoscere").

An answer to the questions raised by friendship and altruism is important for the general interpretation of Epicurus' ethics. Efforts at minimizing the conflicts in his discussion of friendship have been motivated partly, no doubt, by a desire to preserve the "elegant simplicity"[10] of his ethics and of his modes of ethical inquiry.[11] By taking these inconsistencies seriously, however, we can ascribe to Epicurus a considerably more complex, though perhaps less tidy, theory of altruism and of motivation in general.

In many respects, Epicurus' predicament over the relation of pleasure and altruism closely resembles Mill's well-known difficulties in formulating his principle of utility. In attempting to modify the hedonist doctrines of his contemporaries, Mill criticizes orthodox Benthamites for having an excessively narrow conception of human nature and motivation. He complains that missing from Bentham's "Table of the Springs of Action" are other pursuits and ideal ends that are valuable for their own sakes: the desire for self-perfection and for virtue; the love of beauty, of order, and of action; and even the "love of loving" ("Bentham," in *Dissertations and Discussions*). In chapter 4 of *Utilitarianism*, Mill further explains: "The principle of utility does not mean that any given pleasure, as music, for instance, or any given exemption from pain, as for example health, is to be looked upon as means to a collective something termed happiness, and to be desired on that account. They are desired and desirable in and for themselves; besides being means,

10. A. A. Long, *Hellenistic Philosophy* (London, 1974), p. 72.

11. Since the time of Guyau, Epicurus' ethical theory and methods of ethics have been equated with hedonist theories in the British empiricist tradition. Even Epicurus' most sympathetic critics have viewed him as a proto-Benthamite, methodically applying his felicific calculus to all human action. Although these critics mean to differentiate Epicurus' doctrine from less refined sorts of hedonism, they regularly attribute to him a mode of ethical inquiry that is insensitive to common beliefs; they argue that Epicurus rather obsessively attempts to reduce all conduct to fit his hedonist theory by riding roughshod over many central ethical beliefs and intuitions. In this view, Epicurus' hedonism is consistent, but it buys consistency at too high a price: it neglects a large body of evidence and therefore must necessarily fail to capture many important intuitions about morality. Such a view, however, may need modification. At least in his account of friendship, Epicurus seems willing to concede the common belief that friendship requires valuing others for their own sake, even though this creates difficulties for his hedonism. This concession to ordinary beliefs and intuitions may force him into inconsistencies, but it shows that he has at least some sensitivity and respect for the *endoxa*.

they are a part of the end." To give a broader and more plausible conception of happiness than Bentham does, Mill feels constrained to countenance intrinsic ends and sources of value other than pleasure. Strictly speaking, though, this conflicts with the demands of his hedonism by admitting into his theory, as Sidgwick notes, "nonhedonistic grounds of preference."[12]

Epicurus' thoughts on friendship, I would argue, are the expression of an ethical impulse and a philosophical motivation akin to Mill's. In asserting that friendship is *di' heautēn hairetē*, Epicurus recognizes a value and an end other than pleasure. However reluctant, this acknowledgment is not just a casual or momentary lapse into benevolence, nor is it merely an isolated feature of his ethical thinking that should be explained away in the light of his other views. By attending carefully to the conflicting signals in his theory of friendship, we can isolate something of the specific manner in which ethical questions presented themselves to Epicurus and, indeed, to other Hellenistic moral philosophers. Furthermore, by examining the nexus of issues that includes altruism and friendship, we can bring into sharper relief some of Epicurus' most characteristic ethical aims and goals, not all of which are smoothly compatible.

Associationist and Contractual Friendships

At this point, it will be helpful to examine the two accounts of friendship developed by Epicurus' *diadochoi*. Each isolates and further elaborates an important strand of Epicurus' thought on altruism, but not without violating other central features of his theory. One group, whose views Torquatus finds a bit faint-hearted, maintains that an awareness of the intrinsic value of friendship may blossom (*efflorescere*; I.69) from an initial preoccupation with one's own interest.[13] A proponent of this type of associationist theory

12. H. Sidgwick, *The Methods of Ethics*, 5th ed. (London, 1893), pp. 95, 148.
13. "Cum autem usus progrediens familiaritatem effecerit, tum amorem efflorescere tantum ut, etiamsi nulla sit utilitas ex amicitia, tamen ipsi amici propter se ipsos amentur" (*De fin.* I.69). J. M. Guyau, *La morale d'Epicure* (Paris, 1886), p. 136, has been the most influential proponent of this view (reluctantly and inconsistently

might appeal to psychological or to historical criteria to explain the possibility and the origins of altruism. Torquatus' discussion lends itself more readily to psychological interpretation, but scholars have found its requisite historical framework as well. In Lucretius' discussion of the formation of mankind's first communities, there occurs a passage that, on some accounts, gives historical justification for the Epicurean's pursuit of friendship:

> tunc et amicitiem coeperunt iungere aventes
> finitimi inter se nec laedere nec violari,
> et pueros commendarunt muliebreque saeclum,
> vocibus et gestu cum balbe significarent
> imbecillorum esse aequum misererier omnis.
> nec tamen omnimodis poterant concordia gigni,
> sed bona magnaque pars servabat foedera caste;
> aut genus humanum iam tum foret omne peremptum
> nec potuisset adhuc perducere saecla propago.
>
> *(DRN* V.1019–27)

Then neighbors also began to enter into *amicitiem* with one another, eager neither to harm nor suffer harm, and they entrusted their children and the race of women to each other's protection, conveying by means of inarticulate cries and gestures that it was fair for all to have pity on the weak. Nonetheless, total harmony could not be brought about in every case, but a good part, indeed the greater part, would keep their agreements faithfully; otherwise, even then the human race would have been completely destroyed, nor could it have propagated itself down to the present day.

Farrington finds in this passage a historical warrant for the Epicureans' rejection of civil society and their espousal of simple communities based on friendship. On his view, friendship is an attempt to recapture a golden age of innocent reciprocities prior to the evils

---

followed by C. B. Bailey, *The Greek Atomists and Epicurus* [Oxford, 1928], p. 520). In "Vita Prior in Lucretius," *Hermathena* 81 (1953), 59–62, and "Lucretius and Manilius on Friendship," *Hermathena* 83 (1954), 10–16, B. Farrington describes the historical genesis of altruism; H. Usener, *Kleine Schriften* (Leipzig, 1912), p. 234, and D. Konstan, *Some Aspects of Epicurean Psychology* (Leiden, 1973), pp. 42–43, describe the psychology of forming altruistic attachments.

of civil society. Unfortunately, although this passage has been the source of many fertile misunderstandings, it provides evidence for neither the history nor the anthropology of friendship.[14] Clearly, Lucretius is describing only the foundation of justice, the basis of which is a contract for avoiding mutual harm ("nec laedere nec violari"; *KD* 31–3). To the extent that these primitive *foedera* (V.1025) guarantee only mutual noninterference, they do not reflect the mature vision of friendship practiced by the sage.[15] Nevertheless, even though surviving Epicurean texts furnish no clear historical justification of friendship, it is easy to see how such a defense might be formulated on the basis of associationism.

The associationist, similarly, can invoke psychological criteria to explain the growth of altruistic attachments. To a certain extent, these later Epicureans anticipate a kind of Freudian mechanics of desire that takes as its opening premise the psychological and rational priority of egoism. Initially, individuals are endowed with

---

14. Lucretius' use of *amicitia* at *DRN* V.1019 has been the source of considerable misunderstanding. Konstan, p. 43, correctly claims that in this context *amicities* cannot mean friendship (*pace* J. Rist, "Epicurus on Friendship," *Classical Philology* 75 [1980], p. 123). Relying on Lily Ross Taylor and Syme, he argues that *amicities* refers to political alliances, as it regularly does in the literature of the Republic. Such linguistic considerations alone, however, cannot support his position, since *amicitia* covers a wider range of relationships (see P. A. Brunt, " 'Amicitia' in the Late Roman Republic," in *The Crisis of the Roman Republic*, ed. R. Seager [Cambridge, 1969], pp. 199–218).

15. Long ("Pleasure and Social Utility," p. 310) argues that Lucretius is describing the "imagined origins" of friendships at *DRN* V. 1019. I find at least four serious difficulties for this account: (a) Even at this stage, the content of such "friendships" would be exceptionally impoverished. It seems highly implausible to suggest that friendship ever consists in nothing more than friends' leaving each other alone (*nec laedere nec violari*). (b) The expression *nec laedere nec violari* clearly translates the Epicurean formula for justice, *to mē blaptein allēlous mēde blaptesthai* (*KD* 33), and uses terminology familiar from Roman legal texts and inscriptions. (c) The appeal to a prior standard of fairness (*aequum*) in 1023 has no place in Epicurean discussions of friendship, nor does *concordia* (1024) with its implications of widespread societal harmony (on *concordia* see D. O. Ross, *Virgil's Elements* [Princeton, N.J., 1987], p. 209). (d) The process by which these relations are formed is not strictly rational (thus the appeal to sentiment and pity in 1023), nor are its results (the protection of women and children and the propagation of the race) included among the usual aims of Epicurean friendship. Cf. D. Furley ("Lucretius the Epicurean on the History of Mankind," in *Lucrèce*, Fondation Hardt, Entretiens sur l'antiquité classique 24 [Geneva, 1978], pp. 1–27) on the gulf separating Epicurus' developed doctrines from their primitive adumbrations in *DRN* V.

feelings of narcissistic self-love, but as self-love becomes differentiated and more limited, they form external attachments to others.[16] They may come to love friends even without expecting any personal pleasure.[17] Unfortunately, evidence for the actual mechanism of this process is not forthcoming in surviving Epicurean texts, and *efflorescere,* the *vox Ciceroniana,* is too vague to allow any very precise formulations. But associationism is a plausible move for these later Epicureans to make in defending the possibility of friendships that are *di' heautas hairetai.* Given the Epicurean emphasis on self-evident truths based on perception, a defense of altruism grounded in empirically verifiable psychological facts would not be surprising. By a somewhat similar move, Epicurus, in maintaining the truth of hedonism, sometimes merely notes some facts about our psychologies that he takes to be readily apparent to perception. An unkind critic might suggest that these later Epicureans are merely indulging a similar dogmatic impulse.

Despite the rational status of his first principles, Epicurus is quite clear about particular desires, like altruism, and their justification. These later Epicureans neglect their master's continual warnings that all particular first-order desires and impulses must be evaluated carefully and prudently. The important question for Epicurus' ethics is neither the causal origin of a desire nor its empirical description as arising from association. On the contrary, he is concerned with the proper evaluation of each desire and its place in one's life. During the course of our psychological development we may acquire desires to benefit our friends at the expense of our own self-interest, or perhaps such desires grow and become more firmly

16. Aristotle's account at *EN* 1166a1–2 can be fruitfully compared (see C. Kahn, "Aristotle and Altruism," *Mind* 89 [1981], 20–40). Cf. T. Nagel, *The Possibility of Altruism* (Oxford, 1970), pp. 19–20, on the general problem of normative inferences from facts about our psychologies.

17. *Pace* Rist, "Epicurus on Friendship," p. 124, who argues that in this passage *utilitas* means "particular advantages" but not "pleasure." For Rist the associationists sever friendship from advantage (I.69) but not from pleasure. Cicero, however, mirroring Epicurus, moves freely between *voluptas* and *utilitas* in his discussion of self-interested action (cf I.33–4, and Reid *ad loc.*); and it seems clear enough that, for these Epicureans, friends must be willing to value others apart from any hedonic benefit (*etiam omissa spe voluptatis;* II.82). Similarly, associationism makes explicit a final move toward altruism that Epicurus leaves in doubt at *SV* 23 (see below, "Friendship and Pleasure").

rooted in each successive generation. We may, moreover, have good empirical evidence that altruistic sentiment has its origins in imitation, habit, learned psychic dispositions, or institutions. The central question for Epicurus, though, is whether it makes good hedonic sense to satisfy a desire (*SV* 71). Altruistic desires might be necessary, like desires for food and shelter, or they might be merely unnecessary and liable to interfere with one's peace of mind and tranquillity. If, as in the case of ambition or avarice, altruism is unnecessary and harmful, the *sapiens* should eliminate it from his life in accordance with the dictates of the hedonist calculus. Even if indulging in altruism were a psychological necessity, the *sapiens* would want to reduce his concern for others to a minimum, if such concern diminishes his *eudaimonia*. If an Epicurean wants to justify the pursuit of friendship, he is therefore constrained to show how it can contribute to an agent's overall interest.[18] This demand precludes some standard defences of altruism based either on sentiment or on an agent's present aims and goals,[19] but it is hard to see how these later Epicureans might otherwise hope to justify their theory.

Two further difficulties naturally arise in this context, and Cicero quickly notices them. First, he registers the Kantian complaint that sentiment provides too idiosyncratic and contingent a basis for altruism. He argues that an Epicurean's altruistic feelings might soon fade in a friendship devoid of advantage. Later Epicureans may have thought that altruistic emotions are distinguishable from more contingent and transitory emotions such as passionate love, and thus they may have hoped that altruistic emotions, by being ingrained and habituated through association, could become stable enough to provide a foundation for more steady attachments.[20]

18. *Pros pasas tas epithumias prosakteon to eperōtēma touto: ti moi genēsetai an telesthēi to kata tēn epithumian epizētoumenon, kai ti ean mē telesthēi. (SV* 71). See *SV* 46; *Ad Men.* 132a: "the pleasant life is produced by sober reasoning searching out the motives for all choice and avoidance."

19. D. Parfit gives an account of the present-aims theory and its justification of altruism in *Reasons and Persons* (Oxford, 1984), pp. 127–30.

20. See L. Blum, *Friendship, Altruism, and Morality* (London, 1980), for a defense of friendship based on stable altruistic emotions. Three basic objections to the emotions that B. Williams describes in Kant find sympathetic anticipation in Epicurus: the emotions are too capricious; they are passively experienced; proneness

Such a development would be intriguing and important in Epicurean thinking about the passions, but it clearly would be a deviation from Epicurus' own conception.

Second, it is possible to dispute the associationists' description of the growth of altruistic desires. Cicero argues that, instead of merely being the result of habit, altruism requires the prior recognition of nonhedonic value. For this reason, the associationist misconstrues both the psychology and the mechanisms of altruistic friendship, since from a desire for pleasure and advantage only expedient friendships will arise (II.82). One does not come to associate altruism and pleasure by experiencing the pleasures of altruism. Nor can we explain the value of friendship merely in terms of the feelings associated with it. Rather, as Aristotle and the Stoics argue, one will find altruism pleasant to the extent that one already independently values its pursuit.

In any case, as Cicero notices (II.82), associationism admits too much. It recognizes pursuits that have value independent of their capacity for producing pleasure. Nor is it enough to argue that altruism arises from habit and association. Merely describing the genesis or explaining the acquisition of a desire gives insufficient reason for further cultivating it.[21] Therefore, the associationism of later Epicureans violates Epicurus' basic demand that we foster our desires reflectively and voluntarily, and we can safely assume that Epicurus himself would reject this development in Epicureanism.

The contractual account of friendship[22] bears witness to a contrary

---

to experiencing them is fortuitiously distributed (see Williams, "Morality and the Emotions," in *Morality and Moral Reasoning*, ed. John Casey [London, 1970]). For the Epicurean, moreover, it may be that no kind of social emotion is natural (Epict., *Disc.* 1.23.3, *In.* 1.21).

21. Epicurus fears the loss of rational control in passionate love (*SV* 18; Plut., *Amat.* 767c, where Epicureans are called *anerastoi*). Similarly, he allows little weight to custom, to habit, or to convention, since he wants our happiness to be securely in our own hands. See Guyau, pp. 136–39, for an account that makes friendship involuntary, instinctual, and mechanical rather than reflective. For a discussion of these issues see J. Narveson, *Morality and Utility* (Baltimore, 1967), p. 60. Also noteworthy in this context is Cicero's use of *amare* and *diligere*, since he uses *amare* only in connection with associationism.

22. *De fin.* II.83 suggests that Epicurus did not hold a contractual theory, and there is no hint of such a view in any of the fragments. *SV* 39 describes the mutual obligations of friendship, without, however, giving a contractual justification of those

attitude in later Epicureanism. Torquatus' statement of its precepts is extremely compressed: "Sunt autem qui dicant foedus esse quoddam sapientium ut ne minus amicos quam se ipsos diligant."(I.70) ("There are also those who claim that wise men make a kind of contract to love their friends no less than themselves"). First, it is important to notice that Epicurus, unlike Locke or Rousseau, allows the idea of contracting, by itself, no independent weight. To the Epicurean, the procedural fairness of a contract's formation is altogether irrelevant in deciding whether one should adhere to it. In his account of justice, Epicurus argues that a contract reflects the nature of justice (*tēn tou dikaiou phusin*) only if it continues to maintain agents' mutual advantage (*KD* 37–38). To a certain extent, then, Cicero is justified in his charge that an Epicurean has few reasons to honor, and no reason to value, an unprofitable commitment. For Epicurus, a contract must explain why a particular kind of behavior is conducive to an agent's overall interest. Consequently, some have supposed that arguments analogous to those for contractual justice can be employed to preserve the egoism of contractual friendship. Just as the sage contracts with society as a whole to refrain from mutual harm, he might form compacts with friends for mutual help.

The arguments, though, are disanalogous in one crucial respect. A sage can form a contract to refrain from mutual harm with no regard for another's sake. If friendship included merely a contract for mutual positive help, it perhaps could be given a similar egoistic foundation.[23] But the requirements of the pact described by Cicero

obligations; Lucretius' expression *vincula amicitiai* (III.83) shows a similar avoidance of the technical vocabulary of contracts. Of the theories that appear in the *De finibus*, only the contract explicitly captures Aristotle's demand for the reciprocity of friendship. The associationist, by failing to take sufficient notice of self-interest, may form friendships unwisely or too readily (see *SV* 28 for Epicurus' strictures against this practice). Perhaps by means of the contract, some later Epicureans attempted to give more formal recognition to the type of sentiment expressed at *SV* 39; or perhaps the ambiguities of *amicitia* facilitated a later conflation of Epicurus' theories of justice and friendship.

23. Rist, in spite of Cicero's testimony, attributes to Epicurus a theory of friendship which is contractual and strictly egoistic. He argues that self-sacrifice can be explained in terms of the sage's loyalty to his contractual partners (*Epicurus*, p. 133; "Epicurus on Friendship," p. 128). But this emphasis on *fides* is not Epicurean (*Lael.* 65); moreover, the contribution of loyalty to one's overall pleasure needs to be rationally explained and defended. Whether or not Rist is correct in arguing that

are noticeably stronger, since a wise man makes a contract to love another as much as himself. In effect, such a contract commits the sage to an inconsistent set of beliefs concerning his *telos*. He must treat both his own and his friend's pleasure as the goal of his actions. This condition is not so strong as the hedonist paradox that requires one to forget one's pleasure completely in order to maximize it; rather, it requires that the sage regard his own and his friend's good as equal parts of an end that he intrinsically desires. It might be argued that in so doing, he maximizes his pleasure. But as Bishop Butler (*Sermons* xii) argues, he no longer can treat his own pleasure as the only *telos*.[24]

Cicero (II.83) exploits this feature of contractual friendship by arguing that if a sage succeeds in loving another as himself, he cannot regard his friend as a means to his own pleasure. Conversely, if he does view friends as a means to his own pleasure, he has not fulfilled the terms of the contract. If a sage values another only as a means, or if he has contracted for the sole purpose of mutual help, he will perhaps adhere to an unprofitable commitment. But, Cicero argues (II.79), he cannot do so without inner frustration or even, perhaps, without longing for his friend's death to release him from an unprofitable tie. In order not to consider such a friendship merely as an impediment to one's *ataraxia*, one must treat friendship as a non-instrumental end and value a friend's pleasure as much as one's own.

On the basis of Cicero's testimony, it is possible to form a fairly plausible picture of the genesis and the motivation of these later Epicurean theories. Almost by itself, the fact that Epicurus' followers give such diametrically opposed assessments of the nature and value of altruism suggests an initial obscurity in his own account.[25] Each

---

a contract for mutual help can always be hedonically justified, the compacts formed by later Epicureans require more than mutual help—they require concern for another's sake.

24. Guyau, pp. 139 ff., defending an associationist position, is similarly inconsistent. He claims that the sage learns through association to maximize his pleasure by valuing others for their own sake. Thus, what the associationist discovers through chance and habit, the contractualist attempts to turn into a reflective strategy.

25. Cicero (I.69) says that *Epicurei timidiores* hold the associationist view. From this, Rist (*Epicurus*, p. 131) concludes that Epicurus was a strict egoist and that later Epicureans elaborated altruistic doctrines in response to criticism from the Sceptics. Rist's historical account relies on disputable claims. He implies that Cicero calls the

of these theories defends and further elaborates commitments that are in an uneasy tension in Epicurus' thought. In accordance with *Gnomologium vaticanum* 23, the associationist allows friendship to float loose as an independent criterion but fails to give a motive for its continued pursuit. The Hobbesian attempts consciously to subordinate friendship to personal gratification but fails to show why friendship is choiceworthy for itself. Both are plausible developments of an impulse that is more obscurely felt in Epicurus' theory. But Epicurus himself is decidedly more reticent about severing friendship from pleasure or subordinating friends to one's own interest.

Friendship and Pleasure

In turning to Cicero's presentation of Epicurus' theory we are faced with an initial exegetical difficulty. Torquatus begins his exposition of Epicurus' view of friendship by denying that friends should value each other's pleasure as much as their own (I.66).[26]

proponents of associationism *timidiores* because they affirm altruism; but their concern for altruism is not the source of their timidity. What distinguishes these Epicureans is their claim that altruism can be severed from self-interest (*etiamsi nulla sit utilitas ex amicitia, tamen ipsi amici propter se ipsos amentur*; I.69). An unwillingness to link altruism to an agent's pleasure is the source of their timidity. Given the general doctrinal conservatism of Epicureans, it is unlikely that, because of Academic criticism, a concern for altruism would have arisen in the face of a strictly egoistic formulation by Epicurus. It is more plausible to assume that these later theories were primarily attempts to explain and defend doctrines of the master that increasingly were seen to be problematic.

26. Scholars have been troubled by this initial premise. Rist (*Epicurus*, p. 129), following Madvig, finds the development of the argument problematic. He denies that this premise accurately reflects Epicurus' view. But it surely is consonant with Epicurus' widespread commitments to egoism and hedonism; moreover, Cicero clearly presents it as part of one united position. Evidence from Plutarch (*Non posse* XV.1097a) is sometimes adduced in this context: *tou eu paschein to eu poiein ou monon kallion alla kai hēdion einai*. But the use of this passage in discussions of friendship is misleading. Bailey, *The Greek Atomists*, p. 520, correctly argues that it is without parallel and not supported by argument elsewhere. *SV* 44 suggests that if by chance a wise man gets many possessions, he can distribute them to win the gratitude of his neighbors. It is more pleasurable to give to one's neighbors because the sage needs nothing from them, except to be left alone (see *De fin.* I.52 for benevolence

He then proceeds somewhat paratactically to the claim that the *sapiens* will feel exactly toward his friends as he does toward himself and will exert himself as vigorously for his friend's pleasure as for his own (I.68). This move is not precisely explained, and one might suspect Cicero of offering up a potpourri of Epicurean doctrine or perhaps of giving a wry caricature of Romans who do not quite see the full implications of espousing Epicureanism. Closer examination, however, shows that Cicero rather neatly captures the unresolved philosophical tensions that surface in Epicurus' writings.

Given his general theoretical commitments, there are two ways that Epicurus can move from his initial egoistic premise to an affirmation of altruistic friendship. The general strategy of the first is already familiar. Pleasure is our sole aim in life, and friendship is an especially productive means of attaining it. A necessary condition for maintaining reliable friendships, however, is that we treat friends as we treat ourselves. In order to gain the maximum hedonic benefits from friends, therefore, we must treat them altruistically. As in the contractual theory, this strategy attempts to preserve important and generally accepted requirements of friendship along with egoism. But the attempted reconciliation of egoism and friendship suffers from the same inconsistency and psychological implausibility[27] as does the contractual theory. To regard his friend's pleasure as his own, the sage must hold beliefs that are inconsistent for a hedonist: he must regard both his own and his friend's pleasure as the final goal of his actions. This first option, then, collapses into a less formal version of the contractual theory. For that reason it fails as an interpretation of Epicurus, since we know that he does

---

not associated with friendship). Although this passage may explain other sorts of benevolence, it is not compatible with the requirements of friendship; one must treat a friend's pleasure as one's own (I.68). Nor is it clear how this passage would be a threat to altruism if it merely shows that we get more satisfaction by doing something for others (cf. W. Frankena, *Ethics* [Englewood Cliffs, N.J., 1963], p. 20). For the pleasure of giving to be strictly egoistic, we need the further claim that one's sole aim in giving is one's own pleasure (see *EN* 1120a6–1121a9).

27. It is in one's interest not actually to value another as oneself but to seem to do so (*De fin.* II.78). Given Epicurus' emphasis on inner states of character, as opposed to rule-directed behavior, such an egoistic strategy would threaten to engender constant inner frustration.

not hold a contractual theory. Moreover, because it treats friendship only as a means to a further end, it does not explain why Epicurus would call friendship *di' heautēn hairetē*.

A second option brings us back to Mill and the claim that something can be valued as a means to an end as well as for itself, as part of an end. Perhaps Festugière intends to attribute to Epicurus a position akin to this when he asserts that Epicurean friendship is an "end in itself, an integral part of wisdom, a way of life equivalent to happiness."[28] Although Festugière does not explain how we are to understand these claims in a hedonist context, his conflation of pleasure and its sources is instructive. Such a reconciliation of altruistic action with egoism depends on a slide from "sources of happiness or pleasure" to "parts of happiness or pleasure." An illegitimate move from "pleasurable pursuits" to "pleasures" led Mill to the belief that a hedonist could value things other than pleasure as parts of an end.[29] The confusion that Sidgwick diagnoses in Mill's discussion trades on an ambiguity, which Greek[30] shares with English, based on the idea that if something is pleasant, it is a pleasure. If friendship is a pleasurable pursuit, and hence a pleasure, it can be regarded as *di' heautēn hairetē*, since pleasure clearly is choiceworthy for itself. Epicurus' hedonism is especially vulnerable to this kind of conflation because, like Mill, he consistently fails to separate pleasure from the pursuits that give rise to it. There are many indications of this problem in his accounts of pleasure, but perhaps the most important is that he does not consistently

28. A.-J. Festugière, *Epicure et ses dieux* (Paris, 1946), p. 37.

29. Sidgwick, p. 93, for Mill. See the discussions of T. H. Irwin, *Plato's Moral Theory* (Oxford, 1977), pp. 255, 341, and B. J. Diggs, "Rules and Utilitarianism," *American Philosophical Quarterly* 1 (1964), 44. M. Hossenfelder ("Epicurus—Hedonist malgrè lui," in *The Norms of Nature*, ed. M. Schofield and G. Striker [Cambridge, 1986], pp. 245–63) senses a tension between Epicurus' particular choice of pleasure as the end and his general eudaemonist project, which attempts to show that happiness consists in "reaching all of the goals" that agents have chosen for themselves. An important source of this tension for the hedonist lies in the ambiguity of "reaching all of one's goals," which may suggest (wrongly) that one's particular aims, activities, and goals can be included as intrinsically valuable components of one's final good. See below, note 33.

30. Cf. C. C. W. Taylor, *Plato: Protagoras* (Oxford, 1977), p. 168; T. H. Irwin, *Plato: Gorgias* (Oxford, 1979), p. 200; J. C. B. Gosling, *Pleasure and Desire* (Oxford, 1969), pp. 8–10.

attempt to isolate and describe a special, uniform quality of feeling; rather, he ranks various pleasurable activities on the basis of their immunity from chance interference and frustration.[31]

A comparison with Aristotle might help to clarify both the temptations and the difficulties that such a conception of the good presents for Epicurean hedonism. Epicurus regularly argues that without a reference to an agent's interest, we cannot understand an action (*De fin.* I.32). But a reference to an agent's interest is not necessarily incompatible with altruism. We might claim, for instance, that our ultimate interest, or happiness, consists of various parts or ingredients. Clearly, some of these may be nonsolipsistic. If my happiness is composed of various activities desired for themselves, I might value friendship as an intrinsic element or ingredient of my happiness. My friends' interests, therefore, can be treated as part of a way of life that I value for its own sake. Such a view is available to Epicurus from Aristotle, who makes friendship a component of happiness. Friendship retains, for Aristotle, an egoistic reference to an agent's ultimate interest or *eudaimonia*. In itself, however, this position does not preclude altruism, since he conceives of happiness as consisting of parts, some of which are altruistic. Analogously, by confusing pleasure and its sources Epicurus can treat happiness as if it consists of various parts[32] and therefore allow noninstrumental concern for another's sake.

At *De finibus* I.69, Torquatus closely links friendship to an agent's pleasure. Inasmuch as Epicurus regularly argues that pleasure is a necessary and sufficient condition for happiness, a severe difficulty remains for him. If happiness is a pleasurable solipsistic state to which all other actions contribute instrumentally, it cannot include nonsolipsistic components. A component conception of happiness

31. In defending qualitative differences between sensual and more lofty pleasures, Mill must rely on nonhedonistic grounds of preference. Similarly, Epicurus relies on a nonhedonic criterion when defending his view of pleasure against the sensualists (*Ad Men.* 130): he prefers pleasures that are completely up to us (*par' hēmas*) and not subject to chance.

32. For example, *KD* 28 (*SV* 13) may reflect a component view (*tou holou biou*) and the influence of Aristotle (see *De fin.* II.19 for component conceptions of the final good and Epicurean attitudes toward them). Epicurus' formulation (treating another as oneself) makes both a component conception and a slide from pleasure to its sources attractive.

might explain, though it does not justify, an Epicurean's regarding his own and his friend's good as equal parts of an end. However accommodating to altruism, though, such a view of the good conflicts with the rigid instrumentalism of the rest of Epicurus' doctrines. Thus, like Mill, Epicurus claims that something can be valued both as a means to an end and also for itself, as a part of an end; but it is not clear how a hedonist can defend this position.[33]

Before proceeding, we should note briefly the relative weight given to the interests of others in Epicurus' formulation. Torquatus mentions two conditions:

(a) I treat my friend's pleasure as my own.
(b) I treat my friend exactly as myself.

We may wonder what relation he sees between these two claims. Perhaps we move from hedonic benevolence (a) to a wider conception (b). But (a) needs to be limited by (b), since (a) alone might generate a problem: if I can view my friend's pleasure as my own, why can I not view my pain as *his* own? If it is rational for me sometimes to choose a pain of mine for the sake of a future pleasure, would it not be rational to choose a pain for my friend in order to procure my future pleasure? For Cicero, though, even (b) is inadequate. He complains (*Lael.* 56) that the mere symmetry of treatment in Epicurean friendship is insufficient for altruism: "Quam

---

33. Long, "Pleasure and Utility," pp. 305–306, disagrees and suggests that eudaemonism can allow for something to be both instrumentally and intrinsically good. This proposition is true, I think, of eudaemonist theories such as Plato's and Aristotle's, which take happiness to consist of ingredients and activities not strictly reducible to pleasurable states. For a eudaemonist theorist who embraces hedonism, however, it is, as Sidgwick remarks, "mere looseness of phraseology" to treat activities such as friendship as intrinsically valuable components of happiness or pleasure. It is perhaps worth quoting Sidgwick in full on this point: "It is more remarkable to find J. S. Mill (*Utilitarianism*, chap. iv.) declaring that 'money'—no less than 'power' or 'fame'—comes by association of ideas to be 'a part of happiness,' an 'ingredient in the individual's conception of happiness.' But this seems to be mere looseness of phraseology, venial in a treatise aiming at a popular style; since Mill has expressly said that 'by happiness is intended pleasure and the absence of pain,' and he cannot mean that money is either the one or the other. In fact he uses in the same passage—as an alternative phrase for 'parts of happiness'—the phrase 'sources of happiness' and 'sources of pleasure': and his real meaning is more precisely expressed by these latter terms" (*The Methods of Ethics*, p. 93, n. 1).

multa enim, quae nostra causa numquam faceremus, facimus causa amicorum!" ("How many things we do for the sake of friends that we would never do for our own sakes!") Some recent theorists, such as Nagel, who defend altruism on the basis of objective reasons, might find Cicero's motives for giving greater weight to a friend's interests overly paternalistic or, perhaps, even egoistic. But Cicero clearly is drawing on a common and important intuition about the requirements of altruism. As Aristotle's discussion of friendship shows, these considerations generate interesting puzzles about the possibility of friendships between unequals, the sage's attitudes to unvirtuous or unwise friends, and so on, but perhaps a more pressing question is why an Epicurean should engage even in limited forms of altruism.

Friendship, Happiness, and Invulnerability[34]

From Seneca (*Ep. Mor.* 9.1) we learn that against Stilpo and the Academics, Epicurus argued that the wise man[35] will seek friends

---

34. This section is greatly indebted to an unpublished paper by T. H. Irwin, "The Good Will in Greek Ethics," and to discussions with J. Whiting. Difficulties for an adaptive conception of happiness are taken up by Irwin in "Socrates the Epicurean?" *Illinois Classical Studies* (forthcoming).

35. Unfortunately, it is not altogether clear whether Epicurus limits altruistic friendships to the wise. In contrast to Aristotle, who argues that too many friends are an impediment to living nobly (*EN* 1170b26–27), we find the claim that Epicurus numbered his friends (presumably not all wise) by cities (cf. *De fin.* I.65: *amicorum greges*; and D.L. X.9). This has led some to argue that a spirit of universal friendship developed in Epicureanism; see A. Tuilier, "La notion de *philia* dans ses rapports avec certains fondements sociaux de l'épicurisme," in *ACGB 1968* (Paris, 1969), pp. 318–29, who claims that Epicureans, under the influence of Alexander's political syncretism, moved away from Aristotle's more exclusive and polis-bound conception of friendship. But *SV* 78 claims that the *gennaios* will be most concerned about wisdom and friendship; *KD* 27 and *De fin.* I.65 suggest that wisdom alone is productive of friendship. Torquatus mentions the *sapiens* in only two accounts of friendship: I.68 (which says that a wise man will treat his friend exactly as himself, but does not claim that his friend must be wise) and I.70 (which restricts contracts to the wise). Torquatus' account thus has a marked tendency to limit Epicurean friendships exclusively to the wise. It would be useful to know the extent to which this restriction reflects a distinction made by Epicurus, and whether the bond between wise men is different from that of ordinary friends (II.84). One senses Aristotle's discussion lurking in the background, but in Epicurus' ethics there are strong reasons as well for making the *sapiens* the sole possessor of knowledge, hence of *eudaimonia* and friendship.

even though he is self-sufficient. Similarly, the Epicurean gods form friendships, although they need nothing and harbor no traces of insufficiency.[36] In Greek ethics there is a long tradition of attempting to account for this seemingly paradoxical relation between friendship and self-sufficiency. For Epicurus, though, the problem arises in an especially acute form because his commitment to the self-sufficiency of the *sapiens* is further entangled with a belief that the happiness of a sage is entirely invulnerable to the incursions of fortune. To understand his reasons for defending the pursuit of friendship, it will be useful to begin by examining some general features of his ethical theory.

Epicurus thinks that *eudaimonia* consists, at the very least,[37] in the satisfaction of all of an agent's aims or desires. Some of these are first-order desires (for food, shelter, etc.), while others are second-order desires focused on these first-order desires. We may have to restrict the scope or strength of our first-order desires in order to ensure that they are all satisfied. If we fail to eliminate unsatisfied desires, however, we will be frustrated and hence unhappy. Moreover, Epicurus thinks that all of our particular desires are extremely flexible, as he insists that we can adjust their strength to any situation by means of reason (*KD* 26). The *Epistola ad Menoeceum* constantly reiterates his belief that the pleasant life is achieved through reason, "which makes every choice and rejection tend toward one's final good." Reason, therefore, is the most reliable means to the good life. "Reason has controlled the wise man's greatest and most important affairs, controls them throughout his life, and will continue to control them" (*KD* 16). To see the strength of Epicurus' rationalism, one need only compare the sanguine call to happiness that introduces the *Epistola ad Menoeceum*[38] with Aristotle's more pessi-

36. M. Slote, *Goods and Virtues* (Oxford, 1983), p. 133, questions the coherence of such a view, for reasons that have much in common with associationism. He wonders how a self-sufficient being can come to value friendship without having first experienced the dependency of a prolonged childhood.

37. Epicurus thinks that the consciousness that our future desires also will be satisfied is an important element in *eudaimonia*. For purposes of the present discussion, however, it perhaps will be sufficient to concentrate on the problems friendship raises even for this less complicated demand about the satisfaction of desire.

38. "Let no one while young delay in philosophizing nor when old grow weary of philosophy. For no one is too young or too old for a healthy soul. Anyone who says

mistic attitude in the *Nicomachean Ethics*. The whole missionary appeal of Epicurus' philosophy, his exhortation to mend evil habits, his belief in a good life available to everyone based on the rational selection of pleasures and the knowledge of the nature of things— all these reflect an optimistic, rationalist account of human action. At *Gnomologium vaticanum* 16, he even affirms the Socratic paradox by suggesting that no desire is too difficult to master. For Epicurus, then, all our desires and wants can be modified by reason and focused on our final good.

We may reasonably question his Socratic[39] denial of incontinence, the possibility of occasional indifference, and his claim that we always can eliminate unsatisfiable desires. His motivation, however, is fairly straightforward and shows the essential link between his rationalist moral psychology and his conception of happiness. At *Ad Menoeceum* 131, Epicurus argues that those with extremely flexible desires will be unafraid of chance, *pros tēn tuchēn aphobous*. This is a reaction to Aristotelian and, perhaps, Platonic[40] conceptions of *eudaimonia*, which make even the most competent deliberators vulnerable to chance. By including external goods as necessary ingredients in happiness and maintaining that happiness must meet exacting objective standards, Aristotle suggests that there are cer-

---

that the time for philosophizing is not yet come or has already passed is like one who says that the time for happiness is not yet come or has already passed" (*Ad Men.* 122).

39. *SV* 17, 21, 46. See Giovanni Reale, *Storia della filosofia antica* (Milan, 1979), 3:169–170, for some general connections between Socrates and Epicurus. The only exception to this rationalism is a somewhat dubious report by Plutarch (*De tranqu. an.* 466a), which suggests Epicurus thought that one may be better off giving in to thoroughly entrenched desires for political gain. This passage completely neglects Epicurean claims about the natural limits of desires and probably has been conflated with Stoic *persona* doctrines. Epicurus' emphasis on the memorization of the *stoicheiōmata* of his thought (cf. D. Clay, *Lucretius and Epicurus* [Ithaca, N.Y., 1983], pp. 56–60) has implied to some a strong Epicurean concern with molding and habituating (unconscious) desires. But this process is more rational and less hypnotic than it sometimes is taken to be by those attempting to reconstruct Epicurus' doctrines on the basis of social practices in Epicurean communities. One can readily explain repetition and memorization as parts of Epicurus' materialist view of memory. Repeated exposure to doctrine will fix memory traces more securely in one's mind. This is strictly a rational process that does not involve training one's desires (see *DRN* III.514–25). More important, if our desires required long and careful training and were not susceptible of rapid modification, we would become vulnerable to chance.

40. See J. Annas, *An Introduction to Plato's "Republic"* (Oxford, 1981), pp. 316–17.

tain conditions in which *eudaimonia* is impossible.[41] Epicurus strongly disagrees, contending that no real harm can come to wise men (cf. *De fin.* I.62–63), since their happiness cannot be diminished by chance (*SV* 47; Porph., *Ad Marc.* 30).[42]

There is, perhaps, an initial plausibility in Epicurus' conception of *eudaimonia*. If I am hungry and there happens to be no cheese (cf. U. 182) but a ready supply of bread (U. 181), it seems reasonable for me to adjust to my situation and eat bread. All things being equal, I will be happier than individuals with inflexible desires for cheese who refuse or are unable to redirect their desires. Those with inflexible desires incur more frustration, are more vulnerable to chance features of the world, and will perhaps begin taking dangerous risks to gain their satisfactions. Epicurus' view of flexible desires has the merits of making happiness up to us, *par' hēmas*. If I am unable to adjust and redirect my desires, I give up control over my life and my happiness in important ways.

Flexibility is a plausible criterion to build into an account of happiness. Without limits, however, this demand for the flexibility of desires can become pernicious and destructive. Epicurus' view becomes far less attractive if it gives only reasons for restricting and eliminating desires. Epicurus vacillates (*Ad Men.* 128) between two different conceptions of desires and their satisfaction. He is crucially obscure about whether happiness requires a broad range

41. For an opposing view, see J. Cooper, *Reason and Human Good in Aristotle* (Cambridge, 1975), p. 123 (but see *EN* 1095b32–1096a2).

42. Long ("Pleasure and Social Utility," p. 306) thinks that we should not overestimate the Epicurean sage's invulnerability to fortune and argues that the "Epicurean wise man should not be equated with his Stoic counterpart." At *De fin.* I.62, however, Torquatus makes this equation explicit and claims that the Epicurean wise man is always happy (*sapiens semper beatus*). Furthermore, although the *sapiens* may in a trivial way be interfered with by chance, his *happiness* is invulnerable (Plutarch, *Non posse* 1088b, 1090a; *Tusc. disput.* II.17). In the same passage that Long cites to show the vulnerability of the sage (*Ad Men.* 135), we find the claim that Epicurean doctrine makes it possible for us to live as gods among men. See also *Tusc. disput.* V.27, where Cicero attributes to Metrodorus a version of Epicurus' proud boast at *SV* 47: "Occupavi te, inquit, Fortuna, atque cepi omnisque aditus tuos inclusi, ut ad me aspirare non posses." See D. Clay, "Individual and Community in the First Generation of the Epicurean School," in *Syzētēsis: Studi sull' epicureismo greco e romano offerti a Marcello Gigante*, Biblioteca della Parola del Passato 16 (Naples, 1983), pp. 260–63, for a judicious account of the relation between these two passages. See Diogenes Oen., frag 41.

of desires or just the fewest possible desires.[43] This obscurity is partially polemical: Epicurus thinks that most people have too many demanding desires that force them into competition and continual frustration. But more important, his equivocation reflects a concern to make *eudaimonia* entirely up to us. Epicurus cannot require that we cultivate and always satisfy a broad range of desires without making us vulnerable to possible frustration and unhappiness. Thus, guided by his determination to ensure that we can achieve happiness in any situation, he allows the scope of happiness to expand and contract to fit individual circumstances.

Adapting ourselves to every situation, however, might not lead to anything we would be inclined to call happiness. For instance, Epicurus, as opposed to Aristotle (*EN* 1153b19–21), claims that even on the rack the *sapiens* will be happy. If wise men can adjust their desires so thoroughly that they can find happiness on the rack, we may wonder whether Epicurus really is giving us a recipe for happiness. Adjusting our desires to some conditions will not necessarily secure happiness. Under extreme conditions (concentration camps, torture, etc.), those who still can envisage and desire a better state of affairs are better off. Epicurus might claim, of course, that those with less flexible desires, even in extreme conditions, are just compounding their misery with more frustration. But at this point, it is no longer clear why frustration and unsatisfied desires are to be avoided. Some discontent with camp life would be a hopeful sign, as would unsatisfied desires to be out of the camp. Those in a concentration camp who still can recognize that their desires are being frustrated and their lives diminished are better off and happier[44] than those who, recalling past pleasures, feel completely

43. This helps to explain the different conceptions of Epicurus—as quietist, ascetic, vitalist, sensualist, and so on—that appear in the doxography. We might think of *ataraxia* and *aponia* as desireless states in the sense of a total removal of desires. (For the difficulties in this view, see M. C. Nussbaum, "This Story Isn't True: Poetry, Goodness, and Understanding in Plato's *Phaedrus*," in J. Moravscik and P. Temko, *Plato on Beauty, Wisdom, and the Arts* [Totowa, N.J., 1981], pp. 79–124.) But it is also possible to regard them as states in which one's desires are continually satisfied. Presumably we do not have friends to remove totally a desire for friendship.

44. One might, of course, attempt to sever connections between well-being and happiness by arguing that even though contented camp victims might be less well off, they are still happier. Epicurus cannot allow happiness and well-being to become

content with camp life.[45]

To see the real force of Epicurus' claim here, we should remember that he argues not only that one can be happy on the rack but he also is commited to the claim that one can be just as happy on as off the rack. In effect, Epicurus can give no reason derived from our own happiness for us to prefer being out of a concentration camp or released from torture. To give a more plausible characterization of *eudaimonia*, therefore, Epicurus needs to set limits to the flexibility of our desires.[46] But in so doing, he would have to qualify his claim that happiness is entirely *par' hēmas* and modify his conception of *eudaimonia* based on the mere satisfaction of desires.

Part of the initial plausibility of Epicurus' model of happiness stems from an unclarity about the relation of desires and their objects. The objects of some desires are easily interchangeable. If I am hungry, for instance, it would be irrational to hold out very long for a particular type of food when other foods are readily available. The objects of other desires, however, more clearly reflect an agent's long-term deliberations, values, and goals;[47] hence they are not so easily substituted. Since friends are not readily substituted, nor are relations with them entirely *par' hēmas*, it is difficult to see how altruistic friendships[48] can conform to Epicurus' view of flexible and easily eliminable desires.

---

separated in this way, however, since he argues that *eudaimonia* is our ultimate and complete good.

45. We might reasonably claim that part of what gives some goods (youth, life, etc.) their value is the very fact that they are vulnerable to loss and destruction. Thus, that a particular desire is vulnerable to frustration might make its satisfaction just that much more valuable.

46. It might seem that, in order to practice the virtues, the Epicurean needs at least some minimal constraints on the flexibility of desire. However, Epicurus attempts to revise ordinary conceptions of the virtues, including justice, to fit his conception of happiness. The aim of all the virtues is to control desires rationally and thus ensure their satisfaction. This task need not be entirely negative: *temperantiamque expetendam non quia voluptates fugiat sed quia maiores consequatur (De fin.* I.48). Nevertheless, the virtues are parasitic: they control our desires and adjust their strength, but they cannot ensure that the range of our desires in certain situations will not collapse to a level unacceptable for happiness.

47. Cf. Slote, p. 44, for further difficulties in regarding goods such as friendship as ends of action for which we can reasonably plan.

48. As Aristotle notices (*EN* 1156a19–20), friendships based on pleasure or advantage are more easily broken off or formed to fit circumstances.

These general considerations are important for his account of *philia*. Epicurus urges us in the strongest possible terms to develop friendships. But what if we decide to exclude all concern for others and cultivate a very narrow range of desires that are easily satisfiable? Or what if we rather monomaniacally decide to focus on just one easily satisfiable pursuit? Can he show that we are less happy or any worse off living without friends? At times, Epicurus gives an expansive view of the sage's happiness, and many of his remarks anticipate Butler's admonition that a selfish and narrow character is not promising for attaining happiness. For example, at *Ad Menoeceum* 135, he recommends that Menoeceus practice his doctrines with another like himself (*homoion seautōi*). Similarly, he insists that it is more important to find someone to eat with than to find something to eat (Seneca, *Ep. Mor.* 19.10; U.542). Presumably, he does not mean merely feeding in the same place, as cattle (Arist., *EN* 1170b13–15). Rather, like Aristotle, he implies that being fed is less important than is active participation in a shared pursuit.

These features of Epicurus' account suggest motivations akin to Aristotle's[49] for his espousal of altruistic, as opposed to strictly exploitative, friendships. Given his conception of the final good, however, it is difficult to see how Epicurus can successfully introduce such noninstrumental considerations into his account of *eudaimonia*. Joint activities are not entirely under our own rational control. Furthermore, as Cicero objects (II.83–4), these elements of friendship cannot be justified strictly on the basis of their hedonic worth, since the value of shared pursuits cannot be reduced completely

49. Zeller ascribes such sentiments to Epicurus' "effeminacy" and the need for Epicurean friends to ground the truth of their convictions in mutual approval (*Die Philosophie der Griechen* [Leipzig, 1903], 3:467). A kinder construal would point to Aristotle's emphasis on shared activities and the corresponding gains in self-knowledge that depend on the knowledge of one's friends (*EN* 1169b3); see J. Cooper, "Aristotle on Friendship," in A. O. Rorty, *Essays on Aristotle's Ethics* (Berkeley, Calif., 1980), pp. 301–40. Philodemus (*De dis* 3 frag. 84, col. 13.36–39 Diels) finds conversations and mutual contemplation to be central elements in divine friendship. Cicero describes this aspect of human friendship at II.85 ("At quicum ioca, seria, ut dicitur, quicum arcana, quicum occulta omnia"). Interestingly, in contrast to associationism, on this account altruism becomes psychologically prior to self-esteem (cf. J. Annas, "Plato and Aristotle on Friendship and Altruism," *Mind* 86 [1977], 532–54).

into terms of pleasantly invulnerable psychological states. If we are deceived into thinking that someone is a friend or if we are falsely content and wrongly confident about our friend's help, it is not clear that Epicurus would think that such states are still pleasurable. Friendship, like happiness, is not just a matter of casual belief or subjective satisfactions (*KD* 28, *SV* 28, 34; cf. *SV* 54); our beliefs about friends and the pleasant states consequent upon these beliefs must be veridically grounded. Therefore, friendship for Epicurus cannot remain strictly a matter of subjective psychological states.[50]

A still deeper difficulty confronts Epicurus' account of friendship. Given his view of the sage, it becomes difficult to see how he can give even a purely instrumental defense of friendship's contribution to the pleasant life. Epicurus claims, for instance, that for the sake of friendship we should run risks, *dei de kai parakinduneusai charin philias* (*SV* 28). It is unclear, however, that he can justify any risk-taking given his model of pleasure and rational agency. If opportunities for making friends are abundant, perhaps the desire for friendship can be easily satisfied and will involve no trouble. Friendship, however, is among the external goods (*tōn ektos agathōn*) that Aristotle suggests will make one more vulnerable to chance (*EN* 1169b10–11). For Epicurus this feature of friendship is problematic and presents an awkward dilemma. If friendships are crucial for happiness, he must admit that the sage can be vulnerable. By developing friendships we become more vulnerable to chance, pain, and betrayal.[51] Even if Epicurus denies that friendship makes one vulnerable in this sense, he must admit that without friends a sage's

---

50. Contrast Long, above n. 33.

51. Friendship is a source of security, but a riskier source than justice, since if a sage suffers injustice it will not upset his whole life. Epicurus by no means downplays the role which *asphaleia* plays in friendship, but when he counsels Menoeceus to practice Epicureanism with a friend, he echoes Aristotle's emphasis on the importance of shared activities. This emphasis on *asphaleia* is not necessarily inconsistent with the claim that friendship is valuable for itself. There is no reason why something valuable for itself cannot be valued for other benefits as well. But if friendship were merely a matter of security, it would be safer for the sage to cultivate justice. In distinguishing the pleasures of altruistic friendships and ordinary friendships of advantage, Epicurus would need to either (a) rely on a non-hedonistic ground of preference of the sort he elsewhere denies or (b) show how the desire for altruistic friendship is more easily satisfied and requires fewer risks than ordinary friendships. Neither alternative is very promising.

happiness will be somehow incomplete.[52] Epicurus does not think that a sage's happiness can be augmented or diminished, and he carefully avoids distinguishing gradations in the happiness of sages in the manner of Antiochus (*De fin.* V.84). The strength of his claim, however, successfully undermines any justification for forming friendships. Instrumental appeals for developing friendships lose their force if the sage's happiness is completely invulnerable.

If friendship is necessary for happiness, happiness can no longer be entirely *par' hēmas*, nor can we always avoid the frustration of our desires. Epicurus, then, must either modify his account of *eudaimonia* and rational agency or weaken his commitment to friendship. By doing neither he is forced into an inconsistency. He defends the pursuit of *aponia* and *ataraxia* based on his model of happiness as the satisfaction of desire. But in trying to add friendship as an additional requirement for happiness, he undermines this defense. Accordingly, Epicurus needs an independent evaluative criterion for justifying the possible frustration and loss of rational control involved in friendship. He must appeal, moreover, to sources of value in activities that are independent of their ability easily to satisfy desire. This need for an independent criterion explains, perhaps, why Epicurus is led to call friendship *di' heautēn hairetē*.

Rist[53] claims that although the gods are self-sufficient and enjoy the purest katastematic states, they form friendships for the sake of kinetic pleasure. Would a similar argument be available to justify human friendship? If I can enjoy complete katastematic pleasure without friends, do I have reasons for cultivating friends for the sake of richer kinetic experience? Such a defense is unlikely, as Epicurus neither gives a rational method for ranking kinetic pleasures nor claims that we have any rational concern for kinetic pleasures, since they are not *par' hēmas*. If I can enjoy the highest katastematic state on bread and water, and the kinetic pleasures of

52. Philodemus recognizes, for instance, that the gods' happiness would be less complete without friendship (*De dis* 3, frag. 84, col. 1.2–4). For Epicurean attempts to account for this requirement of completeness, see Annas, "Epicurus on Pleasure and Happiness," *Philosophical Topics* 15 (1987), 5–21.

53. Rist, *Epicurus*, p. 154. The relevant passage in Philodemus is *De dis* 3, frag. 84, col. 1.2–9, 15–16 Diels.

cheese merely vary[54] but do not increase my satisfaction, I have no reason for wanting anything but bread and water if they are more readily available. If different kinetic pleasures cannot increase my happiness, I may perhaps try cheese on a whim, if it involves no risks. But Epicurus cannot justify taking risks for the sake of kinetic pleasures. Nor, since they are mere variations, would it matter much if I make mistakes in my evaluations of them. As we have seen, however, Epicurus thinks that friendships involve risks and must be evaluated very carefully. Similarly, at *Ad Menoeceum* 130, he claims that those who least need luxuries are best able to enjoy them; he does not claim, however, that the wise man gets more pleasure from such luxuries. The sage, then, has no reason to prefer one kinetic pleasure to another. If friendship is merely a kinetic pleasure, the sage has no grounds for valuing his friends any more than a nice salad or a fine wine.

Epicurus, of course, has no systematic program for eliminating all desires. In fact, he encourages us, if the opportunity presents itself, to indulge harmless desires. Lucretius (proem to *DRN* VI) even suggests that the growth of such desires was crucial to the development of a society that made Epicurean philosophy possible. But the Epicurean cannot assign such pleasures any value, since to do so would threaten the sage's complete happiness. By distinguishing kinetic and katastematic pleasures in this way, Epicurus creates a difficulty familiar from Stoic and Kantian ethics, the problem of rationally comparing incommensurable values. If katastematic and kinetic pleasures are incommensurable, there can be no

---

54. For the sake of the argument, I follow the Diano-Rist account of the relation between kinetic and katastematic pleasures. Corresponding problems in justifying friendship on the basis of kinetic pleasure would be generated by other accounts as well. For instance, Giannantoni ("Il piacere cinetico nell'etica epicurea," *Elenchos* 5 [1984], 25–44) argues that kinetic pleasures arise only from the satisfaction of unnecessary desires; but in that case, the pleasures of friendship, if they were kinetic, would be unnecessary. Similarly, Merlan's view that kinetic pleasures are merely momentary (*Studies in Epicurus and Aristotle* [Wiesbaden, 1960]), would give no justification for cultivating lasting, stable relations. J. C. B. Gosling and C. C. W. Taylor (*The Greeks on Pleasure* [Oxford, 1982], pp. 365–396), think that kinetic pleasures fall into the same class as katastematic pleasures. Such an account might avoid problems of incommensurability, but it still would not show why the particular pleasures of friendship should be cultivated, if they are vulnerable to chance and future frustration.

way of comparing them rationally, since they are not on a uniform scale of value. Hence the preference for the right katastematic state cannot be a rational one. Although Epicurus is perhaps ready to admit this in the case of katastematic pleasure, he can no longer give a rational defense of his attitude toward kinetic pleasures. Therefore, any attempt to base friendship on kinetic pleasure not only trivializes friendship but also precludes the possibility of recommending friendship on the basis of reason. As we have seen, for Epicurus altruism requires just such a rational defense.

At *Ad Menoeceum* 127–28, Epicurus claims that of the necessary desires, some are necessary for happiness, others for the repose of the body, and others for life itself. Unfortunately, we do not know which desires Epicurus thinks are necessary for happiness. If he argues that the satisfaction of a broad range of desires is necessary for happiness, it would have important implications for his ethical theory. It would allow him to build in certain limits to the flexibility of our desires. For instance, I may want many friends, but if I were in a situation that offered few opportunities for friendship, I could have a few friends and still be happy. But I could not be happy without any friends at all, since my desires are flexible only within certain limits. If Epicurus maintains that friendship is a necessary desire, however, his dilemma returns in another form. By including desires for an external good like friendship among those necessary for happiness,[55] he would make the sage vulnerable to chance and frustration. Again, Epicurus would have to revise his conception of happiness by admitting intrinsic values other than satisfaction and rational control.

Conclusion

We have seen the various tensions in Epicurus' ethical thinking that force him into inconsistencies. This problem is partly of his-

---

55. Epicurus might limit the flexibility of desires by describing an underlying structure of desires whose mutual dependence makes their satisfaction interentailing. If I have a set of desires (a, b, c, d) that I try to restrict by satisfying only (a) and (b), I will not realize that the satisfaction of (a) and (b) depends on the satisfaction of (c) and (d) as well. But this attempt would also fall prey to the same objection: it would make me vulnerable to chance and frustration if, say, (c) and (d) could not be satisfied.

torical interest, inasmuch as it shows a hedonist's attempt to return to Socratic conceptions of rational agency and control over individual happiness. Epicurus attempts to make happiness invulnerable to chance. He seems simultaneously attracted, though, to an Aristotelian conception of *eudaimonia* that includes *philia* as an essential ingredient of happiness. His position is philosophically instructive as well. Like Mill, Epicurus believes that we can value something for its own sake apart from its instrumental contribution to our satisfaction. This position is inconsistent with the claims of his hedonism, but it shows that any hedonist who wants to give a plausible account of happiness must appeal to intrinsically desirable sources of value and concede that the achievement of happiness is not entirely in our own hands.

In Epicurus' analysis of friendship, we find the realization that, to a certain extent, we must relinquish control over our happiness if we are to find it worth possessing. This discovery creates an observable tension in his thought about the ultimate good. Indeed, in the context of the central preoccupations of Hellenistic moral thinking such a discovery is almost paradoxical. Epicurus' solution to the problem of friendship represents, as does the parallel Stoic discussion of preferred indifferents, a distinctive attempt to account for important elements of our ethical beliefs and practices while making *eudaimonia* an invulnerable psychic state. Like the Stoics, moreover, Epicurus adopts a Socratic moral psychology and shows little reluctance in abandoning the complexities of Platonic and Aristotelian views of moral motivation. Interestingly, though, he reveals some unease with a conception of happiness based strictly on the satisfaction of desire, and he appears reticent about giving up all the benefits of an Aristotelian account of the final good. In many ways, his attempt to reconcile the demands of a strictly rationalistic moral psychology with a more expansive conception of happiness is paradigmatic of the kinds of problems bequeathed to Hellenistic moral philosophers by their predecessors. Moreover, Epicurus' account of *philia* shows the limits moral psychologies can place on conceptions of happiness and exemplifies the difficulties that beset Hellenistic philosophers in fitting their moral psychologies to plausible accounts of happiness.

4

Reason, Responsibility, and the
Mechanisms of Freedom

In a famous passage, Lucretius admits to being seized by a divine
pleasure and dread (*divina voluptas ac horror*; *DRN* III.28–29) when
contemplating the discoveries of Epicurean natural philosophy. Not
least among these discoveries is the possibility that everything in
the world of our ordinary experience might be stripped away[1] to
reveal the mute, impassive workings of atoms in the void. For a
wide variety of thinkers, the implications of such an atomistic reduction have been more an unmixed source of dread than of pleasure or consolation.[2] Indeed, ethical philosophers of many
denominational loyalties have found it chilling to contemplate the
possibility that the items of our ordinary experience might share,
at best, a shadowy, second-class ontological status. If our lives, goals,
histories, and even momentary pleasures are in some fundamental
sense less specifiably real than the material parts that constitute
them, we might begin to suspect that in treating ourselves as moral

1. This renders the Epicurean locution *perihairesis* (*Ad Hdt.* 55). Cf. D. Clay for
a sensitive analysis of Lucretian language and poetic tactics for "stripping the phenomenal world," *Lucretius and Epicurus* (Ithaca, N.Y., 1983), p. 160. Clay's discussion
itself illustrates how hard it is to speak about atoms and void without importing
formal and functional notions that are strictly applicable only at a macroscopic level
of explanation.

2. Cf. F. M. Cornford's passionate outburst against ancient atomism's "pre-
destined goal" to take "Life out of Nature": "Admirable as a tool of research into
inorganic nature, it [atomism] strikes a chill of horror into men of an opposite
temperament, who will not seek the living among the dead" (*From Religion to Philosophy: A Study in the Origins of Western Speculation* [New York, 1912], p. vi).

and causal agents we have made a rudimentary category mistake. That is, if life's true actors are merely its particles and we are merely what our atoms do, it becomes clear that *we* do not really do anything at all; we are merely the activities that the atoms, life's real "agents," perform.[3]

Accordingly, when Lucretius registers his own psychological responses to the existence of atoms and void, we may reasonably wonder whether he has failed to pursue the logic of his argument far enough. What, other than a regrettable failure in explanatory economy or, perhaps, some convenient but imprecise way of talking, allows Lucretius to view himself and his own thoughts as unities with causal and moral efficacy? Why would his pleasure and dread not be better described and understood in terms that make reference solely to underlying atomic patterns and movements? David Furley, for instance, has argued that the most characteristic feature of "matter-in-motion merchants" is precisely the priority they give to explanations in terms of parts.[4] Atomist explanations of wholes begin from the bottom up, and understanding must likewise proceed from the more simple to the more complex.

Scholars have commonly assumed that Epicureans are committed to a radical reductionism that eliminates any need for independent, macroscopic explanations of psychological states or moral goals. David Glidden, for example, argues that Epicurus believes that human well-being consists solely in the smooth functioning of soul atoms. Therefore, questions about happiness and "whether a particular man is fulfilling his human nature [are] in the last resort a question in atomic mechanics."[5] Such an account might explain why, for instance, we hear so little about ethics from Lucretius. If

---

3. For this particular formulation see R. Faber, *Clockwork Garden: On the Mechanistic Reduction of Living Things* (Amherst, Mass., 1986), pp. 3–11.

4. D. J. Furley, "The Cosmological Crisis in Classical Antiquity," in *Proceedings of the Boston Area Colloquium in Ancient Philosophy*, ed. J. J. Cleary (Lanham and London, 1987), 2: 16.

5. D. Glidden, "Epicurus and the Pleasure Principle," in *The Greeks and the Good Life*, ed. D. Depew (Fullerton, Calif., 1980), p. 190. Glidden argues that Epicurus, by focusing on our soul atoms, eliminates the need for moral explanations and for accounts of intentional states. He thinks that Epicurus' attempt to give an account of the pleasurable atomic configurations of souls is a "psychological" theory that bypasses any need for higher-order intentional or moral explanations.

his real task is to understand atomic motions, he might think it superfluous to spend too much time on higher-order ethical explanations that cannot pretend to the kind of mechanical exactness Glidden thinks necessary for an understanding of happiness.

If this picture of Epicurean explanatory ambitions is correct, however, most of my account of Epicurus' ethics to this point will have been superfluous. I have relied on the ongoing assumption, with support from the doxography and Epicurus' own ethical writings, that human beings, in some fundamentally irreducible sense, are autonomous moral and causal agents and that their beliefs, desires, and goals have their own relevant explanatory principles. In analyzing Epicurus' conception of individual and social ends, I have repeatedly appealed to psychological and to teleological criteria in explaining human action. And these explanations, like those of Epicurus, have rather conspicuously avoided mentioning the motions and combinations of atoms in the void.

If, however, Epicurus' epistemology and physical theories commit him to the strict reduction of intentional and moral states to the movements of atoms, his ethical theory as a whole obviously will be faced with some very awkward dilemmas. We have seen, for instance, a continual emphasis throughout his ethics on the importance of having our happiness in our own power. Yet if we are merely epiphenomena of material constituents, it is unclear how we could ever exert any control over our happiness. Moreover, Epicurus could hardly hold us responsible, without such control, for failing to change our beliefs in light of Epicurean ethical teachings. In principle, of course, all his ethical doctrines face a common threat from reductionist atomism. Thus, we might attempt to examine his views on the plausibility of analyzing virtuous, friendly, or pleasurable psychic states strictly in terms of their material configurations. However, Epicurus' most considered and self-conscious reflections on the relation of his ethics and his atomic theory occur in the context of his denial that causal determinism is compatible with autonomous, *par' hēmas* action. This feature of his arguments is not surprising, in view of the central role that autonomy plays in his ethics. It is important, however, not to conflate problems of reductionism with those of determinism. Clearly, one can be a determinist and still find mechanistic reductions of human action repugnant. Brand Blanshard, for instance, defends the view that human action is strictly determined by beliefs, intentions, and individual character. Yet, he complains that mechanistic reductionism is an affront to common sense: "What most affronts [the plain man], I think, is the suggestion that he is only a machine, a big foolish clock that seems to itself to be acting freely but whose movements are controlled completely by the wheels and weights inside."[6] Therefore, I propose, at least initially, to keep separate questions of reductionism and determinism, since scholars have sometimes run them together in ways that are unhelpful. First, however, it will be necessary to look in more detail at the general theory of action and responsibility found in Epicurus' ethical works. This will prepare the way for a more extended discussion of the relation of human freedom to both determinism and mechanistic reductionism.

Rationality and Responsibility

Epicurus usually is considered the first philosopher in antiquity to have argued that human freedom is incompatible with determinism. He thus denies that we are to be held responsible for our actions if they are fully determined by antecedent events beyond our own control. But even though he often is given a measure of credit for stirring up worries about the compatibility of responsibility and determinism, and thereby putting libertarianism on the philosophical map, no consensus has emerged about the quality of his arguments or even about the actual details of his position.

At a very general level, though, two features of Epicurus' opposition to determinism seem fairly clear. On the one hand, he attempts to isolate a class of human actions that are *par' hēmas*, up to us, and not completely determined by their antecedent causes. Typically, scholars concentrating on this facet of his argument have attempted to discover those elements of human action for which a denial of strict causal determination seems most plausible. Accord-

---

6. B. Blanshard, "The Case for Determinism," in *Determinism and Freedom in the Age of Modern Science*, ed. S. Hook (New York, 1958), p. 10. Quoted by Faber, p. 5.

ingly, most have agreed that Epicurus hopes to save human action from being fully determined either by postulating uncaused acts of will or perhaps by appealing to uncaused occurrences in the formation of our characters.

On the other hand, Epicurus maintains that the very notion of determinism itself is self-refuting. That is, determinists, in attempting to defend their doctrine, offend against either the logical or the pragmatic requirements of their own argument. For this claim, he offers the following considerations. The determinist holds that all our beliefs are caused solely by antecedent physical events; however, there can be no grounds for distinguishing a rational from a nonrational belief, Epicurus argues, if all our beliefs are caused by prior physical events. There is no reason to think that a belief in determinism can be justified by rational argument any more than a belief in indeterminism can; hence proponents of determinism can neither appeal to reason nor engage in genuinely rational argument in defense of their thesis.[7] For the most part, scholars who have focused on this second strand of Epicurus' argument have been preoccupied with the coherence of his claim that no genuinely rational arguments, and hence no reasonable grounds for accepting determinism, can exist if determinism is true.

At first glance, the connections between these two lines of argument are not readily apparent, since it is difficult to see, at least on standard descriptions of Epicurean indeterminism, how his account of the requirements of rationality can be related to an indeterminist defense of voluntary action. Scholars, for the most part, have been content to treat these two elements of Epicurus' attack on determinism in relative isolation.[8] I would argue that this is a

---

7. This self-refutation argument occurs in *On Nature* (G. Arrighetti, *Epicuro opere*, 34.26–30, and C. Diano, *Epicuri ethica et epistulae*, p. 39) and has recently been the subject of a superb paper by D. Sedley, "Epicurus' Refutation of Determinism," in *Syzētēsis: Studi sull' epicureismo greco e romano offerti a Marcello Gigante*, Biblioteca della Parola del Passato 16 (Naples, 1983), pp. 11–51.

8. A very important exception is Sedley "Epicurus' Refutation." The view of responsibility that Sedley finds in *On Nature* corresponds in key ways to the account that I argue can be reconstructed from Epicurean ethical doctrines as a whole; but I emphasize more strongly the fundamental role that reason and rational control play in Epicurus' conception of responsible *par' hēmas* actions, and I have strong misgivings about his account of upward and downward causation (see notes 68 and 73).

mistake. Epicurus, I think, sees essential connections between these two strands of his argument because he identifies nondetermined, responsible actions with those that are rational. That is, he believes that we are responsible for actions to the extent that they are under our rational control and have an origin in our own rational agency. Consequently, he can maintain that we are subject to praise or blame only to the extent that we are capable of molding our behavior in response to rational arguments. Given these essential connections between responsibility and rational argument, it becomes clear why Epicurus should find it necessary to defend the possibility of rationality itself from the threats he finds posed to it by determinism.

In the course of his discussion of the benefits of *phronēsis* (*Ad Men.* 133), Epicurus makes the following threefold distinction: some events happen by necessity (*anagkēn*), some happen by chance (*tuchēn*),[9] and some are within our own control (*par' hēmas*).[10] This distinction is well documented throughout the doxography, although Aetius (1.29.5) gives a somewhat different account. He suggests that for Epicureans some things are by chance, some by necessity, and others are by *prohairesis*, or deliberation.[11] This iden-

---

9. It is important to distinguish *tuchē* from the swerve. At *De soll. an.* 964e (U. 281), Plutarch appears incorrectly to attribute a mysterious triune aspect to swerves, since they must have no effect on things by *anagkēn*, a purposive effect on human action, and they also must account for chance events in the world. (See Philod., *De signis* 36.7.) A. A. Long ("Chance and Natural Law in Epicureanism," *Phronesis* 22 [1977], 63–88) effectively dismantles Guyau's defense of the claim that *tuchē* is the result of swerves and concludes, "There is no need of any exceptional atomic movement to account for the aimlessness and lack of purposiveness in Epicurus' view of nature" (p. 67). As he points out, indeterminacies for the Epicurean paradoxically are needed to make a contribution to the purposiveness of human actions. (But see E. G. Asmis, *Epicurus' Scientific Method* [Ithaca, N.Y., 1984], p. 280, for a discussion of *De signis* 36.7.) I will disagree, though, with Long's claim that swerves have *macroscopic* chance effects on human action.

10. See *On Nature* (Arrighetti, 34.33.3–4) for Epicurus' distinction between motion that is *di' hēmas* and motion that is *dia tēn phusin kai to periechon*. See also Philodemus, *De signis* 36.14, and Cicero, *De natura deorum* I.69, for action that is *par' hēmas*; Plutarch, *De soll. an.* 964c, for *to eph' hēmin*.

11. What Aetius means by *prohairesis* is problematic, and I certainly would not want to stake too much on possible hints of Aristotelian deliberation in this passage. J. Rist (*Epicurus: An Introduction* [Cambridge, 1972], p. 99) thinks Aetius's use of *prohairesis* roughly corresponds to 'moral personality' or 'character' and cites Epictetus for evidence. Given Rist's general agreement with Furley on the role that fixed dispositions and characteristics play in Epicurean responsibility, such a reading

tification of responsible action with deliberative action in the doxography is by no means misleading. In fact, I would argue that it accurately captures a characteristic feature of Epicurus' account of responsibility, namely, his attempt to link *par' hēmas* action with *phronēsis* and rational deliberation.

I wish to begin with the claim that Epicurus considers us responsible only for actions that are under our own immediate rational control, since many would find it controversial. Most scholars have argued that when it comes to questions of assigning responsibility, Epicurus, unlike Aristotle or the Stoics, sees no relevant distinction between rational and nonrational action. Such a distinction serves no purpose for Epicurus, it is argued, because he is a psychological hedonist. If every living creature pursues pleasure as its ultimate end, there can be no basis for distinguishing, for example, the actions of normal adults from the actions of very young children or animals. Since all living things pursue the same nonrational end and are motivated by the same nonrational desires for pleasure, the distinguishing characteristics of a responsible action must be found elsewhere.[12] Hence, it is claimed, Epicurus is forced to postulate random breaks in causality in an attempt to save our actions from being determined. The overall results of this theory, of course, are hardly attractive, since it is not very satisfactory to hold us responsible for a predetermined course of behavior that is interrupted, occasionally and mysteriously, by random and

would be congenial to his overall theory. However, for a discussion of the general problems in construing *prohairesis* in post-Aristotelian writings, see B. Inwood, *Ethics and Action in Early Stoicism* (Oxford, 1985), pp. 240–42.

12. See D. J. Furley, *Two Studies in the Greek Atomists* (Princeton, 1967), study 2: "Aristotle and Epicurus on Voluntary Action," p. 186: "Aristotle was not much troubled by the idea that the attraction of external objects might be a form of compulsion, so that all actions performed with such an end in view would be exempt from moral appraisal. But for Epicurus the case was more acute. For Epicurus was a hedonist. He held that as a matter of fact men seek what is pleasant and avoid what is painful, and that to obtain pleasure is the whole end of actions. Moreover, he held that pleasure or pain is the *inevitable* accompaniment of every experience. The implication of this might appear to be that a pleasant object *necessarily* arouses feeling, and feeling *necessarily* provokes action. He had to find an answer, therefore to this damaging suggestion." Clearly, a major problem for such a view is that it will extend ascriptions of responsibility in unintuitive ways. For instance, no relevant distinctions can be made on this basis between normal adults, small children, or even wild animals.

inexplicable happenings. Nonetheless, if Epicurus espouses a rigidly mechanistic stimulus-response model of action, indeterminate intrusions might seem to be the only way to modify the causal mechanisms of our response to pleasurable objects.

Several objections can be raised against this particular view of Epicurean hedonism. First, it is not at all obvious that Epicurus should be bothered any more than other eudaemonist theorists by the claim that we all pursue a natural end. Nor is it clear that Epicurus, or any other Greek moralist, would find the fact that we all necessarily pursue happiness a threat to voluntary action. Epicurus merely takes it for granted that we all pursue happiness (*Ad Men.* 122), and it would be very odd to think that he posits indeterminate happenings to enable us to choose or to refrain from choosing *eudaimonia* as our *telos*.

Should the fact that Epicureans identify *eudaimonia* with pleasure, however, create any special problems for their theory?[13] Here the key question to ask is what kind of control we exert over our pursuit of pleasure, the means to our pleasures, and our response to pleasurable objects. If we view pleasant things as somehow having a compulsive attraction for us,[14] or if we are genetically programmed to involuntarily pursue pleasures, it might reasonably be claimed that our choices in such cases will be strictly determined. But it is not at all clear that Epicurus is committed to any of these theses.

In criticizing such a view of hedonic compulsion, Aristotle (*EN* 1110b9–18) maintains that it would be ridiculous to blame external causes or pleasant objects for our actions; rather, we should blame ourselves for being too easily ensnared by pleasant things. He thinks, that is, that our own contribution in choosing and evaluating plea-

13. For instance, at *EN* 1172b35 Aristotle comes close to acknowledging that it is natural to pursue pleasure; but this claim in no way makes the acquisition of states of character involuntary. Cf. R. R. K. Sorabji, "Aristotle on the Rôle of Intellect in Virtue," *PAS* n.s. 74 (1973–4), 107–29.

14. Furley's claim that hedonism poses a special threat to voluntary action fits rather awkwardly with his insistence that Aristotle's account of action in *De motu animalium* is just as "mechanistic" as Epicurus' (*Two Studies*, pp. 215 ff.). If both Epicurus and Aristotle hold a strict stimulus-response model of motivation and desire, then it is hard to see why hedonism should pose any more of a threat to voluntary action than does a peripatetic conception of the *telos*. In both cases, there would be "no break in the chain of causation from stimulus to response" (p. 216).

sures is up to us. We should notice, though, that the Epicurean argues even more strenuously than Aristotle that external goods can exert no compulsive attractions for us.[15] Epicurus' models of desire and rational agency do not take pleasant external objects as their primary focus, since a dependence on external goods and their pleasurable attractions will make us vulnerable to chance. Rather, the Epicurean insists that inner states of *ataraxia* and *aponia* are our highest pleasure. We achieve them by making certain that our desires are flexible enough to find satisfaction in all circumstances. In some ways, then, the Epicurean will be even more free from the external compulsions of external objects than the Peripatetic, since Aristotle includes external goods as instrinsically valuable components of *eudaimonia*. Consequently, Aristotelian agents are more dependent on external conditions and therefore more likely to be susceptible to the attractions of external goods.

Correspondingly, Epicurus can agree with Aristotle that we may not be able to deliberate about *eudaimonia* as our natural *telos*. But we surely can deliberate about the things that are, as Aristotle argues, *pros to telos*.[16] For instance, if it is up to us[17] to deliberate about the sorts of activities and pursuits we take pleasure in, then

15. "[Aristotle's] view was that external objects stimulate *characteristic* responses in us; what we do as moral agents depends not only on the nature of the stimulus but also on our own trained disposition. Could this have been Epicurus' solution too? I think it was. (Furley, *Two Studies*, p. 228). I would agree with Furley in emphasizing the importance of internal responses; however, as I argue below, he attributes to Epicurus a view of characteristic dispositions that is too rigidly mechanistic. In order to guarantee our responsibility for our dispositions, he maintains (p. 234) that swerves are necessary to disrupt our characteristic responses. The latter claim is unnecessary, however, if the wise Epicurean, as Furley himself argues (p. 235), finds his freedom in the fact "that his *psyche* is the product of his own actions and is not unalterably shaped by some 'destiny' from the time before his birth." That is, only if we view dispositions as fully fixed and formed from birth do we need to postulate indeterminate events to rupture causal chains (see Sorabji, *Necessity, Cause, and Blame* [Ithaca, N.Y., 1980], pp. 230–42).

16. For Aristotle, *ta pros ta tele* are not strictly instrumental and may include components of *eudaimonia*. However, even though Epicurus thinks that the virtues, for example, are instrumental means to pleasure, the fact that it is our responsibility to cultivate virtuous states suggests that our acquisition of pleasures will require deliberations for which we can be held accountable.

17. *Ad Men.* 133–34 makes explicit the connection between that which is up to us and ascriptions of responsibility: *to de par' hemas adespoton, hoi kai to mempton kai to enantion parakolouthein pephuken.*

we may be praised or blamed accordingly. Or if it is in my power to cultivate a virtuous life and, as a consequence, live pleasantly, then clearly I can be held accountable for developing or for failing to develop a virtuous character.

It will now be useful to look more generally at Epicurus' account of the contribution made to our actions by these inner aspects—our *pathē*, desires, and character—to see the extent to which he thinks they are *par' hēmas*. For if we are able to exert autonomous control over these inner elements of our actions, we then will have to reject a passive, mechanistic view of the Epicurean's response to pleasures and pleasurable objects. Moreover, our conclusions about these features will strongly influence our views about the overall role that indeterminacies play in Epicurus' explanations of human action.

We can begin with Epicurus' account of the *pathē*, since they might appear to be especially independent of our control. If I burn my hand on a hot stove, my sensations of pain do not seem to be up to me.[18] Or if I am prone to fits of anger or anxiety, I might view myself as a passive victim of states over which I have no control. If our *pathē* or affections are, as their name in Greek implies, just things that happen to us, then we might reasonably argue that the *pathē* of pleasure and pain are merely uncontrollable responses to external stimuli. And we would have to view the occurrences of these pleasurable or painful happenings to us from the perspective of merely passive, though no doubt interested, spectators.

Epicurus' view of the *pathē* wavers on the question of passivity, however. On the one hand, he wants the *pathē* to serve as a preconceptual given waiting to be clothed in conceptual garb. In this way, the *pathē* can have an independent foundational role in moral judgments. At the same time, however, Epicurus thinks that beliefs have

---

18. As Aristotle argues at *EN* 1113b28, it would be pointless as well to try to persuade us not to get hot or distressed or hungry or anything else of this sort, since we will experience these sensations nonetheless. Interestingly, Aristotle does not include pleasure on this list, since he thinks that we can deliberate about the kinds of activities that we take pleasure in. D. Charles (*Aristotle's Philosophy of Action* [Ithaca, N.Y., 1984], p. 161) attributes to Aristotle a 'desire-based' or affective account of action; but he underestimates the importance of rational belief in the Aristotelian's pleasures. If the view of pleasure and belief that I have attributed to Epicurus is right, we can see why he might take a corresponding view of our responsibility for our pleasures.

an active, causal role to play in our *pathē*.[19] Thus, the Epicureans' use of *pathos* is, as Julia Annas has recently argued, extremely elastic inasmuch as it includes both relatively simple sensations and more complex emotions. The latter, especially, have a high degree of conceptual content built into them[20] and are closely connected with the rational element in the soul (*DRN* III.152–60). Furthermore, since the pleasures of the mind are more important than those of the body, and since troubles of the soul are much worse than the body's troubles,[21] these more complex *pathē* with a richer doxastic component are more centrally related to happiness.

Philodemus' *On Anger*,[22] an important text for understanding the structure of Epicurean *pathē*, continually emphasizes the essential role[23] that our beliefs play in our *pathē*.[24] In fact, in Philodemus' ac-

19. J. McDowell, "One Strand in the Private Language Argument" (unpubl.), examines the difficulties of treating states such as 'being in pain' as preconceptual givens that can play a foundational role in perceptual or moral judgments.

20. See Diogenes of Oenoanda, new frag. 10, which includes under the heading of *pathē* the complex emotions experienced by individuals witnessing a disaster. I am indebted to J. Annas for allowing me to see an early draft of her contribution on Hellenistic psychology in the forthcoming *Cambridge History of Hellenistic Philosophy*. For a general discussion of the problem see also A. O. Rorty, "Akrasia and Pleasure: *Nicomachean Ethics* Book 7," in *Essays on Aristotle's Ethics*, ed. Rorty (Berkeley, Calif., 1980), pp. 283–84.

21. See Diogenes of Oenoanda, frag. 38; Annas, "Psychology"; and M. Nussbaum, "Therapeutic Arguments: Epicurus and Aristotle," in *The Norms of Nature*, ed. M. Schofield and G. Striker (Cambridge, 1986), p. 31, for the overwhelming importance for Epicureans of therapeutically treating disturbing *pathē* of the soul.

22. This text has recently received stimulating and detailed examination by Martha Nussbaum, "Therapeutic Arguments," pp. 31 ff., and by Annas, "Psychology."

23. Philodemus does not distinguish between (1) beliefs as causes of emotion and (2) beliefs as part of the content of an emotion. (See I. Thalberg, "Emotion and Thought," *American Philosophical Quarterly* 1 [1964], p. 45, and J. C. B. Gosling, "Emotion and Object," *Philosophical Review* 74 [1965], p. 486, for further discussion of this distinction.) I suspect that, as in the case of the virtues (see chapter 2, "Justice, Psychic States, and the Unity of Virtue"), Epicureans are more inclined to accept (1) because they generally avoid the Stoic strategy of reducing affective states to purely cognitive ones. Philodemus, for instance, argues that a belief that one has been harmed is necessary but not sufficient for being angry (47–50). At the same time, however, the close connections Epicureans see between *pathē* and perceptions might easily lead them in the direction of (2). In either case, beliefs are a necessary condition for having an emotion (*On Nature* 34.26).

24. See chapter 1, "Pleasure and Belief," for further discussion of the relation of pleasure and belief. Whether we agree with A. Manuwald, *Die Prolepsislehre Epikurs*

count the *pathē* become so sanitized and restructured by beliefs that little remains in them that is not amenable to rational correction and control. Some *pathē* like love, superstition, or the fear of death depend entirely on false beliefs; consequently, the removal of the offending belief will completely eliminate the disturbing *pathos*.[25]

For the Epicurean, moreover, even in the case of physical pains, the right beliefs play an important role in our actual response to pain. If we believe that intense pains will be of short duration or if we are able to recall past pleasures, present pains will not be especially disturbing. If I am in a general state of satisfaction and *ataraxia*, the sharp physical pains of, say, having a kidney stone will seem to be merely a momentary and unimportant intrusion. On the other hand, if I am generally disturbed and unhappy, I might take that same physical pain[26] as an overwhelming indication of my overall misery, and, as a consequence, I might find it completely absorbing.

Therefore, although it might be merely arbitrary to hold us responsible for our *pathē* if they were not responsive to our own beliefs and deliberation, we can see how important Epicurus thinks our own contribution is in eliminating, modifying, and engendering

---

(Bonn, 1972), that *prolēpseis* are transmitted culturally through language, or with A. A. Long, who argues that each individual forms his own *prolēpseis* from his own sensory experience and then relates it to language ("*Aisthesis, Prolepsis,* and Linguistic Theory in Epicurus," *BICS* 18 [1971], 114–33), we can still see why Epicurus holds us responsible for the *prolēpseis* we acquire and the way we apply them to our experience. See E. G. Asmis, *Epicurus' Scientific Method,* pp. 19–21, for a lucid account of the general problem of *prolēpseis.*

25. We might reasonably object that this merely shifts problems of therapeutically treating *pathē* from an affective to a cognitive sphere; it does not show why persistent and ingrained beliefs are any more amenable to rational correction than are ingrained desires. The beliefs of a convinced racist may be no more amenable to rational persuasion than the desires of a drug addict. Epicurus' theory, however, shows a corresponding optimism about the corrigibility of beliefs and desires, and for much the same reason. Invulnerability requires both cognitive and affective flexibility. For our ability to control the formation of our beliefs, see *DRN* IV.768–76, and E. G. Asmis, "Lucretius' Explanation of Moving Dream Figures at 4.768–76," *American Journal of Philology* 102 (1981), 138–45.

26. Here we might wonder whether it really would be the same state of pain in these different cases. Our answer, for the most part, will depend on the amount of conceptual content we build into pain. In any case, the Epicurean remedies against pain all require an extensive range of true beliefs about the world as well as human nature, desires, and psychology. Thus, even in the case of physical pain, our beliefs have a crucial role to play.

our *pathē*. At this point, it might be argued that such an account merely shuffles problems of responsibility back to an earlier stage. My beliefs may play a fundamental causal role in my *pathē*, but if they[27] arise from a disposition or character that I have acquired involuntarily, then I still am not really exerting any autonomous, rational control over my *pathē*. Indeed, Philodemus suggests that a particular belief may not by itself be sufficient for having a *pathos*. Our reactions will also depend on our overall character, our set of beliefs, and the general structure of our desires (cf. *On Anger* 32).[28]

For the Epicurean, these additional elements in our responses show a corresponding degree of flexibility and responsiveness to rational control. In order to see this, it might be helpful to begin with some general considerations about Epicurus' view of desires. The Epicurean claims that we have certain necessary desires such as hunger. Clearly, ascriptions of responsibility in such cases will depend on our views about one's ability to cope with these necessary desires. For instance, one reason we tend to think that wild animals are not responsible for their actions is that they lack the requisite control over their desires.[29] The desires that they do possess merely

---

27. See for instance, Furley, *Two Studies*, p. 202, on the role of *prolēpsis*, *epibolē*, and *doxa*. Furley argues that our beliefs play a regular causal role in action and that there is no reason to assume that beliefs, which at the atomic level are motions of the soul, are indeterminate motions. This thesis is true in the sense that not every belief is necessarily accompanied by a swerve. If we view beliefs as being certain atomic movements of the soul, however, it is surely possible that there might be indeterminacies in these motions as well. If swerves are to be random, we must allow that they can happen anywhere in the causal mechanisms that explain actions. This requirement vitiates the attempts of Bailey, and more recently, D. Fowler ("Lucretius on the *Clinamen* and 'Free Will,' " in *Syzētēsis: Studi sull' epicureismo greco e romano offerti a Marcello Gigante*, Biblioteca della Parola del Passato 16 [Naples, 1983], 2:329–52) to stipulate a particular moment for swerves to intervene in these mechanisms. It is important, therefore, to distinguish microscopic and macroscopic explanations of beliefs. At the macroscopic level, Epicurus treats beliefs as arising in an intersubjective context in which agents hear advice, are praised or blamed, and deliberate about various courses of action. It is these features of the rational acquisition of our beliefs that make us responsible. How these macroscopic properties of our beliefs are related to atomic events is a separate question (see below, "Indeterminism and the Swerve").

28. Cf. Annas, "Psychology."

29. Cf. P. Huby, "The Epicureans, Animals, and Free Will," *Apeiron* 3 (1969), p. 17, for a discussion of a passage in *On Nature* (Arrig. 34.25.21–34) that suggests that Epicureans distinguished wild and tame animals and thought that the latter

impel[30] them into various kinds of behavior. By contrast, rational adults can exert a remarkable amount of control over their desires, at least according to the Epicurean's optimistic rationalism.

Suppose, then, that I am hungry. Nothing in Epicurus' writings even vaguely hints that I could be compelled by a necessary desire for food to eat whatever is set in front of me. Even necessary desires are subject to a wide variety of controls. I may, for instance, have a desire to eat; nonetheless, it is clearly up to me to choose simple,

---

could be blamed and admonished to some degree for their actions. This is because the actions of tame animals are not completely determined by their initial constitutions. Presumably, one indication of this is that we expect tame animals to learn to show some control over their immediate desires in response to our admonitions. I am not convinced, however, that Epicureans would consider such actions by animals as full-blown cases of responsibility, since even tame animals are not able to deliberate about the kind of desires they acquire. Of course, an animal's action may be *voluntary* in the wider sense of initiating its own movements (as *DRN* II.263 clearly shows). But our ability to evaluate rationally our desires is what characterizes human responsibility.

KD 32 has suggested to some the possibility that Epicurus extended ethical notions such as contractual justice to animals: *Hosa tōn zōiōn mē edunato sunthēkas poieisthai . . . pros tauta outhen ēn dikaion oude adikon; hōsautōs de kai tōn ethnōn hōsa. . . .* " Sedley, for instance, attempts to link *KD* 32 with the *On Nature* passage ("Epicurus' Refutation," p. 38). This argument has some rather odd results, however. It is by no means clear that *tame* creatures are particularly adept at forming contracts (bees, ants, packs of wolves, etc. are not tame, but can be appealed to for examples of natural 'social contracts'; see Xenophon, *Hipparch.* 4.19–20, Aelian *NA* 3.16, 8.14). Given the strong connections Epicurus sees between contracts and psychic harmony, I think the first clause of this passage may be restricted to humans, who alone among *zōia* are able to form Epicurean contracts. The second clause, then, refers to contracts between different human groups.

30. *DRN* II.256 ascribes *voluntas* to living creatures (*animantibus*) and not just to men, raising questions about the relation of voluntary action and responsible action in Epicurus' theory as a whole. There is evidence for resisting the claim that Epicureans merely identify responsible with voluntary action, since they pick out additional features of *par' hēmas* action that distinguish the actions of rational adults from those of very young children and animals. As I will argue, Epicurus' account of *par' hēmas* actions relies on connections between our rational control and evaluation of our desires and our responsibility. In many ways, Epicurus' problems about the relation of responsibility and voluntariness parallel difficulties in Aristotle's account. For Aristotle see T. H. Irwin, "Reason and Responsibility in Aristotle," in *Essays on Aristotle's Ethics*, ed. A. O. Rorty (Berkeley, Calif., 1980), pp. 117–55, and S. Sauvé, "Aristotle's Causal Discriminations: Teleology and Responsibility" (Ph.D. diss., Cornell University, 1987). Sauvé suggests that Aristotle conflates 'being up to an agent' with 'voluntariness' because of an ambiguity in his conception of how actions have their origin (*archē*) in agents. She further argues that Aristotle establishes only that character formation is voluntary, not that it is 'up to us.'

healthful fare as opposed to luxurious and harmful foods. Even if practical reasoning involves the strictly technical question of choosing means to an already determined end, in this case the satisfaction of hunger, we can be held responsible for choosing harmful rather than healthy foods. If I give you strong arguments demonstrating how bread and cheese clearly benefit you and fit into your plan for a happy life, presumably I can blame you for neglecting my advice and eating harmful foods, since you at least have control over these particular kinds of choices.[31]

Indeed, Epicurus makes even stronger claims about the powers of reason and its efficacy in modifying, correcting, and eliminating desires. Reason can also fix the relative strength of our various particular desires. Suppose that I am an Epicurean who strongly values friendship and has a corresponding desire to benefit my friends. At the same time, there happens to be a famine in which even Epicureans can no longer satisfy their hunger. I find myself down to my last few loaves of bread, while my friend is completely without food. At this point, I have two conflicting desires, my desire to benefit a friend and my desire for food.[32] I know that my friend will starve without my help; however, we both can survive a bit longer on the bread that I have left, even though I will be in a painful state of continual hunger. Epicurus would claim that I can be held responsible for this kind of choice, because he thinks that

31. To take a popular example from contemporary literature on problems of free will, suppose we think of the kinds of control we can exert over our yielding to a particular reflex such as coughing (cf. D. J. O'Connor, *Free Will* [New York, 1971], p. 122). We might cough voluntarily to announce our presence, or we might be able to resist the urge to cough until a particular aria is over, or we might be completely unable to exert any control at all during a fit of coughing. Neither an inflexible deterministic model of human action nor an extreme libertarian position seems adequately to capture this sense of the varying degrees of control that we can or cannot exert over our actions. Epicurus, I would argue, in trying to distinguish actions that are *par' hēmas* from those that are necessary or random, is concerned precisely with the kinds of rational control we can exert over our desires.

32. This particular example is doubtlessly somewhat artificial, especially since Epicurean friends are self-sufficient and it is not clear that an Epicurean would be benefiting others by prolonging their lives. This sort of example, however, can perhaps bring out the extreme control and mastery that Epicurus thinks we are able to exert over our desires. He believes, moreover, that determinism is unable to account for some obvious differences between those actions that are forced and those that, as in this example, Aristotle would call 'mixed' (*On Nature* 34.29).

I can rationally evaluate and adjust the strength of my various desires in light of some more general aim.[33] Even a necessary desire such as hunger is extremely flexible. In the case of an unnecessary and harmful desire like passionate love, we can eliminate the offending desire completely.

These features of Epicurean hedonism are important because they show that we are not merely compelled by our desires nor do we merely form rational plans to satisfy the desires we happen to have. Epicurus expects us, as rational creatures, to reflect on the desirability of our desires themselves and to develop critical attitudes toward our first-order desires (*Ad Men.* 132; *SV* 71).[34] Furthermore, Epicurus plausibly links responsible action with our ability to order and modify our desires in light of an end that, in a real sense, we rationally articulate.[35] That is, we progressively give an overall form and structure to our desires and in so doing endow our general search for pleasure with its particular shape. If we were merely compelled by our *pathē* and desires to act in various ways, we would not be held responsible for our actions. But if reason has the power that Epicurus suggests it has, we can be blamed for the particular way that we order our desires and aim at our final good. Like Aristotle[36] and the Stoics, therefore, Epicurus has a strong motivation for distinguishing rational from irrational action. So far, however, he appears to have no need to postulate macroscopic indeterminacies to free us from being compelled by our *pathē*, our desires, or even our ultimate goal, pleasure. Reason gives us sufficient control over these to warrant ascriptions of responsibility.

We are now in a somewhat better position to turn to the problem of our responsibility for our character as a whole. If our beliefs

33. Cf. Irwin, "Reason and Responsibility," p. 129, for a discussion of these varieties of rational control and the Aristotelian background.

34. See H. G. Frankfurt, "Freedom of the Will and the Concept of a Person," *Journal of Philosophy* 68 (1971), 5–20, for a discussion of the close links between the capacity for forming second-order volitions and conceptions of freedom and responsibility. On the importance of second-order *desires* in Epicurus' conception of personal identity, see chapter 1, "Pleasure, *Ataraxia*, and *Aponia*."

35. Cf. Alexander Aphrod., *De anima* II.19.

36. Epicurus' views of reason and responsibility can be usefully compared with Aristotle's 'complex' view as reconstructed by Irwin ("Reason and Responsibility," p.126).

and desires depend on our overall character, and if our characters are either rigidly predetermined or merely acquired randomly, it is not clear why we ultimately should be held accountable for our actions. But even if we believe that it is somehow up to us deliberately to fashion the sorts of characters that we want, we still might seem to be involved in the following regress. My responsibility for my present actions depends directly on my responsibility for acquiring my present character, which depends in turn on my responsibility for my earlier actions, which in turn were the outcome of my earlier character, and so on until I reach the moment of my birth or even earlier.[37] As Sorabji notes,[38] this type of argument continually shuffles the problem of responsibility back to an earlier stage.

At the same time, it blurs the distinctions we are inclined to make between the actions of normal adults and those of small children. And in the manner of the sorites paradox, it strongly challenges attempts to distinguish between properties or states by asking us to identify an exact moment of transition between them. That is, it forces us to specify a precise point of transition or shift from nonresponsible to responsible action. By the same token, however, the argument also affirms that we can account for continuities in the development of human character without any ruptures in causality. We seem to be caught in a dilemma.[39] Either there are no breaks in causality and our characters are strictly determined by

37. In Plato's *Republic* and Samuel Butler's *Erewhon* ("Birth Formulae") for instance, we find disembodied souls choosing to be born into different sorts of lives; in such cases, then, responsibility may even precede birth. We might ask what makes these disembodied souls responsible for their choices, since their present state of character would be susceptible to the same sort of regress argument. Indeed, one common way of arguing against this regress is to show the kinds of unattractive consequences it might have: responsibility for character would begin at the moment of birth, of conception, or, on some theories of the soul, even earlier. But in all these cases, it merely shuffles the problem of responsibility back to an earlier stage without showing what specific criteria are needed for ascriptions of responsibility.

38. See R. Sorabji, *Necessity, Cause, and Blame: Perspectives on Aristotle's Theory* (Ithaca, N.Y., 1980), p. 230, for this problem and an account of Aristotle's response.

39. "There is both continuity and discontinuity. The character of the person is to some extent still determined by the initial constitution of his *psyche*. . . . But to a much greater extent his character is adaptable" (Furley, *Two Studies*, p. 234). I would argue that at a macroscopic level of explanation, the Epicurean ascribes these continuities and discontinuities in our character formation to reason and rational argument, not to indeterminate events.

their initial causal conditions, in which case there would seem to be no way of specifying a point of transition between childhood and adult actions, or there must be a precise moment of transition between non-responsible and responsible states of character. On this second view, we are challenged to explain how causal continuities are suddenly ruptured and how our characters can be modified in ways that do not causally depend on any prior states of character.

Faced with this regress, two questions arise about Epicurus' theory that should be kept separate. First, we must ask whether he is aware of these problems, especially since one strong motivation for ascribing indeterminacies to his account of character formation relies on the assumption that he feels the force of this regress argument.[40] Second, it is important to see whether Epicurus' theory really is vulnerable to this kind of regress.

For several reasons, we should expect Epicurus not to shuffle the problem of responsibility back to an earlier stage in this way. The whole tenor of his ethical philosophy suggests that anyone at any age, no matter how corrupt, can come to enjoy the good life, because we can modify our desires and change our characters in light of deliberative arguments. Unlike Aristotle, who is often extremely gloomy about the possibility of reforming character,[41] Epicurus believes that anyone, no matter how old, can still become happy. Again in direct opposition to Aristotle, Epicurus does not stress the importance of noncognitive training for the student of ethical philosophy, nor does he give habituation and unreflective enjoyment a central position in moral education. There is a brief suggestion

40. See Furley (*Two Studies*, pp. 193–94) for Aristotle's alleged failure to see the force of this regress (but see Irwin, "Reason and Responsibility," p. 154). Furley also argues that Epicurus fails to consider the process of character formation (p. 235). This contention is misleading if it suggests that Epicurus is not worried about how we come to have the characters that we have (cf. *SV* 80; *SV* 64; *SV* 62; *SV* 15; *Ad Men.* 122).

41. Aristotle suggests that individuals can be so badly brought up that they can never come to enjoy *eudaimonia*. Furley (*Two Studies*, p. 235) infers from this suggestion that Aristotle's view of character formation is susceptible to the regress argument. See R. Sorabji, (*Necessity, Cause,* and *Blame*, p. 231) and Irwin ("Reason and Responsibility," pp. 140–41) for very different attempts to save Aristotle's position by showing how he may not need to view the character of adults as fully formed or incapable of being influenced by deliberative arguments.

(*SV* 80) that our early training may be important: Epicurus warns that we must watch carefully over the young so that they do not develop maddening desires.[42] But he nowhere maintains that habits and dispositions can become so ingrained that they cannot be thoroughly reformed (*SV* 46, 64). Moreover, for Epicurus, knowledge alone is able to effect our reformation (*SV* 16; *Ad Men.* 122). Consequently, he believes that our characters are not fully formed when we are young and that they never become completely fixed.[43]

Given that Epicurus insists that we can reform, how are we to view the process of reformation? There would seem to be two options. He might defend the libertarian claim that there are actions not caused by an agent's character. On this view, no matter how thoroughly one has become, say, a miser, it is still possible to rise above one's character and perform a generous action. Epicurus' second option would be to argue that although one may modify one's character, one cannot act uncharacteristically. That is, a miser may become generous, but a miser cannot act generously, that is, uncharacteristically.

The account I have given of Epicurus' theory of rational agency suggests that he would neither want nor be able to argue for the claim that there are actions that are not causally continuous with character. Modern libertarians often appeal through introspection to a metaphysical self or "continuant" to explain choices that are not an expression of one's character.[44] It is not clear, however, how

42. See M. Nussbaum, "Therapeutic Arguments," for a general discussion of the respective differences between Aristotelian and Epicurean educational methods, assumptions, and views of ethical argument.

43. Furley suggests that freedom for both Aristotle and for Epicurus (*Two Studies*, p. 235) consists not in constant choices between alternatives but in performing actions consistent with one's character. I have argued that such a view of Epicurus is misleading if it precludes the possibility of radical reformations of character in the light of Epicurean beliefs. But what of the convinced Epicurean? Will the sage merely respond to the world from a fixed and unchanging disposition, as Furley implies (p. 235)? Epicureans achieve a sense of self-sufficiency and autonomy by continually evaluating, caring for, and exerting control over their desires. Thus, even the sage is expected to monitor and evaluate every desire carefully, since the desirability of having particular desires may change in shifting circumstances. The Aristotelian values the stability of a virtuous character, but in doing so makes agents more vulnerable to chance. In contrast, the Epicurean's wish to insure his invulnerability prevents his forming a completely fixed and unchanging disposition.

44. See C. A. Campbell, "Is 'Freewill' a Pseudo-Problem?" *Mind* 60 (1951), pp.

such a shadowy or causally mysterious account could be derived from Epicurus' view of the soul. For Epicurus, the rational soul is not a metaphysical entity that transcends ordinary macroscopic laws and relationships in some special way. Its overall workings are susceptible of rational explanation at a phenomenal level.

In some fragmentary passages of *On Nature*, Epicurus apparently tries to account for the ways in which character can be modified. He describes the effects that knowledge has on the configuration (*sustasis*) of particular souls or characters. He suggests, as we would expect from the account of reason found in his ethical writings, that knowledge changes the configuration of one's character or soul. There are no hints that macroscopic indeterminacies effect these changes,[45] nor is there any suggestion that reason and knowledge are inadequate for the task.[46] A parallel passage in Lucretius confirms these claims about the powers of reason: "In many other respects the various natures and characteristic habits of mankind necessarily differ; . . . but in these matters I see that there is one thing that I can affirm: so slight are the remaining traces of our different natures that reason [*ratio*] is unable to expel from us, that nothing hinders us from living lives worthy of the gods" (*DRN* III.314–15, 319–22). We may have been born with a high proportion of heat atoms, thus being prone to anger, but *ratio* is able to mold and modify character. Our overall character is up to us

---

441–65, and "Self-Activity and Its Modes," *Contemporary British Philosophy*, 3d series, ed. H. D. Lewis (London, 1956), pp. 83–115, for two classic statements of this view. Sedley suggests ("Epicurus' Refutation," p. 29) that a much-disputed section of the self-refutation argument (*On Nature* 34.30.7–15) relies on introspective data. But I take it that the Epicurean appeal to our 'consciousness of freedom' (if, indeed, a notion this strong can even be derived from the phrase *elathon heautous*) is a long way from the claim that we have introspective access to an uncaused, metaphysical self. For an interesting attempt to show how such 'consciousness of freedom' might arise, see P. Slezak, who argues that machines might come to have a conception of a nonphysical self by attempting to account for their own Gödel limitations ("Descartes' Diagonal Deduction," *British Journal for the Philosophy of Science* 34 [1983], 13–36).

45. For a different account, see Rist, *Epicurus*, p. 96.

46. Arrighetti 34.21.17; 34.24.24–29; 34.25.6; 34.25.25–29. Cf. Usener, *GE*, p. 648. For a contemporary defense along very similar lines of the rational modification of character and our consequent liability for our actions, see D. Wiggins, "Towards a Reasonable Libertarianism," in *Essays on the Freedom of Action*, ed. T. Honderich (London, 1973), pp. 33–61.

and emerges from our own rational deliberations. Through reason and by responding to rational argument, we can change our characters so that anger does not interfere with our attainment of happiness; one can change from being irascible (*orgilos*) and can develop a disposition free from anger (*aorgetos;* Philodemus, *On Anger* 32). We may have been endowed with a certain character at birth, but our character is not determined, nor does it unfold deterministically from an original configuration. Similarly, Epicurus does not suggest that only one initial configuration of soul at birth will enable us to lead a pleasant life. *Ratio* is able to mold any initial inheritance into a pleasurable one. Consequently, Epicurus thinks that we can deliberate effectively about our characters and rationally modify our natural endowments accordingly.

By the same token, we can see why Epicurus' account is not susceptible at this juncture to the regress argument. At no time do our characters become so fixed that it is impossible for us to deliberate about the sorts of characters we may be advised to acquire. Epicurus' fluid conception of character denies both premises of the regress argument. Character is never so fully fixed that it compels action. Nor do our choices as children necessarily doom our characters and completely determine our later actions. As adults we still can deliberate about our characters and we can be praised or blamed for the results of these deliberations.[47] Character is acquired neither by chance nor by necessity; it remains continually *par' hēmas*.

We might still object at this point that Epicurus' account of reason and hence of character remains vulnerable to further attack by the determinist. If our rational deliberations are merely the product of causal processes outside of our own control, then we might suppose that our autonomy and control over these deliberations are mere illusions. We have seen how Epicurus, in attempting to avoid the conclusions of the regress argument, must rely on a kind of Archimedean point that is neither *apo tuchēs* nor *dia tēn anagkēn*.[48]

47. We may wonder whether Epicurus restricts responsible action to normal, rational adults. He might be expected to hold responsible those agents whose powers of rational deliberation have not been impaired by accident, disease, and so forth. His more optimistic views about rationality, however, might incline him to blame agents we might normally excuse.

48. For criticism of the possibility of such a separate viewpoint on causal pro-

But in so doing, he appeals not to uncaused macroscopic occurrences but to the powers of reason. Consequently, he must defend
the autonomy of rational deliberation and, indeed, of reason itself
from determinism.[49]

There is evidence that Epicurus makes such an attempt in arguing
that determinism is self-refuting.[50] For present purposes, it might
be helpful to limit our examination of his argument to one critical
premise,[51] namely, that determinism precludes the possibility of
genuine reasoning. Epicurus makes the initial assumption that determinism could be true only if a mechanistic or physicalist account
of human thought and action is true.[52] Thus, as Sedley argues,

cesses, see P. Gasper, "Intentionality, Reference, and Knowledge: A Defence of
Physicalism" (Ph.D. diss., Cornell University, 1986). I am greatly indebted to his
general discussion of the relations between physicalism and determinism. I have
similarly benefited from S. Sauvé's arguments.

49. Epicurean accounts of future contingents and their denial of bivalence (*De
fato* 18, 21, 37–38; *Academica* II.97) display a similar concern with insulating human
rationality from determinism and fatalism (see R. Sorabji, *Necessity*, p. 109). It might
be objected that if Epicurus' account of our rationality preserves human action from
chance, it can do so only by succumbing to determinism. Suppose, for instance, that
I am trying to complete a long geometric proof. The more complete my rational
grasp of the problem is, the less freedom of choice I have in formulating the proof.
In fact, we might think that someone without a sure grasp of the solution will be
freer to choose different approaches to the problem. If rationality is the hallmark
of human action, it would appear that as our actions become more rational they
become less free. Epicurus' denial of logical determinism is meant to guard against
this deterministic alternative. Human rationality too must be neither *apo tuchēs* nor
dia tēn anagkēn. (See Long, *Hellenistic Philosophy* [Berkeley, Calif., 1974], pp. 58–59.)

50. It might be argued that the connections that I am drawing between Epicurus'
account of character formation and his defense of the possibility of rational argument
is merely a gift to him, since there is little explicit evidence about Epicurus' views
of the possible connections between these two strands of his argument. His account
of the self-refutation argument in *On Nature*, however, is embedded in his account
of character formation. The concluding expression of 34.30, *peri hou legōn ex archēs
eis to tauta parekkathairein aphikomēn apodidonai*, implies only that these two elements
are loosely connected in this particular presentation of doctrine. It does not necessarily deny that Epicurus sees deeper connections between the arguments.

51. See Sedley, "Epicurus' Refutation," for a richly detailed and wide-ranging
discussion of the passage as a whole.

52. *SV* 40, however, seems to have in its sights a more limited target. For discussion of the claim that physicalism and determinism somehow require each other,
see Gasper; for the claim that physicalism is self-refuting, see H. Putnam, "Why
Reason Can't Be Naturalized," in *Realism and Reason* (Cambridge, 1983), pp. 229–
47.

Epicurus' attempt to show that determinism is self-refuting also becomes an attempt to defend atomism from the "internal rot of reductionism,"[53] that is, from an eliminative materialism that rejects the explanatory efficacy of notions such as desires, reasons, and intentions.[54] For Epicurus, these macroscopic explanatory entities are a prerequisite for rational debate and hence, for rationality itself.

Sedley suggests that one of Epicurus' targets may be atomists in the Democritean tradition, such as Nausiphanes, who were aiming to reduce mental states to atomic configurations.[55] Epicurus' initial objection to such an undertaking is that if mental states were mere epiphenomena, they could have no practical, causal effect on the world nor, indeed, could they ever affect one another.[56] In many respects, this closely corresponds to Popper's worry that physicalism would make all of our beliefs, feelings, and thoughts the "superfluous byproducts" of physical events.[57] Like Popper, Epicurus thinks that determinists may perforce concede that we have such inner experiences, but at the same time they must treat our beliefs and thoughts as mere illusions that are not causally effective.[58] This initial Epicurean line of argument against the determinist and physicalist is unlikely, however, to move either opponent. The determinist who resists mechanism can simply argue that our beliefs and thoughts will be causally effective only if determinism is in fact true. It is only when causal agency is transferred to our material parts that our beliefs become ineffectual illusions. By the same token, a central claim of physicalism is that our beliefs and feelings either are identical to material states or are entirely constituted by matter.

53. Sedley, "Epicurus' Refutation," p. 35.

54. The explicit evidence for connections between determinism and physicalism in this argument are unfortunately rather slight, although elsewhere in *On Nature* (35.11.1–5 Arrighetti), the self-refutation argument seems to be aimed at physicalism (see Sedley, "Epicurus' Refutation," p. 32).

55. Cf. Sedley, "Epicurus' Refutation," p. 33, and Democritus 68.B.7, 9, 125.

56. Such a view is perhaps reflected in 34.29.20 of the *On Nature* passage.

57. K. Popper, "Of Clouds and Clocks," in *Objective Knowledge* (Oxford, 1972), pp. 217–23. See J. Trusted, *Free Will and Responsibility* (Oxford, 1984), pp. 59, 123; and Gasper.

58. See 34.30. Cf. Trusted, p. 132, and G. Strawson, *Freedom and Belief* (Oxford, 1986,) pp. 74–76, for discussion of this consequence of determinism.

Thus, the physicalist can argue that mental states have causal efficacy precisely because they are physical states.[59] If our mental states were not material states, then and only then might there be problems with their causal efficacy. Thus Epicurus' initial objection is not very effective against either opponent.

Epicurus' main line of defense is considerably more interesting, however. He grants to the physicalist and the determinist that beliefs have causal efficacy and that we consciously reason from premises to their conclusions. If the conclusions we come to through reasoning are causally necessitated, however, he argues that they fail to be cases of *genuine* reasoning.[60] It is important to notice that Epicurus' attempt to run a self-refutation argument here only works against an extreme form of determinism, namely, fatalism.[61] That is, it requires that we accept particular conclusions of arguments regardless of their merits or truth. Only the fatalist, however, is committed to claiming that we must accept the conclusion of a particular argument simply because we would have accepted it no matter what. Determinists can insist that the truth of propositions will certainly influence the processes and outcomes of their reasoning. In fact, they easily can agree with Epicurus that fatalism precludes rationality, since it fails to show the requisite sensitivity to the merits or truth of particular arguments. But determinists can plausibly maintain that they merely would have drawn a dif-

59. For further discussion see Gasper, and P. S. Churchland, "Is Determinism Self-refuting?" *Mind* 90 (1981) 99–101.

60. See R. Trigg for a recent restatement of this argument. In a chapter devoted to 'caused belief' he argues: "Determinism makes the process of arriving at truth a haphazard one. In a nondeterminist system the whole point of reasoning and assessing evidence is to decide what is true, and even though mistakes occur, it is not an accident that beliefs are true or that knowledge is gained. Determinism cannot adequately explain this. . . . Even when I think the belief rests on sound evidence, I must acknowledge that my assessment of the evidence as good is itself causally produced" (*Reality at Risk: A Defence of Realism in Philosophy and the Sciences* [Sussex, 1980], pp. 148–49).

61. In this way the strategy of the argument is parallel to Lucretius' refutation of scepticism about knowledge (*DRN* IV.469–499), which is similarly aimed at and only effective against the extreme sceptic. For Epicurean reactions to Diodorus' 'Master Argument,' see D. Sedley, "Diodorus Cronus and Hellenistic Philosophy," *Proceedings of the Cambridge Philological Society* 23 (1977), 74–120. Sedley, "Epicurus' Refutation," pp. 28–29, tends to run together questions of fatalism and questions of determinism in this passage. I am indebted to Gasper for this clarification.

ferent conclusion if the truth or merits of an argument had been different. So long as the causes that fix belief are appropriately sensitive to the relations that obtain between the processes and conclusions of our arguments, then they do not undermine the rationality of a belief.[62] The physicalist will offer a similar account of the relations between the mechanisms that fix belief and the relations that obtain between the processes and conclusions of arguments.[63] Therefore, the self-refutation argument may allow Epicurus to save his account of rationality from the threats of fatalism, but he still needs a stronger defense against determinism and mechanism.

We will need to return to these issues in further assessing Epicurus' attempts to save the autonomy of ethical explanations. At this point, though, let us turn to an examination of his motivations for further appealing to indeterminacies in his attack on determinism and physicalism.

Indeterminism and the Swerve

Although evidence for the swerve is extremely fragmentary, few scholars today[64] would deny that Epicurus believed that there were random events at the atomic level that kept all atomic motions and configurations from being thoroughly necessitated. It remains a matter of speculation, however, how these random atomic happenings are supposed to affect human action. It has usually been assumed that random or uncaused events at the atomic level issue in random or uncaused events at the macroscopic level of human

62. For a general discussion of these issues, especially the relation of belief-fixing mechanisms to rationality, see D. Dennett, "Mechanism and Responsibility," in *Essays on the Freedom of Action*, ed. T. Honderich (London, 1973), pp. 159–84.

63. Cf. Putman for a spirited denial of this physicalist claim. For an opposing view see R. Boyd, "Scientific Realism and Naturalist Epistemology," in *P.S.A. 1980*, ed. P. Asquith and R. Giere (East Lansing, Mich., 1980), 2:613–62.

64. One of the last scholars to deny that the swerve was Epicurus' invention was A. Brieger, *Die Urbewegung der Atome bei Leukippos und Demokritos* (Halle, 1884). However, the combined evidence of Lucretius, Philodemus, Diogenes of Oenoanda, Cicero, Plutarch, Galen, and Plotinus makes the case for attributing it to Epicurus himself overwhelming.

action. Yet even Epicurus' most sympathetic critics concede that such an account would raise fundamental problems for his treatment of human action and responsibility. If our decisions or our characters are prey to random happenings that render our desires, beliefs, and intentions erratic and causally ineffective, we should not be held responsible for our actions. If action is to be intelligible and responsible, our desires and beliefs must directly influence our actions without the mysterious intervention of chance happenings. Similarly, our characters must develop without inexplicable intrusions if we are to be held liable for them.

Accordingly, Epicurus' postulation of indeterminate events in human action would seem puzzling. It seems even more perplexing, however, when viewed against the broader framework of his ethical theory. As we have seen, throughout his ethical writings Epicurus needs and espouses accounts of action, character, and practical reasoning that do not seem to be influenced by any indeterminacies. By itself, of course, this tendency hardly shows that swerves do not have indeterminate macroscopic effects that ultimately are important in ethical explanations. But these general features of Epicurus' ethical thinking at least provide some initial grounds for questioning whether he thinks that indeterminacies at the atomic level are accompanied by corresponding macroscopic indeterminacies. After all, Epicureans usually insist that different explanatory levels have their own specific properties: atoms do not laugh, cry, perceive, or think, whereas macroscopic entities are neither indestructible nor eternal, nor do they continually move at high speeds. Why then should we suppose that in the case of indeterminacy, there are strict analogies between the characteristics of atomic motions and of human actions?

Since it has been such a well-entrenched assumption that there must be a direct correspondence between these different explanatory levels, it will perhaps be helpful to survey briefly the difficulties that any indeterminist account will face in giving a coherent explanation of human action at a phenomenal level. Consider the following mundane case: I am sitting in a restaurant having dinner, when a waiter asks me if I want dessert. On one version of indeterminism, if my decision is to be free, I must be able to choose between contracausal alternatives: either I will or will not order a dessert. That is, if my decision is caused by antecedent factors such as habits, dispositions, and character, it is not free in the sense required for responsibility. I must have the so-called freedom of spontaneity to choose either alternative. More simply, there must have been a moment at which it was true that I could have ordered dessert and that I could not have ordered it.

Contracausal accounts along these lines have been attributed to Epicurus; however, immediate difficulties arise in attempting to correlate such a view of responsible human action with atomic indeterminacies.[65] Bailey, for instance, suggests that an indeterminate gap, or atomic swerve, is required before every free action to break the causal chains that would make action necessitated. But, to return to our example, suppose that the last link in the causal chain is my thinking, "I will not order any dessert," then a swerve occurs that removes the possibility of my thought's causally influencing my action, and I order dessert. Granted, a swerve might efficiently break causal chains and keep my action from being determined, but it also makes action unintelligible and attributions of responsibility problematic. To illustrate further difficulties for this view, suppose that the last link in the causal chain is my thinking, "I will order dessert," then a swerve occurs, and I order dessert. It is still reasonable to object that this random intrusion has not made my action any more free, at least to the extent that it has not provided me with any power or control over my action that I would otherwise lack. If I am disconnected from my actions so that I have no influence over them, one must concede that the gap of indeterminacy has made my will powerless and my action random and involuntary. My contribution to the action seems trivial.[66] If someone were to ask me, "Why did you order dessert?" my reply, "It

65. C. Giussani, *Studi lucreziani* (Turin, 1896), and C. B. Bailey, *The Greek Atomists and Epicurus* (Oxford, 1926); more recently, a version of this view, especially as it relates to Aristotle's theory of action, has been defended by E. G. Asmis, "The Epicurean Theory of Free Will and Its Origins in Aristotle" (Ph.D. diss., Yale University, 1970), and in W. Englert's *Epicurus on the Swerve and Voluntary Action* (Atlanta, 1987), which had not yet appeared as this book was going to press.

66. Nor would it help matters much to suggest, as Bailey and Giussani sometimes seem to, that we can somehow control the microstates of our minds and select the right atomic event to trigger a macroscopic volition. Apart from questions about how we could possibly have conscious or unconscious access to these atomic happenings, further difficulties arise in setting up a direct correlation between macroscopic choices and supposedly random atomic events.

just sort of happened that I did," would be puzzling. And we would find it difficult, as a consequence, to justify ascriptions of responsibility on such a basis.[67]

Worse still, it is even harder to see how such an account can be made consistent with the demands of Epicurus' physical theory. Such a view requires a direct correspondence between individual volitions and swerves. If swerves are instantaneous, minimal, and totally random, however, there might be several swerves among various soul atoms at the same time. Which of these would initiate a particular volition? Or if one swerve occurs and frees my choice from causal chains, why should another swerve not occur between a volition and an action? Similarly, if we can regularly count on a swerve to happen before each of our decisions, we can no longer call it random. As a consequence, the determinist can include such 'indeterminacies' in explanations of actions by claiming that swerves are causally regular features of every action.

Would it help matters any if we locate indeterminacies elsewhere? Would we be any more accountable if swerves occurred ten minutes, one month, or twenty years before a particular decision? There is a certain oddity, of course, in even attempting to situate supposedly random happenings more plausibly. The whole point about atomic indeterminacies is that they can happen, as Epicureans insist, at any time and at any place. They are uncaused and completely random.[68] If, however, as Furley suggests, Epicurus postulates

---

67. In all fairness, it should be noticed that few indeterminists have claimed that every choice involves an uncaused event. C. A. Campbell, for instance, argues that indeterminism can explain special cases such as a coward performing a brave action when there is nothing in his past history which seems to explain it causally ("Is 'Freewill' a Pseudo-Problem?"). T. Saunders ("Free Will and the Atomic Swerve in Lucretius," *Symbolae Osloenses* 59 [1984], 37–59) argues that the Epicurean swerve has a special role to play in such "effortful" situations. We might reasonably object, however, that there are no grounds for this restriction. Why should spontaneous, uncaused decisions take place only in special cases when, say, duty and inclination conflict? Epicurus would face an even more difficult challenge if he held such an account. It would be highly implausible to suggest that supposedly random atomic swerves should occur at just the right moment to insure the possibility of uncharacteristic action. If I am trying to stop smoking and I finally stop, it is merely arbitrary to claim that this has been effected by a *random* swerve.

68. Cicero (*De fato* 22) suggests that Epicurus was hesitant to admit this con-

swerves not to break the causal chains involved in particular decisions but to free our characters as a whole from being determined
by external causes and our genetic inheritance, they need not be
such regular or frequent events. In fact, it is better for this theory
if they are not too frequent, since they may have disruptive effects
on our overall character. Again, however, it is difficult to see how
claims about the frequency or timing of swerves can be anything
other than merely arbitrary.

What, then, could induce Epicureans to attempt to correlate
swerves with the development of our characters? In Furley's view,
Epicurus begins, sensibly enough, with a theory of action closely
modeled on Aristotle's. For both Aristotle and Epicurus, he argues,
actions flow from our dispositions and characters in a regular causal
way. We are therefore responsible for actions to the extent that we
are responsible for the acquisition of our characters. Moreover, if
actions are causally dependent on character, Epicurus will not need
to argue that freedom depends on contracausal alternatives. So
long as our characters are not strictly determined by causal chains
stretching back beyond our personal history, we can be held re-
ponsible for actions that flow from them.

To go back to our example, suppose that sometime in the past I
decided never again to eat dessert and my avoidance of desserts becomes a settled habit. I can be held responsible for my present decision if I have voluntarily acquired the habit of avoiding dessert.
Even if the habit of avoiding desserts has become so ingrained that
I could never change it and, as a consequence, no longer really have
contracausal alternatives when faced with making a decision, I still
am responsible for my present choice of refraining from dessert.

At this point, however, Epicurus' theory begins to get into trouble,

---

sequence of his doctrine. But it is not clear how much should be read into his claim
(especially given Cicero's own admission at *De fin.* II.15 that he finds such discussions
about natural philosophy obscure). Sedley argues, however, that macroscopic intentional states can in some sense bring about swerves and that only in a cosmogonic
context do swerves occur *nec tempore certo nec regione loci certa.* Lucretius (*DRN* II.259–
60) clearly thinks, however, that such a restriction is unwarranted. For him, swerves
are completely uncaused. Moreover, if swerves could in some sense be caused, they
would present no obstacle to determinists, who could easily factor them into their
accounts.

if it is to be consistent with his physical doctrines. If our responsibility for our characters depends on past choices that in turn depend on our characters, Epicurus will need to postulate indeterminate events in an agent's biography in order to guarantee that inherited characteristics do not compel action.[69] Furley claims that Epicurus can thus espouse a more moderate indeterminism, which preserves our responsibility for our characters. He suggests that one random swerve in an agent's psychic configuration of atoms would be enough to disrupt inherited genetic motions and free individual character from both an inner genetic destiny and compulsion from external factors.

It is still unclear on this theory, however, why we should be held responsible for our characters. Our characters may be freed from causal chains because of the swerve, but their formation still is not strictly *par' hēmas*;[70] it depends on chance interruptions of an inherited genetic mixture, and, as a consequence, our own contribution to this process is not causally sufficient. If I have inherited a certain character that determines my behavior, and then a random swerve suddenly modifies my character so that I am compelled to pursue different actions, it seems merely arbitrary to hold me responsible for my new course of action. This is hardly a cheerful view of the possibilities of human freedom, but Furley finds a kindred difficulty in Aristotle's account of character. Both Epicurus and Aristotle, he argues, fail to ask themselves hard questions about character development and never notice that our upbringing at the hands of teachers and parents may be considered as an external cause of our characters.

I think we have seen reasons to doubt this particular view of Epicurean character formation. But for the sake of argument, suppose

69. It is worth noticing how Furley's account gives in to the demands of the regress argument by specifying an exact moment of transition between voluntary and involuntary states. See above, "Rationality and Responsibility," for questions about the regress and Epicurus' susceptibility to it.

70. Furley (*Two Studies*, pp. 234–35) ascribes to swerves merely the negative role of breaking causal chains, and he suggests that we will then develop in a regular causal way with experience, praise and blame, and so forth, making their respective contributions to the formation of our characters. Nonetheless, a necessary condition of our responsibility for this development is a random macroscopic interruption of our normal experience.

that Epicurus attempts to account for the regress argument in the way that Furley suggests. It still would leave Epicurus with the extremely implausible task of fitting such an account to his physical doctrines. If swerves are random, what guarantees Epicureans that their characters will be freed from genetic compulsion in their youth? Or what if someone experiences a first swerve at forty or perhaps never at all? By the same token, this theory demands effects from the swerve that seem implausibly holistic. If I experience a swerve in one of my soul atoms, why should we suppose that it will have any influence at all on the vast majority of causal chains that make up my inherited character? Even if a single swerve could affect some localized bit of behavior,[71] it still seems highly improbable that it could free my character as a whole from its previous causal influences. Moreover, in the absence of any empirical tests for random swerves, what are we to make of a criminal who claims that his soul atoms never swerved or, perhaps, swerved too often?

Any effort to set up direct parallels between macroscopic events and atomic happenings will harbor similar implausibilities. More important, such attempts get Epicurus' doctrine and his motivation exactly backward. On these theories, swerves have random effects on human action, but they cannot really occur at random times and places; they must intervene in decisions or in the formation of our characters at the appropriate moment for the requisite theory. I would argue that the opposite must be the case. Epicurus nowhere relies on macroscopic indeterminacies in his ethical theory; consequently, Epicurus may think that swerves have nonrandom effects on human agency and character. At the same time, a general account of the swerve is required that preserves indeterminacy at the level of microscopic explanations;[72] it must remain a continual fea-

71. For recent criticism of the claim that subatomic indeterminacies could affect the much bigger chemical and electrical events of the brain, see Trusted, pp. 56–57.

72. I take these to be two morals that we can safely draw from *DRN* II.251–93. Lucretius says that *voluntas* is guaranteed by swerves. But he makes no explicit statement here or anywhere else that swerves have a random effect on macroscopic human action. Many have argued that Lucretius' phrase at 259 (*declinimus item motus nec tempore certo . . .*) suggests a strong parallel between macroscopic and microscopic indeterminacy. Sedley disagrees ("Epicurus' Refutation," p. 48), arguing that we can "grant Lucretius the persuasive force of the echo without squeezing it too hard for precise theoretical content." Sedley is correct, I think, since Epicureans are often

ture of atomic explanations that swerves can occur at no fixed time or place.[73]

Varieties of Reduction

After his account of the swerve, Lucretius pauses to give two analogies to illustrate the relation of atomic motion to our ordinary world of experience (*DRN* II.308–32). He says that sheep can be playing on the hillside, but from a great distance they collectively appear (*videatur*) as a kind of whiteness at rest on a hill. Similarly,

---

careful to distinguish the properties of different explanatory levels. Sometimes, to be sure, their use of analogy in arguments for *adēla* leads them to see stronger correlations between atomic and macroscopic properties. Epicurean arguments for atomic shapes, for instance, tend to import phenomenal structural or functional properties to the atomic level (sweetness is caused by smooth atoms and bitterness by rough, hooked atoms; *DRN* IV.658–62). Thus it is difficult to tell how much Lucretius means to be packing into II.259. Epicurus, however, suggests that the properties of intentional states differ sharply from the properties of their atomic constituents (*On Nature* 34.22). And in the rest of *DRN* II, Lucretius takes great pains to differentiate phenomenal and atomic properties. For a discussion of similar problems in Philodemus' defense of inferences by *anaskeuē* and *homiotēs*, see Asmis, *Epicurus' Scientific Method*, pp. 197 ff., esp. pp. 207–11.

73. D. Sedley, "Epicurus' Refutation," pp. 39–40, offers a more sophisticated account of the relation between mental events and atomic happenings that, I think, fails for a similar reason. Sedley argues that there is no reason in principle why secondary properties of atomic configurations could not affect their constituent atoms. In one sense this is true. We might reasonably argue that higher order intentional systems can create changes in microscopic atomic structures (compare Dennett). However plausible such a view might be for some nonreductionists, it will hardly work for Epicurus; if a swerve is a material consequence of some higher-order activity, it can no longer be random or uncaused. Only if it stands in some weaker relation, such as coincidentally accompanying every choice, could it be taken into account as a reliable statistical element that might be factored into higher-order explanations. But it would then no longer be random in the required sense. Thus Sedley's claim that volitions actualize "the ever-present possibility of swerving" (p. 49) does not seem to me to preserve sufficiently the randomness of swerves. Nor does his primary evidence for such a view, *On Nature* 34.22 (*eita anadidōsi euthus mechri tōn prōtōn phuseōn*), unambiguously show the direct causal intervention of conscious processes on micro-states. *Anadidōsi* is compatible with indirect influence; for example, my eating a certain food may be accompanied by certain microscopic changes in my blood, but I do not directly or consciously exert control over these changes. My macro-level choices certainly affect micro-states, but only indirectly.

from a place on a high mountain, even the movements of great armies appear to be but a shining speck at rest on the plain below.[74] Analogously, the world of atoms is in constant motion, yet the world of our experience appears for the most part to be orderly and stable. We might be tempted to draw either of two conclusions from these examples. We might think that macroscopic phenomena are strictly identical to their atomic constituents—that is, macroscopic stillness just *is* constant atomic motion. Or we might make the more radical claim that reference to the world of our ordinary experience should be eliminated entirely in favor of atomic explanations—that is, we may have illusions of macroscopic stillness, but we are mistaken since nothing really has any ontological status except matter in motion. These two common forms of materialism, an identity theory and eliminativism, have often been attributed to Epicureans. But, interestingly, Lucretius avoids suggesting in this passage that our sensory experiences in such cases are mere illusions that we might better explain by separately identifying their discrete components.[75] He makes use of these analogies only to show that there need not be any direct correspondences between the properties of phenomena and their material constituents.[76] Macroscopic appearances may have different characteristic properties, but that in no way undermines their integrity or the veracity of our perceptual

74. P. Conway rightly stresses the way that Lucretius' argument takes phenomenal evidence as proof for atomic events, instead of the other way around ("Epicurus' Theory of Freedom of Action," *Prudentia* 13 [1981], p. 87). For the Epicurean principle that the swerve does not conflict with macroscopic experience, see Philodemus, *De signis* 36.7–17, and Diogenes of Oenoanda 32.

75. C. Taylor describes this possibility of fashioning explanations in the form of discrete units of information, each of which is separately identifiable from its connections with any of the others (*The Explanation of Behaviour* [London, 1964], ch. 1).

76. Illud in his rebus non est mirabile, quare,
omnia cum rerum primordia sint in motu,
summa tamen summa videatur stare quiete,
praeterquam siquid proprio dat corpore motus.
omnis enim longe nostris ab sensibus infra
primorum natura iacet: quapropter, ubi ipsa
cernere iam nequeas, motus quoque surpere debent;
praesertim cum, quae possimus cernere, celent
saepe tamen motus spatio diducta locorum. (*DRN* II.308–16)

experience. In fact, any attempt to cast general doubt on our perceptual experience is itself self-refuting (*DRN* IV.469–77).[77] Consequently, the Epicurean defense of the unity and integrity of *aisthēsis* indicates that macroscopic entities themselves have a visible order[78] that enters into explanations of that order.

We may reasonably wonder, of course, how these two elements of Epicurus' theory are meant to fit together.[79] But it is first important to notice how these theoretical commitments will affect his general account of the relation between intentional and materialist explanations. If we take Lucretius' analogies seriously,[80] they suggest that human action can be viewed from two different perspectives, neither of which is strictly equivalent or reducible to the other. At one level of explanation, human action may be viewed as atoms of various shapes and sizes in constant and sometimes random motion. At a macroscopic level, however, our actions are orderly, regular, and rational, or at least responsive to reason. This level is not a mere illusion, however, nor is there any reason to suppose that there must be any direct correspondences between macroscopic and microscopic properties.

I have argued that a satisfactory account of the swerve must satisfy

77. See M. F. Burnyeat, "The Upside-Down-Back-to-Front Sceptic of Lucretius iv 472," *Philologus* 122 (1978), 197–206. For the general background of this attack on scepticism, see M. F. Burnyeat, "Protagoras and Self-Refutation in Later Greek Philosophy," *Philosophical Review* 75 (1976), 44–69.

78. These may include both formal and functional principles of order. For instance, Lucretius explains that parents pass on to their offspring various similar traits (*DRN* III.741–53), which clearly are higher-order principles of organization (see *DRN* I.159–83).

79. The metaphysical basis for these claims is explored with great skill by Sedley in "Epicurean Anti-Reductionism," in *The Bounds of Being*, ed. J. Barnes and M. Mignucci (Cambridge), forthcoming. He argues quite persuasively that although atomic entities may be aetiologically primary, they are in no way ontologically primary. He also makes the important point that for Epicureans, accidental properties are undeniably real but lack "existence at the atomic level." This claim lends strong support to the view that Epicurus is no reductionist.

80. A badly mangled passage (*On Nature* 34.21–22) suggests that Lucretius' analogies might not be strong enough to capture the special differences between intentional states and their material components. Epicurus apparently suggests that such states differ more radically (*kata tina tropon dialēptikon*) from their material components than those properties we see from a different distance (*ou ton hōs aph' heterou d[i]astēmatos*). See Sedley, "Epicurean Anti-Reductionism," for discussion of the terminology and force of this distinction.

at least two general requirements: it must guarantee randomness at the microscopic level, and it must preserve rationality at the macroscopic level of explanation.[81] Clearly, Epicurus faces a difficult initial hurdle if he is to consistently maintain both of these theses. He must show how the discrete movements of individual atoms, which either are *apo tuchēs* or *dia tēn anagkēn*, can blossom into purposive human action. In many ways, his task is similar to that of a cybernetician attempting to give an account of intelligent behavior by introducing randomizing elements in a computer program. It is sometimes claimed that such programs will display nomological regularities that are not strictly determined. Nor are they merely random since their operations are formulable in terms of general laws. Of course, in such examples suspicions quickly arise about the plausibility of making analogies between human rationality and the operations of computers; more to the present point, however, is how we are to understand the exact status and effects of lower-level randomness. We might object that any attempt to connect microscopic indeterminacies with higher-order explanations will be forced to choose between two mutually exclusive alternatives: either (a) micro-level randomness engenders randomness at the macroscopic level, or (b) it has no effect on the macro-level, in which case macro-level actions remain strictly determined. Determinists generally offer incompatibilists this kind of disjunction between determinism and randomness. Cicero, for example, claims that all events are either random or caused, with the further implication that if an event is caused, it is necessitated (*De fato* 26f.).

The Epicurean, we have seen, denies that this disjunction is exhaustive and tries to stake out a special sphere for human action that is *par' hēmas*, and therefore neither *apo tuchēs* nor *dia tēn anagkēn*. In doing so, he must explain the emergence of higher-order properties that are not simply the cooperative effect of the properties

81. One sometimes hears the objection that Epicurus may feel no need for a unified and consistent theory; he may have been able blithely to separate ethical concerns from his physical doctrines. Such a view is highly implausible, given his many attempts to explain the relation of macroscopic experience to atomic happenings. The influence of atomic explanations on his ethical theory is often exaggerated, but it seems to me hard to give anything other than an ethical motivation for his postulation of the swerve. I would agree with Sedley that the swerve's cosmological function (*DRN* II.225) seems almost an afterthought.

of their simpler parts or constituents.[82] For instance, Lucretius attempts to show how properties like colors (*DRN* II.730), sensation (*DRN* II.865), and life itself (*DRN* II.870) arise from inanimate matter. His discussion, however, leaves some very noticeable explanatory gaps. In effect, he argues that nothing in our experience precludes or contradicts the emergence of higher order properties, but he neither attempts nor claims to be able to give a full account of the causal mechanisms of their emergence.[83] A common charge against theories of emergence has been that they posit properties for which they can give no adequate explanation. Like Lucretius, such theorists may take comfort in the fact that their failure to explain emergence does not by itself disprove the brute facts of perception. But in a certain sense, although emergentist theories seek, in Cornford's phrase, to raise the living from the dead, the conjuration itself always remains essentially mysterious.

We are now in a position to return for a final look at the relation of the swerve to human rationality and action. We can agree with Epicurus that the swerve will prevent the material constituents of

82. For this definition of emergent properties and further discussion, see K. Campbell, *Body and Mind* (New York, 1970), p. 123. A passage in *De fato* 23 clearly suggests that the motions of the mind do not strictly correspond to atomic motions. Lucretius (*DRN* III.847–61) might seem to defend a stronger version of nonreductionism than emergence, however. He claims that if all of our material constituents were to come back together in the same configurations after our death, we would not be the same persons. Thus we might infer that it is possible for qualitatively distinct persons to supervene on the identical material constituents, though Lucretius' argument only suggests that persons are individuated by the contents of their beliefs (for a recent defense of this type of view, see T. Burge, "Individualism and Psychology," *Philosophical Review* 95 [1986], 3–46, and "Other Bodies," in *Thought and Object*, ed. A. Woodfield [Oxford, 1982], pp. 99–120). This thesis would still be compatible with an emergentist view of persons.

83. Nunc ea quae sentire videmus cumque necessest
ex insensilibus tamen omnia confiteare
principiis constare. neque id manufesta refutant
nec contra pugnant, in promptu cognita quae sunt,
sed magis ipsa manu ducunt et credere cogunt
ex insensilibus, quod dico, animalia gigni. (*DRN* II.865–70)

For discussion of Epicurean methods of inquiry and proof in this passage, see Asmis, *Epicurus' Scientific Method*, p. 296. For further discussion of the claim that more informative and complete explanations must proceed not from the bottom up, but from the top down, see M. C. Nussbaum, *Aristotle's "De Motu Animalium"* (Princeton, N.J., 1978), essays 1 and 3, and "Aristotelian Dualism: A Reply to Howard Robinson," in *Oxford Studies in Ancient Philosophy* (Oxford, 1984), 2: 198–207.

human action from being strictly determined by their antecendent conditions. But this thesis still leaves Epicurus with the formidable difficulty of explaining how purposive human action can emerge from a combination of determined and random material constituents. In fact, given Epicurus' general problem of explaining emergence, some have wondered whether he needs the swerve at all. That is, if higher-order properties can mysteriously emerge from atomic combinations, why should human rationality and responsible action not similarly emerge from particles of matter whose motions are strictly determined? This objection is akin to Carneades' claim in the *De fato* that Epicureans could have kept atomic motions strictly determined and still made purposive, responsible human actions arise from them.[84] If the motions of the mind are independent and not reducible to atomic motions (*De fato* 23), then it is not immediately clear why Epicurus needs indeterminacies to guarantee the independence of intentional explanations.

The Epicurean, I think, can offer two responses here. The first relies on the incompatibilist worry that if all micro-level states are strictly determined by antecedent causes, properties that emerge from these states will be similarly determined. Even if we cannot systematically trace the causal mechanisms of emergence, we still have reason to suppose that higher-order properties, barring any indeterminacies, will be strictly determined as well. That our explanations of determined macro-states may not be strictly reducible to determined micro-states will not be sufficient in and of itself to free the Epicurean from worries about necessitation, for Carneades' objection still leaves open the possibility that all events happen by necessity, with different governing laws determining the events of different levels. This possibility would be worrisome enough to Epicurus' conception of rationality (*SV* 40) to induce him to postulate causal gaps.

Just as Epicureans can use the swerve in this way to preserve action from the determinist, they can put it to much the same use against the physicalist. Given that the swerve precludes the possibility of giving completely informative explanations at the micro-

---

84. Carneades' suggestion is seconded by Sedley, "Epicurus' Refutation," pp. 50–51.

level, it presents a corresponding barrier to reductionism.[85] That is, it would do the reductionist no good to claim that all macro-level events are reducible to explanations in terms of atomic motions and indeterminate swerves, since such micro-level explanations will be underdetermined and never completely informative. The reduction, therefore, can in principle never be completed. With these difficulties for reductionism at the micro-level, the Epicurean might reasonably expect that emergent properties will display a similar resistance to the reductionist.

Increasingly, it is being argued that the strategy of giving explanations from the bottom up inevitably generates mysteries and explanatory gaps. In one sense, the swerve is a sign of Epicurus' recognition of these difficulties. In attempting to maintain the integrity and unity of intentional explantions, he finds that he must deny the possibility of reducing the ethical realm to the cooperative effects of its simpler parts. The swerve is a useful weapon against the reductionist, since it challenges the claim that such a reduction can in principle be given. What the swerve fails to do, however, is explain how structures of reason and purposive human action can emerge from simpler, insensate properties. But this explanatory failure is not peculiar to the swerve; it is part of Epicurus' wider difficulty of conjuring up life from matter.

---

85. See Sedley ("Epicurus' Refutation," pp. 40–42) for a different analysis. Sedley argues that Epicurus' nonreductionist view of the self requires indeterminacies to allow macro-states causally to affect micro-states. It is unclear to me, however, that the "mere possibility of their [swerves'] occurrence" and not their actual occurrence is what is important for Epicurus. On this view, moreover, micro-states would become causally overdetermined.

Bibliography

Adkins, A. W. H., *From the Many to the One.* Ithaca, 1970.

Annas, J. "Aristotle on Pleasure and Goodness." In *Essays on Aristotle's Ethics*, ed. A. O. Rorty. Berkeley, Calif., 1980. Pp. 285–99.

———. "Doing without Objective Values: Ancient and Modern Strategies." In *The Norms of Nature*, ed. M. Schofield and G. Striker. Cambridge, 1986. Pp. 3–29.

———. "Epicurus on Pleasure and Happiness." *Philosophical Topics* 15, (1987), 5–21.

———. *An Introduction to Plato's "Republic."* Oxford, 1981.

———. "Plato and Aristotle on Friendship and Altruism." *Mind* 86 (1977), 532–54.

———. "Psychology." Forthcoming in *The Cambridge History of Hellenistic Philosophy.*

Anscombe, G. E. M. "Modern Moral Philosophy." *Philosophy* 33 (1958), 1–19.

Arndt, W. *Emendationes Epicureae.* Berlin, 1913.

Arrighetti, G. "Devoir et plaisir chez Epicure." In *Proceedings of the VIIth Congress of the International Federation of the Societies of Classical Studies*, ed. J. Harmatta. Budapest, 1984. Pp. 385–91.

———. *Epicuro opere.* Turin, 1960.

Asmis, E. G. "The Epicurean Theory of Free Will and Its Origins in Aristotle." Ph.D. diss., Yale University, 1970.

———. *Epicurus' Scientific Method.* Ithaca, N.Y., 1984.

———. "Lucretius' Explanation of Moving Dream Figures at 4.768–76." *American Journal of Philology* 102 (1981), 138–45.

Austin, J. "Pleasure and Happiness." *Philosophy* 43 (1968), 51–62.

Bailey, C. B. *Epicurus: The Extant Remains.* Oxford, 1926.

———. *The Greek Atomists and Epicurus.* Oxford, 1928.

167

Bibliography

Bignone, E. *L'Aristotele perduto e la formazione filosofica di Epicuro.* Florence, 1936.

Blanshard, B. "The Case for Determinism." In *Determinism and Freedom in the Age of Modern Science,* ed. S. Hook. New York, 1958. Pp. 3–14.

Bloch, O. "Etat présent des recherches sur l'épicurisme grec." In *ACGB 1968.* Paris, 1969. Pp. 93–138.

Blum, L. *Friendship, Altruism, and Morality.* London, 1980.

Bollack, J. "Les maximes de l'amitié." In *ACGB 1968.* Paris, 1969. Pp. 221–36.

———. *La pensée du plaisir. Epicure: Textes moraux, commentaires.* Paris, 1975.

Bonelli, G. *Aporie etiche in Epicuro.* Brussels, 1979.

Boyancé, P. *Lucrèce et l'épicurisme.* Paris, 1963.

Boyd, R. "Scientific Realism and Naturalistic Epistemology." In *P.S.A. 1980,* ed. P. Asquith and R. Giere. East Lansing, Mich., 1980. 2: 613–62.

Boyle, J. M. et al. *Free Will: A Self-Referential Argument.* Notre Dame, 1976.

Brandt, R. "Happiness." *Encyclopedia of Philosophy,* ed. P. Edwards. New York, 1967.

Brieger, A. *Die Urbewegung der Atome bei Leukippos und Demokritos.* Halle, 1884.

Brunschwig, J. "The Cradle Argument in Epicureanism and Stoicism." In *The Norms of Nature,* ed. M. Schofield and G. Striker. Cambridge, 1986. Pp. 113–44.

Brunt, P. A. " 'Amicitia' in the Late Roman Republic." In *The Crisis of the Roman Republic,* ed. R. Seager. Cambridge, England, 1969. Pp. 199–218.

Burge, T. "Individualism and Psychology." *Philosophical Review* 95 (1986), 3–45.

———. "Other Bodies." In *Thought and Object,* ed. A. Woodfield. Oxford, 1982. Pp. 97–120.

Burnyeat, M. F. "Idealism in Greek Philosophy: What Descartes Saw and Berkeley Missed." *Philosophical Review* 91 (1982), 3–40.

———. "Protagoras and Self-Refutation in Later Greek Philosophy." *Philosophical Review* 75 (1976), 44–69.

———. "The Upside-Down-Back-to-Front Sceptic of Lucretius iv 472." *Philologus* 122 (1978), 197–206.

———. "Virtues in Action." In *The Philosophy of Socrates,* ed. G. Vlastos. New York, 1971. Pp. 209–34.

Campbell, C. A. "Is 'Freewill' a Pseudo-Problem?" *Mind* 60 (1951), 441–65.

———. "Self-Activity and Its Modes." In *Contemporary British Philosophy,* 3d ser., ed. H. Lewis. London, 1956. Pp. 83–115.

Campbell, K. *Body and Mind.* New York, 1970.

Charles, D. *Aristotle's Philosophy of Action.* Ithaca, N.Y., 1984.

Chroust, H. "The Philosophy of Law of the Epicureans." *Thomist* 16 (1953), 82–117, 217–67.

Bibliography

Churchland, P. S. "Is Determinism Self-Refuting?" *Mind* 90 (1981), 99–101.

Clay, D. "Epicurus' *Kuria Doxa* xvii." *Greek, Roman and Byzantine Studies* 13 (1972), 59–66.

———. "Individual and Community in the First Generation of the Epicurean School." In *Syzētēsis: Studi sull' epicureismo greco e romano offerti a Marcello Gigante.* Biblioteca della Parola del Passato 16. Naples, 1983. Pp. 255–79.

———. *Lucretius and Epicurus.* Ithaca, N.Y., 1983.

Conway, P. "Epicurus' Theory of Freedom of Action." *Prudentia* 13 (1981), 81–89.

Cooper, J. "Aristotle on Friendship." In *Essays on Aristotle's Ethics,* ed. A. O. Rorty. Berkeley, Calif., 1980. Pp. 301–40.

———. "Aristotle on the Goods of Fortune." *Philosophical Review* 94 (1985), 173–96.

———. *Reason and Human Good in Aristotle.* Cambridge, Mass., 1975.

Cooper, N. *The Diversity of Moral Thinking.* Oxford, 1981.

Cornford, F. M. *From Religion to Philosophy: A Study in the Origins of Western Speculation.* New York, 1912.

Crönert, W. *Kolotes und Menedemos.* Leipzig, 1906.

Dennett, D. "Mechanism and Responsibility." In *Essays on the Freedom of Action,* ed. T. Honderich. London, 1973. Pp. 159–84.

Dent, N. J. H. *The Moral Psychology of the Virtues.* Cambridge, 1984.

Denyer, N. "The Origins of Justice." In *Syzētēsis: Studi sull' epicureismo greco e romano offerti a Marcello Gigante.* Biblioteca della Parola de Passato 16. Naples, 1983. Pp. 133–52.

De Witt, N. *Epicurus and His Philosophy.* Minneapolis, Minn., 1954.

Diano, C. *Epicuri ethica et epistulae.* Florence, 1946.

———. "Note epicuree." *Studi italiani di filologia classica* 12 (1935), 61–86, 237–89.

———. "La psicologia d'Epicuro e la teoria delle passioni." *Giornale critico della filosofia italiana* 20 (1939), 105–45; (1940), 151–65; (1941), 5–34; (1942), 5–49, 121–50.

Diggs, B. J. "Rules and Utilitarianism." *American Philosophical Quarterly* 1 (1964), 32–44.

During, I. *Aristoteles.* Heidelberg, 1966.

Dworkin, R. "The Original Position." *University of Chicago Law Review* 40 (1973), 500–33.

Englert, W. G. *Epicurus on the Swerve and Voluntary Action.* Atlanta, 1987.

Faber, R. *Clockwork Garden: On the Mechanistic Reduction of Living Things.* Amherst, Mass., 1986.

Farrington, B. *The Faith of Epicurus.* London, 1967.

———. "Lucretius and Manilius on Friendship." *Hermathena* 83 (1954), 10–16.

————. "Vita Prior in Lucretius." *Hermathena* 81 (1953), 59–62.

Festugière, A.-J. *Epicure et ses dieux*. Paris, 1946.

Fowler, D. "Lucretius on the *Clinamen* and 'Free Will.' " In *Syzētēsis: Studi sull' epicureismo greco e romano offerti a Marcello Gigante*. Biblioteca della Parola del Passato 16. Naples, 1983. Pp. 329–52.

Frankena, W. *Ethics*. Englewood Cliffs, N.J., 1963.

Frankfurt, H.G. "The Freedom of the Will and the Concept of a Person." *Journal of Philosophy* 68 (1971), 5–20.

Furley, D. J. "The Cosmological Crisis in Classical Antiquity." In *Proceedings of the Boston Area Colloquium in Ancient Philosophy*, ed. J. J. Cleary. Lanham and London, 1987. 2: 1–19.

————. "Lucretius the Epicurean on the History of Man." In *Lucrèce*, ed. O. Gigon. Fondation Hardt, *Entretiens sur l'antiquité classique* 24. Geneva, 1978. Pp. 1–37.

————. *Two Studies in the Greek Atomists*. Princeton, N.J., 1967.

Gallie, W. B. "Pleasure." *Aristotelian Society Supplementary Volume* 28 (1954), 147–64.

Gasper, P. "Intentionality, Reference and Knowledge: A Defence of Physicalism." Ph.D. diss., Cornell University, 1986.

Gauthier, D. P. "Morality and Advantage." *Philosophical Review* 76 (1967), 460–75.

Gauthier, R. A., and J. Y. Jolif. *Aristote: L'éthique à Nicomaque*. Louvain, 1959.

Giannantoni, G. "Il piacere cinetico nell'etica epicurea." *Elenchos* 5 (1984), 25–44.

Gigante, M. "Philosophia medicans in Filodemo." *Cronache Ercolanesi* 5 (1975) 53–61.

Giussani, C. *Studi lucreziani*. Turin, 1896.

Giusta, M., ed. *I dossografi di etica*. Turin, 1964.

Glidden, D. "Epicurus and the Pleasure Principle." In *The Greeks and the Good Life*, ed. D. Depew. Fullerton, Calif., 1980. Pp. 177–97.

————. "Epicurus on Self-Perception." *American Philosophical Quarterly* 16 (1979), 297–306.

Goldschmidt, V. *La doctrine d'Epicure et le droit*. Paris, 1977.

————. "La théorie épicurienne du droit." In *Science and Speculation*, ed. J. Barnes et al. Cambridge, 1982. Pp. 304–26.

Gosling, J. C. B. "Emotion and Object." *Philosophical Review* 74 (1965), 486–503.

————. *Pleasure and Desire*. Oxford, 1969.

————, and C. C. W. Taylor. *The Greeks on Pleasure*. Oxford, 1982.

Gough, J. W. *The Social Contract*. Oxford, 1957.

Grice, G. R. *The Grounds of Moral Judgment*. Cambridge, 1967.

Griffin, J. *Well-Being: Its Meaning, Measurement, and Moral Importance*. Oxford, 1986.

Bibliography

Guyau, J. M. *La morale d'Epicure et ses rapports avec les doctrines contemporaines.* Paris, 1886.

Hare, R. M. *Freedom and Reason.* Oxford, 1963.

Harman, G. *The Nature of Morality.* Oxford, 1977.

Hossenfelder, M. "Epicurus—Hedonist malgré lui." In *The Norms of Nature,* ed. M. Schofield and G. Striker. Cambridge, 1986. Pp. 245–68.

———. *Die Philosophie der Antike 3: Stoa, Epikureismus, und Skepsis.* Munich, 1985.

Huby, P. "The Epicureans, Animals, and Free Will." *Apeiron* 3 (1969), 17–19.

Inwood, B. *Ethics and Human Action in Early Stoicism.* Oxford, 1985.

———. "Goal and Target in Stoicism." *Journal of Philosophy* 83 (1986), 547–56.

Irwin, T. H. "Coercion and Objectivity in Plato's Dialectic." *Revue Internationale de Philosophie* 40 (1986), 49–74.

———. "The Good Will in Greek Ethics." Unpublished.

———. *Plato: Gorgias.* Oxford, 1979.

———. *Plato's Moral Theory.* Oxford, 1977.

———. "The Pursuit of Happiness." Unpublished.

———. "Reason and Responsibility in Aristotle." In *Essays on Aristotle's Ethics,* ed. A. O. Rorty. Berkeley, Calif., 1980. Pp. 117–55.

———. "Socrates the Epicurean?" Forthcoming in *Illinois Classical Studies.*

———. "Stoic and Aristotelian Conceptions of Happiness." In *The Norms of Nature,* ed. M. Schofield and G. Striker. Cambridge, 1986. Pp. 205–44.

Kahn, C. "Aristotle and Altruism." *Mind* 89 (1981), 20–40.

———. "The Origins of the Social Contract Theory in the Fifth Century B.C." In *The Sophists and Their Legacy,* ed. G. B. Kerferd. Wiesbaden, 1981. Pp. 92–108.

Kelson, H. "What Is Justice?" In *Essays in Legal and Moral Philosophy,* ed. O. Weinberger. Boston, 1973. Pp. 1–26.

Kidd, I. "Moral Actions and Moral Rules in Stoic Ethics." In *The Stoics,* ed. J. Rist. Berkeley, Calif., 1979. Pp. 247–58.

Kleve, K. "Id facit exiguum clinamen." *Symbolae Osloenses* 15 (1980), 27–30.

Kock, T., ed. *Comicorum Atticorum Fragmenta.* Leipzig, 1880–1888.

Konstan, D. *Some Aspects of Epicurean Psychology.* Leiden, 1973.

Kraut, R. "Two Conceptions of Happiness." *Philosophical Review* 88 (1979), 167–97.

Krohn, K. *Der Epikureer Hermarchos.* Berlin, 1921.

Lewis, D. *Convention.* Cambridge, Mass., 1969.

Long, A. A. "*Aisthesis, Prolepsis,* and Linguistic Theory in Epicurus." *BICS* 18 (1971), 114–33.

———. "Chance and Natural Law in Epicureanism." *Phronesis* 22 (1977), 63–88.

Bibliography

———. *Hellenistic Philosophy*. London, 1974.

———. "Pleasure and Social Utility—The Virtues of Being Epicurean." In *Aspects de la philosophie hellenistique*, ed. H. Flashar and O. Gigon. Fondation Hardt, Entretiens sur l'antiquité classique 32. Geneva, 1986. Pp. 283–324.

Lyons, D. *In the Interest of the Governed*. Oxford, 1973.

———. "The Nature of the Contract Argument." *Cornell Law Review* 40 (1974), 1019 ff.

Lyons, W. *The Disapperance of Introspection*. Cambridge, 1986.

McCloskey, H. J. *Meta-Ethics and Normative Ethics*. The Hague, 1969.

McDowell, J. "The Role of *Eudaimonia* in Aristotle's Ethics." In *Essays on Aristotle's Ethics*, ed. A. O. Rorty. Berkeley, Calif., 1980. Pp. 359–76.

———. "One Strand in the Private Language Argument." Unpublished.

Madvig, J. N. ed. *Cicero: De finibus*. Copenhagen, 1839.

Manuwald, A. *Die Prolepsislehre Epikurs*. Bonn, 1972.

Merlan, P. *Studies in Epicurus and Aristotle*. Wiesbaden, 1960.

Mewaldt, J. *Epikur, Philosoph der Freude*. Stuttgart, 1949.

Momigliano, A. *The Development of Greek Biography*. Cambridge, 1971.

Müller, R. *Die epikureische Gesellschaftstheorie*. Berlin, 1972.

———. "Konstituierung und Verbindlichkeit der Rechtsnormen bei Epikur." *Syzētēsis: Studi sull' epicureismo greco e romano offerti a Marcello Gigante*. Biblioteca della Parola del Passato 16. Naples, 1983. Pp. 153–83.

———. "Sur le concept de *physis* dans la philosophie épicurienne du droit." In *ACGB 1968*. Paris, 1969. Pp. 305–18.

Nagel, T. *The Possibility of Altruism*. Oxford, 1970.

———. "Rawls on Justice." *Philosophical Review* 82 (1973), 220–34.

Narveson, J. *Morality and Utility*. Baltimore, 1967.

Nichols, J. *Epicurean Political Philosophy*. Ithaca, N.Y., 1972.

Nussbaum, M. C. "Aristotelian Dualism: A Reply to Howard Robinson." *Oxford Studies in Ancient Philosophy*, ed. J. Annas. Oxford, 1984. 2: 198–207.

———. *Aristotle's "De Motu Animalium."* Princeton, N.J., 1978.

———. "Therapeutic Arguments: Epicurus and Aristotle." In *The Norms of Nature*, ed. M. Schofield and G. Striker. Cambridge, 1986. Pp. 31–74.

———. "This Story Isn't True: Poetry, Goodness, and Understanding in Plato's *Phaedrus*." In *Plato on Beauty, Wisdom, and the Arts*, ed. J. Moravcsik and P. Temko. Totowa, N.J., 1981. Pp. 79–124.

O'Connor, D. J. *Free Will*. New York, 1971.

Parfit, D. *Reasons and Persons*. Oxford, 1984.

Penelhum, T. "The Logic of Pleasure." *Philosophy and Phenomenological Research* 17 (1956–57), 488–503.

Pesce, D. *Saggio su Epicuro*. Bari and Rome, 1974.

Philippson, R. "Die Rechtsphilosophie der Epikureer." *Archiv für Geschichte der Philosophie* 23 (1910), 289–337, 433–46.

Bibliography

Place, U. T. "The Concept of Heed." In *Essays in Philosophical Psychology*, ed. D. Gustafson. New York, 1964. Pp. 206–26.

Popper, K. "Of Clouds and Clocks." In *Objective Knowledge*. Oxford, 1962. Pp. 206–55.

Putnam, H. "Why Reason Can't Be Naturalized." In *Realism and Reason*. Cambridge, 1983. Pp. 229–47.

Rackham, H. ed. *Cicero: De finibus*. Cambridge, 1914.

Rawls, J. *A Theory of Justice*. Cambridge, Mass., 1971.

Reale, G. *Storia della filosofia antica*. Milan, 1979.

Reid, J. S. ed. *Cicero: De finibus i-ii*. Cambridge, 1925.

Ring, M. "Aristotle and the Concept of Happiness." In *The Greeks and the Good Life*, ed. D. Depew. Fullerton, Calif., 1980. Pp. 69–90.

Rist, J. *Epicurus: An Introduction*. Cambridge, 1972.

———. "Epicurus on Friendship." *Classical Philology* 75 (1980), 121–29.

Rorty, A. O. "Akrasia and Pleasure: *Nicomachean Ethics* Book 7." In *Essays on Aristotle's Ethics*, ed. A. O. Rorty. Berkeley, Calif., 1980. Pp. 267–84.

Ross, D. O. *Virgil's Elements*. Princeton, N.J., 1987.

Ryle, G. *Dilemmas*. Cambridge, Mass., 1954.

———. "Pleasure." *Aristotelian Society Supplementary Volume* 28. London, 1954. Pp. 135–46.

Saunders, T. "Free Will and the Atomic Swerve in Lucretius." *Symbolae Osloensis* 59 (1984), 37–59.

Sauvé, S. "Aristotle's Causal Discriminations: Teleology and Responsibility." Ph.D. diss., Cornell University, 1987.

Scanlon, T. M. "A Contractualist Alternative." In *New Directions in Ethics*, ed. J. P. De Marco. New York, 1985. Pp. 42–57.

Schmid, W. "Epikur." *Reallexikon für Antike und Christentum* 5: cols. 681–819.

Schneewind, J. B. *Sidgwick's Ethics and Victorian Moral Philosophy*. Oxford, 1977.

Sedley, D. "Diodorus Cronus and Hellenistic Philosophy." *Proceedings of the Cambridge Philological Society* 23 (1977), 74–120.

———. "Epicurean Anti-Reductionism." Forthcoming in *The Bounds of Being*, ed. J. Barnes and M. Mignuci. Cambridge.

———. "Epicurus and the Mathematicians of Cyzicus." *Cronache Ercolanesi* 6 (1976), 23–54.

———. "Epicurus: *On Nature* Book xxvii." *Cronache Ercolanesi* 3 (1973), 5–83.

———. "Epicurus' Refutation of Determinism." In *Syzētēsis: Studi sull' epicureismo greco e romano offerti a Marcello Gigante*. Biblioteca della Parola del Passato 16. Naples, 1983. Pp. 11–51.

———. "The Structure of Epicurus' *On Nature*." *Cronache Ercolanesi* 4 (1974), 89–92.

Sen, A. "Choice, Ordering, and Morality." In *Practical Reason*, ed. S. Korner. Oxford, 1974. Pp. 54–67.

Bibliography

————. "Isolation, Assurance, and the Social Rate of Discount." *Quarterly Journal of Economics* 81 (1967), 112–24.

Sidgwick, H. *The Methods of Ethics.* 5th ed. London, 1893.

Slezak, P. "Descartes' Diagonal Deduction." *British Journal for the Philosophy of Science* 34 (1983), 13–36.

Slote, M. *Goods and Virtues.* Oxford, 1983.

Smart, J. J. C. "Extreme and Restricted Utilitarianism." *Philosophical Quarterly* 6 (1956), 344–54.

Smith, M. F. *Thirteen New Fragments of Diogenes of Oenoanda.* Vienna, 1974.

Sorabji, R. R. K. "Aristotle on the Rôle of Intellect in Virtue." *Proceedings of the Aristotelian Society* n.s. 74 (1973/74), 107–29.

————. *Necessity, Cause, and Blame: Perspectives on Aristotle's Theory.* Ithaca, N.Y., 1980.

Steckel, H. "Epikuros." In Pauly-Wissowa, eds., *Real-Encyclopädie*, suppl. xi (1968), cols. 579–652.

Strawson, G. *Freedom and Belief.* Oxford, 1986.

Striker, G. *Kritērion tēs Alētheias.* Nachrichten der Academie der Wissenschaften in Göttingen, Phil.-Hist. Klasse, 1974, 2: 47–110.

————. "Origins of the Concept of Natural Law." In *Proceedings of the Boston Area Colloquium on Ancient Philosophy*, ed. J. J. Cleary. Lanham and London, 1987. 2: 79–94.

Sudhaus, S. *Philodemi volumina rhetorica.* Leipzig, 1882.

Taylor, C. *The Explanation of Behaviour.* London, 1964.

Taylor, C. C. W. " 'All Perceptions Are True.' " In *Doubt and Dogmatism*, ed. M. Schofield, J. Barnes, and M. Burnyeat. Oxford, 1980. Pp. 105–24.

————. *Plato: Protagoras.* Oxford, 1977.

Thalberg, I. "Emotion and Thought." *American Philosophical Quarterly* 1 (1964), 45–55.

Trigg, R. *Reality at Risk: A Defence of Realism in Philosophy and the Sciences.* Sussex, 1980.

Trusted, J. *Free Will and Responsibility.* Oxford, 1984.

Tuilier, A. "La notion de *philia* dans ses rapports avec certains fondaments sociaux de l'épicurisme." In *ACGB 1968.* Paris, 1969. Pp. 318–29.

Usener, H. *Epicurea.* Leipzig, 1887.

————. *Glossarium Epicureum.* Ed. M. Gigante and W. Schmid. Rome, 1977.

————. *Kleine Schriften.* Leipzig, 1912.

Vander Waerdt, P. A. "Hermarchus and the Epicurean Genealogy of Morals." Forthcoming in *Transactions of the American Philological Association* 118 (1988).

————. "The Justice of the Epicurean Wise Man." *Classical Quarterly* n.s. 37 (1987), 402–22.

Vlastos, G. "Happiness and Virtue in Socrates' Moral Theory." *Proceedings of the Cambridge Philological Society* 30 (1984), 182–213.

————. *Platonic Studies.* Princeton, N.J., 1973.

Bibliography

Von der Muehll, P. *Epicurus: Epistulae tres et ratae sententiae.* Stuttgart, 1923.

Von Wright, G. H. *The Varieties of Goodness.* New York, 1963.

Westman, R. *Plutarch gegen Kolotes: Seine Schrift "Adversus Coloten" als philosophiegeschichtliche Quelle.* Acta Phil. Fenn. 7. Helsingfors, 1955.

White, N. P. "Rational Prudence in Plato's *Gorgias.*" In *Platonic Investigations,* ed. D. J. O'Meara. Washington, D.C., 1985.

Whiting, J. "Friends and Future Selves." *Philosophical Review* 95 (1986), 547–80.

Widmann, H. *Beiträge zur Syntax Epikurs.* Stuttgart, 1935.

Wiggins, D. "Towards a Reasonable Libertarianism." In *Essays on the Freedom of Action,* ed. T. Honderich. London, 1973. Pp. 33–61.

Williams, B. "Morality and the Emotions." In *Morality and Moral Reasoning,* ed. J. Casey. London, 1970. Pp. 1–24.

Zeller, E. *Die Philosophie der Griechen in ihrer geschichtlichen Entwicklung.* Leipzig, 1903.

———. *Stoics, Epicureans, and Skeptics.* Trans. O. Reichel. London, 1880.

Index Locorum

Aelian
  NA
    3.16: 141n29
    8.14: 141n29
Aetius
    1.29.5: 134
Alexander Aphrodisias
  De an.
    II.19: 144n35
    II.22: 62n9
Aristotle
  EN: 66, 119
    1095b32–1096a2: 120n41
    1097a15–1098b8: 16n18
    1110b9–18: 136
    1113b28: 138n18
    1120a6–1121a9: 112n26
    1144b19–21: 71
    1152a2: 100n6
    1152b26–35: 22n33
    1153a13–16: 22n32
    1153b19–21: 121
    1154b4: 21n29
    1154b27–32: 45n90
    1156a19–21: 122n48
    1169b3–1170b19: 123n49
    1156b7: 99n2
    1156b31: 99n2
    1166a1–2: 107n16
    1169b10–11: 124
    1170b13–15: 123
    1170b26–27: 117n35
    1172b9–15: 40
    1172b35: 136n13
    1175a11: 21
    1175a21–22: 22n33
    1175a21–b1: 21
  Meta.
    1021b13–14: 25n41

Pol.
    1280b10: 66
Rhet.
    1380b36: 99n2
Top.
    103a6: 61n5
Athenaeus
    XII.547a: 62n10

Bishop Butler
  Sermons
    xii: 111
Butler, Samuel
  Erewhon: 145n37

Cicero
  Acad.
    II.97: 150n49
  De fato
    18: 150n49
    21: 150n49
    22: 157n68
    23: 164n82, 165
    26f: 163
    37–38: 150n49
  De fin.: 8, 65n18, 69, 100n6, 109n22
    I: 7
    I.23: 14n9
    I.29: 16, 16n15
    I.30: 12, 40n75, 41
    I.31: 44n89, 81n51
    I.32: 115
    I.32–33: 28
    I.33–34: 107n17
    I.37: 27, 32n57, 49n99
    I.38: 35
    I.39: 32n56, 49n99
    I.40–43: 82n53
    I.42: 62n10

Index

Cicero *(cont.)*
    I.42–54: 53, 64n15
    I.42–55: 69
    I.43: 63, 70
    I.44: 90n73
    I.46: 75
    I.47: 61n7, 70
    I.48: 28, 122n46
    I.49: 70, 71
    I.50: 69, 70, 77, 95
    I.52: 70, 112n26
    I.52–53: 69, 87
    I.53: 77, 77n39, 78n43
    I.55: 31, 39, 55
    I.58–62: 63n12
    I.61: 62n10
    I.62: 63n11
    I.62–63: 120
    I.63: 24
    I.65: 100n4, 100n6, 117n35
    I.65–70: 102
    I.66: 112
    I.68: 100, 112n26, 113, 117n35
    I.69: 104, 107n17, 111n25, 115
    I.70: 89n70, 110, 117n35
    II: 8
    II.9: 31, 47n95, 49n99
    II.10: 49n99
    II.15: 157n68
    II.16: 49n99
    II.19: 115n32
    II.22: 51
    II.27: 37
    II.28: 83
    II.29–30: 15n11–12
    II.31: 45n92
    II.31–32: 40n75
    II.38–44: 30n52
    II.45–78: 69
    II.50: 61n5
    II.51–59: 82n53
    II.60: 72, 76n37
    II.70: 62n10
    II.71: 90n73
    II.74: 111
    II.77: 33n59
    II.78: 99n2, 113n27
    II.80: 100n4
    II.80–81: 102n7
    II.82: 102n9, 107n17, 109
    II.83: 100n6, 109n22, 111
    II.83–84: 123
    II.84: 100n4, 117n35
    II.85: 123n49
    II.86: 30n52

    II.87: 30n52
    II.87–88: 24n38
    II.88: 24, 26
    II.89: 88n67
    V.55: 41n80
    V.84: 125
  De leg.
    I.40–43: 82n53
  De nat. deor.
    I.69: 134n10
  De off.
    II.41–42: 85n61
    III: 69
    III.9: 90n73
    III.117: 61n7, 74
  Lael.
    24: 100n4
    56: 116
    65: 110n23
  Resp.
    III.13: 89n71
  Tusc. disp.
    II.17: 120n42
    III.49: 60n3
    III.47: 15n11
    V.27: 120n42

Damoxenus
  Frag. (Kock)
    2: 48
Democritus
  Frag. (D.–K.)
    68.B.7: 151n55
    68.B.9: 151n55
    68.B.125: 151n55
    68.B.245: 92n77
Diogenes Laertius
    II.87: 17n20
    II.87–88: 11n1
    X.9: 117n35
    X.28: 63n13
    X.120b: 88n10
    X.120b2–3: 61, 71
    X.121: 27n43
    X.121b: 82n54, 99, 100n4
    X.130: 62n10
    X.137: 41
    X.138: 62n10, 64n15, 88n67
    X.138.4: 60n3
Diogenes of Oenoanda
    10: 139n20
    21: 92n77
    26.1.2: 61n5, 64n15
    32: 161n74

38: 139n21
41: 120n42

Epictetus
Disc.
I.23.3: 108n20
In.
I.21: 108n20
Epicurus
Ad Hdt.
38: 43
55: 129n1
75: 84n56
82.5: 43
Ad Mat. (Arrighetti)
72.29–40: 2n2
Ad Men.: 7, 64, 65n18, 118
122: 11, 16n18, 118, 136, 146n40,
147
123: 70n30
127: 17, 32n56, 51, 62n10
127–28: 36n67, 127
128: 15, 30–32, 32n56, 52n102,
120
128–29: 15
129: 14n9, 26, 40n77, 42, 42n82,
44, 100n6
130: 16, 28, 32n56, 115n31, 126
130b: 31
130–31: 31, 36n67
131: 27n43, 32n57, 62n10
131a: 16
132: 30, 53, 60n3, 61, 69n28,
71n32, 75, 100n6, 144
132a: 31, 42, 43n85, 43, 108n18
133: 27n43, 43, 63n12, 64n16,
70n30, 134
133–34: 137n17
135: 1, 63n11, 120n42, 123
Fragments (Bailey)
37: 27n43
64: 88n67
65: 88n67
76–77: 63n11
80: 64n15
93: 90n73
KD: 7, 64, 65n18
1: 83
3: 27n43, 27
4: 26
5: 61n5, 64n15
6: 83, 89
7: 53, 100
8: 39, 53, 83
9: 28n47, 62n10

10: 32n56, 62n10
10–13: 53
11: 32n56, 37n68, 41n78, 55,
62n10
12: 32n56, 37n68, 55, 62n10, 72
13–14: 100
15: 32n56, 83
16: 43n85, 63n11, 118
17: 63, 64n15, 64, 77, 90
18: 25, 27, 27n43, 27n45, 31, 32,
36n67, 47n95
19: 24, 26, 88n67, 99
20: 24, 25
21: 83
22: 41, 41n78
25: 30
26: 118
27: 100n6, 117n35
28: 115n32, 124
29: 17, 43n85
Σ29: 31
30: 32n57, 43n85
31–33: 106
32: 141n29
32–33: 78n42
33: 32, 78n42, 106n15
34: 77
35: 77, 90n73
36: 77
37: 77, 80, 90n75
37–38: 110
38: 80, 90n75, 94
40: 83
Nat. (Arrighetti)
34.22: 159n72, 160n73
34.21.17: 148n46
34.21–22: 162n80
34.24.24–29: 148n46
34.25.6: 148n46
34.25.21–34: 141n29, 148n46
34.26: 139n23
34.26–30: 133n7
34.29: 143n32
34.29.20: 151n56
34.30: 150n50, 151n58
34.30.7–15: 148n44
34.33.3–4: 134n10
35.11.1–5: 151n54
Peri telous: 62n10
SV: 7, 64, 65n18
13: 115n32, 119n39
15: 146n40
16: 43n85, 73n35, 75, 100n6, 119,
147
18: 109n21

Index

Epicurus *(cont.)*
    21: 17, 119n39
    23: 100, 102, 107n17, 112
    28: 109n22, 124
    33: 31, 32, 88n67
    34: 124
    39: 109n22
    40: 166
    42: 150n52
    44: 16, 88, 95, 112n26
    46: 108n18, 119n39, 147
    47: 120
    51: 62n10
    54: 37n68, 79n45, 124
    56: 100n5
    59: 43n85
    62: 146n40
    64: 146n40, 147
    68: 32n56, 83
    69: 32n56
    71: 30, 32n56, 108, 144
    77: 16
    78: 31, 117n35
    79: 83
    79–81: 77n40
    80: 32n56, 146n40, 147
    81: 32n56
Usener, H.: *Epicurea*
    68: 48n97, 50n100
    70: 62n10
    181: 120
    182: 120
    281: 134n9
    398: 40n75
    417–22: 30
    419: 15n11
    420: 32n58
    422: 36n65
    508: 61n5
    515: 62n9
    516: 61n6
    518: 64n17
    530: 89
    533: 90n73
    542: 123

Gellius
    IX.5.2: 48n97

Hobbes, Thomas
  Leviathan
    Pt. I, ch. 11: 52
    Pt. I, ch. 13: 67, 78
    Pt. I, ch 15: 78
    Pt. II, ch. 21: 80n46

Hume, David
  Enquiry: 92n77
  Essays
    Pt. II, no. 12 ("Of the Original
      Contract"): 84n58

Lactantius
  Institutiones Divinae
    III.17.42: 98n1
Lucretius
  DRN
    I.159–83: 162n78
    II: 82n54, 159n72
    II.14–36: 32n56
    II.225: 163n81
    II.256: 142n30
    II.251–93: 159n72
    II.259–60: 157n68
    II.263: 141n29
    II.308–32: 161
    II.730: 164
    II.865: 164
    II.870: 164
    III.28–29: 129
    III.83: 109n22
    III.152–60: 139
    III.258–322: 71n33
    III.314–15: 148
    III.319–22: 75n36, 148
    III.514–25: 119n39
    III.741–53: 162n78
    III.830: 25
    III.830–977: 26n42
    III.847–61: 164n82
    IV: 41n79
    IV.469–677: 162
    IV.469–99: 152n61
    IV.627–29: 48n96
    IV.658–62: 159n72
    IV.768–76: 140n25
    V: 98, 106n15, 126
    V.925–1457: 83–94
    V.962: 88n55
    V.1019–27: 105
    V.1120–35: 53
    VI: 126
Lycophron
  Frag. (D.–K.)
    83.B.3 (= Ar., *Pol.* 1280b8):
      66n19

Mill, John Stuart
  Dissertations and Discussions ("Ben-
    tham"): 103

Index

Utilitarianism
  Ch. 4: 103–104, 116n33

Origen
  Contra Celsum
    III.80: 50n100
    V.47: 61n6, 64n17

Philodemus
  De dis (Diels)
    3 frag. 84, col. 13.36–39: 123n49
    3 frag. 84, col. 1.2–4: 124n52
    3 frag. 84, col. 1.2–9: 125n53
    3 frag. 84, col. 1.15–16: 125n53
  De ira: 139
    32: 141, 149
    47–50: 139n23
  De signis
    36.7: 134n9
    36.7–17: 161n74
    36.14: 134n10
  Rhet.
    24.26: 90n75

Plato
  Crito
    47d4: 78n44
  Euthyd.
    218d: 62n10
  Gorg.: 52
    507b8–c7: 61n5
  Lach.
    192b–194a: 72n34
  Leg.
    658e–659a: 40
  Phileb.
    20c: 51
  Protag.
    333d5: 74
  Rep.: 94, 145n37
    358e–360e: 82
    583c–585a: 15n12
    Bk.II: 66, 82, 83n55
    Bk.IV: 92

Plutarch
  Adv. Colot.
    1111b: 99
    1117b–c: 2
    1123a: 32n58

1124: 86
1127d: 90n75
  Amat.
    767c: 109n21
  An recte
    1130c: 89n96
  De soll. an.
    964c: 134n10
    964e: 134n9
  De tranqu. an.
    466a: 119n39
  Vita Sol.
    3: 64n14
  Non posse
    1088b: 120n42
    1090a: 120n42
    1097a: 112n26

Porphyry
  Ad Marc.
    30: 120
  De abstin.
    I.7–12: 80n48, 90n74
    I.8.4: 92
    I.10.2: 89n70
    I.51: 31

Seneca
  De benef.
    III.4.1: 30n52
  Dial.
    VII.6.3: 60n3
  Ep Mor.
    9.1: 117
    19: 123
    85.18: 61n5

Sextus
  PH
    III.194: 40n75
  M.
    V.96: 40n75

Stobaeus
  Flor.
    17.35: 36n65
    43.139: 89

Xenophon
  Hipparch.
    4.19–20: 141n29

Index of Modern Scholars

Adkins, A. W. H., 100n6
Annas, J., 12n5, 16n18, 39n74,
    119n40, 123n49, 124n52, 139,
    139n20–21, 141n28
Anscombe, G. E. M., 59n1
Arrighetti, G., 18n22
Asmis, E., 43n86, 84n56, 134n9,
    134n24, 140n25, 155n65, 159n72,
    164n83

Bailey, C. B., 62n10, 65n18, 81–82,
    89n72, 96n85, 104n13, 112n26,
    141n27, 155n65, 156n66
Bentham, Jeremy, 5, 13, 103–104
Bignone, E., 65n18
Blanshard, B., 132
Blum, L., 108n20
Bollack, J., 100n6
Bonelli, G., 12n3, 68n24
Boyd, R., 153n63
Brandt, R., 18n23
Brieger, A., 153n64
Brunschwig, J., 14n9, 18n22, 40n75,
    40n77, 41n80, 42n82, 44
Brunt, P. A., 106n14
Burge, T., 164n82
Burnyeat, M. F., 14n7, 41n79, 64n15,
    162n77

Cambell, C. A., 148n44, 156n67
Cambell, K., 164n82
Charles, D., 138n18
Chroust, A. H., 81n52
Clay, D., 64n14, 77n41, 119n39,
    120n42, 129n1
Conway, P., 161n74
Cooper, J., 120n41, 123n49
Cornford, F. M., 129n2, 165
Crönert, W., 65n18

DeLacy, P., 90n75
Dennett, D., 152n62, 160n73
Dent, N. J. H., 59n2
Denyer, N., 66n19, 81n52, 82n53,
    84n56, 89n72, 90n75
Depew, D., 18n23
Descartes, René, 6
DeWitt, N., 99n3
Diano, C., 48n96, 49n99, 125n54,
    133n7
Diggs, B. J., 114n29
Dworkin, R., 80n46

Englert, W., 155n65

Faber, R., 130n3
Farrington, B., 104n13
Festugière, A-J., 114
Fowler, D., 141n27
Frankena, W., 112n26
Frankfurt, H. G., 144n34
Furley, D., 10, 25n39, 100n15, 130n4,
    134n11, 135n12, 136n14, 137n15,
    141n27, 145n39, 146n40–41,
    147n43, 158n69–70, 158–159

Gallie, W. B., 21n31
Gasper, P., 150n48, 150n52, 151n57,
    152n59, 152n61
Gauthier, D. P., 80n49
Giannantoni, G., 125n54
Giussani, C., 65n18, 155n65, 156n66
Giusta, M., 40n75
Glidden, D., 37n68, 43n86, 46, 130
Goldschmidt, V., 65n18, 66n19,
    77n40, 80n48, 81n52, 86n63, 89n72
Gosling, J. C. B., 14n7, 14n9, 15n12,
    20n26, 22n32, 24n38, 28n47, 29n50,
    30, 40n76, 45n91, 48n96, 49n99,
    64n15, 125n54, 139n23

Index

Gough, J. W., 80n47
Grice, G. R., 92n79
Griffin, J., 18n21
Guyau, J. M., 5, 12, 103n11, 104n13, 109n21, 111n24, 134n9

Harman, G., 95n84
Hegel, Georg Wilhelm, 3
Hobbes, Thomas, 17, 51, 66, 68n25, 87–89, 101–102, 112
Hossenfelder, M., 15n13, 17n20, 27n45, 114n29
Huby, P., 141n29

Inwood, B., 36n67, 68n25, 134n11
Irwin, T. H., 16n15, 52n101, 66n21, 72n34, 73n35, 91n76, 114n29, 117n34, 142n30, 144n33, 144n36

Kahn, C., 84n57, 107n16
Kant, Immanuel, 108, 108n20, 126
Kelsen, H., 92n77
Kidd, I., 68n25
Konstan, D., 81n52, 82n53, 90n73, 90n74, 104n13, 106n14
Kraut, R., 23n36, 38n71, 39n72

Lewis, D., 88n68
Locke, John, 13, 17, 79–80, 110
Long, A. A., 10, 25n40, 34n62, 34n63, 39–40, 47n95, 49n99, 62n29, 89n72, 100n6, 103, 106n15, 116n33, 120n42, 124n50, 134n9, 139n24, 150n49
Lyons, D., 32n57, 80n46

McClosky, H. J., 96n85
McDowell, J., 139n19
Manuwald, A., 76n38, 139n24
Merlan, P., 15n10, 33n60, 45n90, 125n54
Mewaldt, J., 15n10
Mill, John Stuart, 5, 17n19, 54n104, 95n84, 103–104, 114, 116, 128
Momigliano, A., 2
Müller, R., 80n48, 100n6

Nagel, T., 55n106, 80n50, 107n16, 117
Narveson, J., 109n21
Nichols, J., 52n101
Nussbaum, M. C., 2, 42n84, 121n43, 139n21–22, 147n42, 164n83

O'Connor, D. J., 143n31

Parfit, D., 108n19
Penelhum, T., 14n8, 20n26, 21n30, 34n64
Pesce, D., 16n15
Philippson, R., 77n41
Place, U. T., 21n31
Popper, K., 151n57
Putnam, H., 150n52, 153n63

Rackham, H., 36n65
Rawls, J., 81n51, 82n53, 90n73, 90n74, 104n13, 106n14
Reale, G., 119n39
Reid, J. S., 107n17
Ring, M., 18n23
Rist, J., 42, 42n82–83, 45n92, 47n95, 49n99, 81n52, 100n6, 106n14, 107n17, 110n23, 111n25, 112n26, 125, 134
Rorty, A. O., 139n20, 142n30
Ross, D. O., 106n15
Rousseau, Jean Jacques, 79–80, 110
Ryle, G., 14n8, 21n30, 34n64

Saunders, T., 156n67
Sauvé, S., 142n30, 150n48
Scanlon, T. H., 95n84
Schneewind, J. B., 13n6
Sedley, D., 10, 25n40, 27n44, 133n7, 133n8, 148n44, 150n51, 151n53–55, 152n61, 157n68, 159n72, 160n73, 162n79–80, 165n84, 166n85
Sen, A., 85n59
Shields, C., 42n81
Sidgwick, H., 13–14, 14n9, 15–16, 18n22–23, 20n26, 32n57, 33–34, 54, 63n11, 96n85, 104, 114n29, 116n33
Slezak, P., 148n44
Slote, M., 118n36, 122n46
Smart, J. J. C., 63n11
Sorabji, R. R. K., 71n31, 136n13, 137n15, 145, 146n41, 150n49
Stawson, G., 151n58
Striker, G., 10, 11n2, 43n86, 68n25

Taylor, C., 161n75
Taylor, C. C. W., 44n88
Thalberg, I., 139n23
Theodorides, Ch., 2n2
Trigg, R., 152n60
Trusted, J., 151n57–58, 159n71
Tuilier, A., 117n35

Index

Usener, H., 65n18, 100n6, 104n13, 148n46

Vander Waerdt, P. A., 80n48, 81n52, 90n75
Vlastos, G., 18n23, 62n10, 95n84, 99n2

White, N. P., 55n106
Whiting, J., 52n101, 56n108, 117n34
Wiggins, D., 148n46
Williams, B., 108n20

Zeller, E., 3–4, 12, 90n75, 123n49

Library of Congress Cataloging-in-Publication Data

Mitsis, Phillip.
    Epicurus' ethical theory : the pleasures of invulnerability / Phillip Mitsis.
    p. cm.—(Cornell studies in classical philology : v. 48)
Bibliography: p.
Includes index.
ISBN 0-8014-2187-X (alk. paper)
    1. Epicurus—Ethics. 2. Ethics, Ancient. I. Title. II. Series. B573.M58 1988
171'.4'0924—dc19   88-47746